TITO'S YUGOSLAVIA

DUNCAN WILSON

CAMBRIDGE UNIVERSITY PRESS

CAMBRIDGE

LONDON · NEW YORK · MELBOURNE

Published by the Syndics of the Cambridge University Press
The Pitt Building, Trumpington Street, Cambridge CB2 1RP
Bentley House, 200 Euston Road, London NW1 2DB
32 East 57th Street, New York, NY 10022, USA
296 Beaconsfield Parade, Middle Park, Melbourne 3206, Australia

First published 1979

Printed in Great Britain by
Western Printing Services Ltd, Bristol

Library of Congress Cataloguing in Publication Data
Wilson, Duncan, Sir.
Tito's Yugoslavia.

Bibliography: p.
1. Yugoslavia – Politics and government – 1945 –
2. Yugoslavia – Economic policy – 1945–   3. Tito,
Josip Broz, Pres. Yugoslavia, 1892–   I. Title.
DR370.W54   320.9′497′02   79–11009
ISBN 0 521 22654 4

For Betty with love

Contents

Preface

The scope of this book is defined in the opening chapter. It is intended primarily for the reader with a general interest in contemporary history and international affairs, but with no particular knowledge of Yugoslavia. I hope none the less that it can stand up to some specialist criticism.

It is my pleasant task to acknowledge a number of debts, first to the Foreign and Commonwealth Office, who posted me twice to Yugoslavia, in 1951–3 as Counsellor of Embassy, and in 1964–8 as Ambassador, and allowed me subsequently to look at my own official despatches from Belgrade. The Yugoslav Embassy has been most helpful in providing me with Yugoslav official publications and background material over recent years. Sir Dugald and Lady Stewart in March–April 1977 had me to stay for an unconscionable time at the British Embassy, Belgrade, and arranged many contacts for me. Then, as often before, Desa Trevisan was generous with time and information. Richard Kindersley of St Antony's College, Oxford, Fred Singleton, of the Centre for Yugoslav Studies at Bradford University, and Christopher Cvijić of *The Economist* have made helpful comments on various stages of the text, and Lilian Bainbridge has been most patient and efficient in typing a great deal of illegible manuscript. None of these, of course, has any responsibility for the final product.

My editors at the Cambridge University Press, Patricia Williams, William Davies and Iain White have been throughout very encouraging and helpful.

Perhaps my greatest debts are indirect ones, to my wife and family for sharing my interest in our Yugoslav environment, to our many friends there from 1951 onwards, to the staff of the British Embassy and their families during my periods of service in Belgrade, and to the 'club' of British people in various walks of life, starting with Sir William Deakin and Sir Fitzroy Maclean, who might be termed 'Yugo-British' and have on so many occasions discussed with me Yugoslav impressions and affairs.

Notes on spelling and pronunciation

I have used Serbo-Croat spellings (Latin script) in all cases except where it would look affected to do so ('Beograd' for Belgrade). The following are brief notes on the pronunciation of Serbo-Croat words:

a   somewhere between 'a' in father and 'u' in luck.

c   as 'ts' in rats (Cer = 'Tser').

ć   a soft 'tch', or as 'tu' in picture (Bihać = 'Bihatch').

č   a rather harder 'tch', or as 'ch' in church (Čačak = 'Tchatchak').

dj   as 'gi' in giraffe.

dž   a rather harder version of the same sound, or 'J' in James.

i   as 'ee' in been, but rather shorter.

j   as 'y' (Kragujevac = 'Kraguyevats'); after a, j is used to produce the sound ie in English tie (Kajmak = 'Kiemak').

lj, nj   except at the end of words, 'j' softens 'l' or 'n' audibly, and is pronounced together with the consonant (Ljuba = 'lyuba', the 'lyu' being sounded as in the English pronunciation of lieu; Njegoš = 'Nyegosh', the 'nye' being sounded much as 'gne' in the French *insigne*, but rather more firmly). At the end of words, the 'j' only very slightly softens 'l' or 'n'; again the French '*gne*' is the nearest equivalent.

š   as 'sh' (Šabac = 'Shabats').

zh   as 'j' in French jour, or 'si' in English vision.

h   something like Scottish 'ch' in loch, but rather softer, and thus often omitted at the beginning of Serbo-Croat words ('Ajduk' for 'Hajduk').

u   as 'oo' in moon, but rather shorter.

Abbreviations

AVNOJ	Parliaments summoned by Tito during the war.
CC	Central Committee.
CP	Communist Party.
CPY	Communist Party of Yugoslavia.
CPSU	Communist Party of the Soviet Union.
COMECON	Council for Mutual Economic Assistance (of Warsaw Pact Countries).
CTY	Confederation of Trade Unions of Yugoslavia.
EEC	European Economic Community.
FEC	Federal Executive Council.
FTT	Free Territory of Trieste.
GATT	General Agreement on Tariffs and Trade.
GIF	General Investment Fund.
IMF	International Monetary Fund.
KGB	Soviet secret police.
LCY	League of Communists of Yugoslavia (= CPY after 1952). In the text the synonym 'Party' is often used.
NATO	North Atlantic Treaty Organization.
NDH	Croatian National State (wartime).
NKVD	former title of Soviet secret police (KGB).
OAU	Organization of African Unity.
OZNA	former title of Yugoslav secret police (UDBA).
RIS	Russian Intelligence Service.
SAWPY	Socialist Alliance of the Working People of Yugoslavia.
SUNFED	Special United Nations Fund for Economic Development.
UAR	United Arab Republic.
UDBA	Yugoslav secret police.
UNCTAD	United Nations Conference on Trade and Development.
UNIDO	United Nations Industrial Development Organization.
UNRRA	United Nations Relief and Rehabilitation Administration.

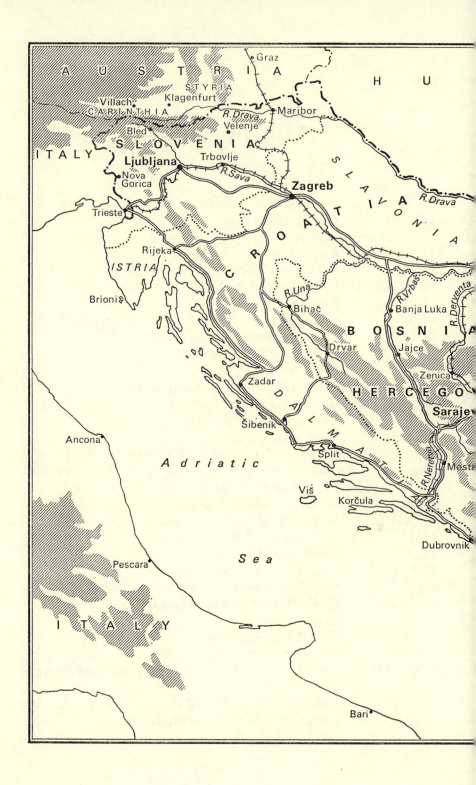

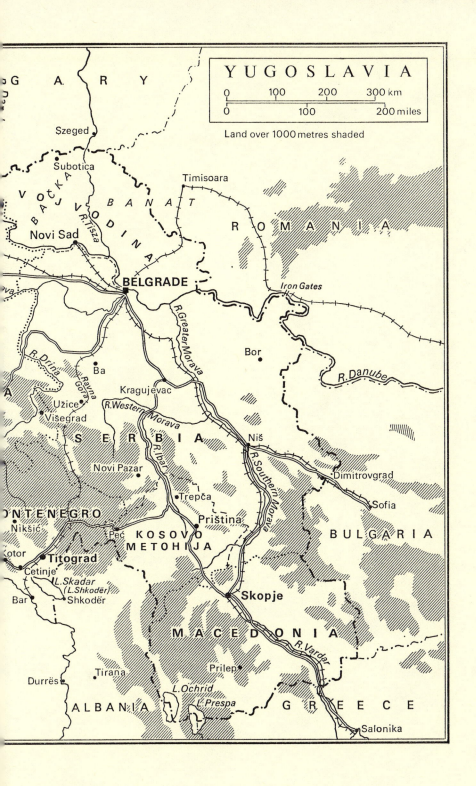

YUGOSLAVIA

0   100   200   300 km
0   100   200 miles

Land over 1000 metres shaded

I

Introductory

The aim of this book is to provide non-experts – the 'Intelligent Man' or 'Woman' of Bernard Shaw's titles – with a brief account of Communist Yugoslavia from 1945 onwards. Not for the first time the South Slav lands are a centre of international attention, as an area over which the interests of great powers or alliances can easily clash. The Ottoman and Habsburg Empires met and fought on this ground from the sixteenth to the nineteenth centuries. The rivalry of the Habsburg and Russian Empires here led to the First World War. Here Stalin's imperial policies met with a vital check in 1948. It is easy to envisage further Soviet attempts to increase their influence, particularly after Marshal Tito's disappearance from the political scene, and such attempts could lead to an East–West confrontation in the area, or even on a European scale.

The fact that Eastern and Western interests could clash in the Yugoslav area is of course not in itself sufficient reason for a detailed study of the political and economic development of Yugoslavia. Even in a shrinking world, Yugoslavia may appear to many as a remote Balkan country, whose policies can be of little interest to Britain. However various aspects of these policies have been of much importance both in themselves and in their direct and indirect effects on the international scene of the last thirty years.

In the field of foreign policy, Tito's defiance of the Cominform, his various partial reconciliations with the Soviet Union, and his attitude to the emergence of Eurocommunism in recent years have had effects important for the Soviet Union and for East–West relations as a whole. His pursuit of 'non-alignment' and efforts to co-ordinate the policies of non-aligned (mainly Asian and African) states have also had their importance on a world scale. They have to some extent determined the shape of confrontation or co-operation between 'North' and 'South' – the more and less developed countries of the world – on questions of international investment and trade. The Yugoslav leaders have also played an influential part in determining how far 'non-alignment' should be equated with the anti-imperialist and anti-colonial movement, which in effect has meant how far it has been acceptable to the Soviet leaders. In 1961 'non-alignment' seemed on this count to be very close to 'near-alignment'; in 1979 Yugoslav and Soviet/Cuban ideas about the proper direction of non-aligned policy in Africa are very different.

Admitted that Yugoslavia may be important not merely as an 'object' of the foreign policies of other states, but also as an actor with a considerable role on the international scene, the further question remains whether its internal affairs are worth studying in detail. Again there is a double answer to such doubts. If Yugoslav foreign policy is important, Yugoslav internal policy must also have at least a secondary importance, since it is closely linked with foreign policy, each influencing and being influenced by the other. The Yugoslav 'way to socialism' and development of the philosophy and practice of self-management might have been forced on Tito anyhow by economic necessities after the break with the Cominform in 1948. However it was also deliberately developed as an anti-Stalinist, anti-étatist political philosophy. As such, it insists that the Communist Party, even though it retains a political monopoly, should advise and stimulate rather than direct and administer. This is an heresy unacceptable to the Russian leaders, and particularly to Khruschev's successors. The more positive side of Yugoslav philosophy, the development of 'self-management' at all levels of society, has also been a stumbling-block for the Russians. 'Self-management' in domestic affairs leads naturally to 'self-management' or independent action for each state at national level. This fact has had implications for the solidarity of the 'Eastern bloc' which the Romanians have been very ready and the Russians very unready to accept.

There is of course a two-way interaction between Yugoslav foreign and domestic policies. The international context determines internal developments as well as vice versa. Djilas' advocacy of a multi-party system at the end of 1953 was no doubt premature and would probably have come to nothing anyhow. But its speedy failure was doubly assured by the international context of that time. Tito's reaction can only be fully understood in the light of the fact that after Stalin's death in March 1953 he was anxious for a reconciliation with Soviet Russia, hopeful of social developments within it, and unwilling to give the Soviet leaders any further cause to say that Yugoslavia had deserted the road to Communism. Similarly the action taken by the Yugoslav authorities in 1975 against 'neo-Marxist' writers and philosophers was motivated partly by a desire to provide proof to the Soviet leaders of Yugoslav orthodoxy on essential matters of political philosophy, and thus to keep the balance of Yugoslav foreign policy even between East and West.

On Yugoslavia's Western front, the policies of de-control, allowing the profit motive to operate, and adapting Yugoslavia's price structure and pattern of industry to the world market – the total package originally labelled as Economic Reform in 1965 – have *de facto* operated strongly in favour of closer economic links with Western Europe which themselves have important implications for Yugoslav foreign policy. The interaction here between foreign and domestic policies is typically complex. It is the comparatively developed industries of Croatia and Slovenia which have normally had the greater share of increased trade with the West. One result of this is that Croatia and Slovenia have become prosperous in relation to, for instance, Bosnia and Macedonia. The gap between 'North' and 'South', more developed and less developed Republics, has increased within Yugoslavia. This has tended to stimulate demand in the 'South' for more central control of the economy, and government with a 'firm hand', which approximates more closely to the Soviet model. And, if demand for a 'firm hand' intensified, it might attract more or less direct support from the Soviet Government. The process of argument is of course here much simplified, but is further proof of the close inter-relation between Yugoslav domestic policies and Yugoslavia's external relations with East and West.

It can reasonably be claimed also that for the student of politics, Yugoslav internal policies are of considerable interest in themselves, quite apart from their interaction with the world of international politics. In many respects of course Yugoslavia is unique; but the story of Tito's experiments is relevant to the study of certain political-economic problems which are of widespread occurrence today. How can the minimum of cohesion and central direction be assured in a multiracial and highly confederate state? How, in the economic field, can monetary incentive be most effectively combined with some general direction of investment, and the maximum of 'workers' participation' with either? Is the existence of one and only one political party necessary for the adequate solution of these two problems? And, if so, is the existence of such a party compatible with democratic freedoms as usually conceived in Western countries? Can the claims of Kardelj, Yugoslavia's senior political philosopher, be justified, that Yugoslavia is not a 'one-party state', in spite of the existence of only one political party, and that under the new Yugoslav Constitution and implementing acts there is a genuine 'plurality of interests' in operation, which ensures for the Yugoslav 'working-class' much more real control over their environment than can be given under 'bourgeois democracy'? Or is a single political party, whatever the theoretic controls on its action, bound sooner or later to misuse its monopoly position and to deteriorate into tyranny under the temptations of power? Finally and not least how far has the shape and direction of Yugoslav policies, domestic as well as external, been determined by President Tito himself? How far have the results of his charismatic leadership been institutionalised against the day when he himself is no longer at the head of affairs?

The author does not attempt in this book to answer such questions systematically, in spite of the conviction that, even in their specifically Yugoslav form, they are of general importance. His hope is rather that this book will provide historical material from which readers can draw their own conclusions.

2

The Kingdom of Yugoslavia

Yugoslavia throughout its short history has been a multinational, multi-racial, and multicultural state, with problems which cannot be understood without reference to a more distant past. The most constant of these has been what is called the 'nationalities problem', and the dimensions of this must be indicated at the start. Recent estimates of population (for 1977) show the following figures for the six Constituent Republics:

		Nos (in thousands)
Bosnia		4,082
Croatia		4,551
Macedonia		1,811
Montenegro		572
Serbia*		5,467
	Kosovo	1,486
	Vojvodina	1,992
Slovenia		1,806
	Total	21,767

* 'Restricted territory', i.e. excluding the Autonomous Provinces listed immediately after 'Serbia'.

The figures conceal further complications. The Bosnians are not considered to have a nationality of their own and include a good number of Serbs and Croats. On the other hand, the Moslem religion (often in conjunction with certain racial characteristics) has been widespread in Bosnia and has differentiated it to a large extent from the other five Republics. Within these Republics there are racial minorities, of which the most important are the Serbs in Croatia. The Albanians, amounting to 1.3 million in 1971 (or 6–7% of the whole population, with a high birth-rate) are concentrated mainly in the Autonomous Province of Kosovo-Metohija, but spread over into Macedonia. The

Autonomous Province of the Vojvodina, north of the Sava and the Danube east of Belgrade, contains a mixture of races, the Magyar minority constituting over a quarter of its total population. These are the basic facts of Yugoslavia's 'nationalities problem'. Their importance is enormously enhanced by the history that lies behind them.

The crucial historical boundary within Yugoslavia lies between those regions which formerly lay within the bounds of the Austrian Empire and those which for centuries formed part of the Ottoman Empire in Europe. This corresponds very roughly to the division between Slovenia, Croatia and Dalmatia on the one hand, and Serbia, Bosnia and Macedonia on the other. The division between Serb and Croat has been and is of vital importance. There is no obvious racial difference between Croats and Serbs, both descendants of tribes that penetrated south-eastern Europe in the late sixth century A.D. There is however a great difference in history and culture. The Croats were attached first to Hungary, then to the Habsburg Empire, from 1102 to 1918, and the great majority of them were Catholics. The Serbs built up a considerable Balkan Empire in the fourteenth century, were conquered by the Turks at the end of it, but reconquered freedom for themselves in the nineteenth century. Their religious loyalty was to the Orthodox Church. Serb and Croat speak and read what is virtually the same language, but the differences in their history and culture are symbolised by the fact that the Croats use the Latin and the Serbs the Cyrillic alphabet. These differences have given rise to political tensions which still cause difficulties in Yugoslavia today and were the crucial political fact of Yugoslavia between the wars.

2

The new Kingdom was faced from the start with three crucial problems which had not been adequately solved by 1941, when it was sucked into the vortex of the Second World War, and persist in modified forms today. There was the question of frontiers and minorities; the continuous tension between centralists (mainly Serb) and federalists or confederalists (mainly Croat); and the general poverty of Yugoslavia, together with major economic and social differences between its people and classes. All these problems contributed to the emergence of Yugoslavia in its present form, and are still important.

Yugoslavia in 1919 as today had seven nation-neighbours – Italy, Austria, Hungary, Romania, Bulgaria, Greece and Albania. With Italy the new state had difficult frontier problems, a legacy from the old

Venetian supremacy on the Adriatic coast, and of the newly-united Italy's ambition to replace Austria-Hungary as the dominant power in Trieste, Istria and Dalmatia. In Trieste itself and in most of the coastal strip for 50 miles south and east of Trieste the majority of inhabitants were Italian, and elsewhere in the region Italians formed at least substantial pockets of the population. Latin–Slav antagonism in this area was sharp. It was to prevent Italian territorial gains that Croat and Slovene troops had until 1918 fought with determination for Austria-Hungary on the Isonzo front. The Italian Government on their side resented the virtual abrogation of the secret Treaty of London (the price of their entry into the First World War in 1915) and from the first took their chances to undermine the unity of the new Yugoslav state. By 1920 d'Annunzio had seized for them the important harbour of Rijeka (Fiume).[1] Italy's war-time Allies acquiesced in d'Annunzio's coup, and it was legalised by the Treaty of Rapallo (November 1920), under which Italy received the whole of the Istrian coast, the town of Zara and the island of Lagosta. The desire to regain this territory was one of the few political sentiments that united the citizens of the new Yugoslavia.

Elsewhere it had substantial minority problems which other neighbours could exploit. Slovenia had been linked more closely than Croatia with Austria – in consequence its economic and educational standards were the highest in Yugoslavia, but disentanglement from Austria was difficult. In October 1920 a plebiscite determined the border of Slovenia and Austrian Carinthia along the Karawanken mountain range, but left a minority of some 50,000 Slovenes within Austria.

The former Hungarian province of the Vojvodina, north of Belgrade, had been largely settled in 1690, after the expulsion of the Turks, by Serb immigrants in a great northward migration from southern Serbia; but by 1919 it also contained over 500,000 Germans, 468,000 Magyars and 231,000 Romanians, apart from smaller racial minorities. The Germans and Magyars alone comprised over 8% of the total population of Yugoslavia in 1921, and could not be regarded as loyal citizens, particularly in the international setting of the late thirties.

Another important minority, acquired by Serbia as the result of the victorious Balkan wars of 1912–13, and reacquired in 1919 by Yugoslavia, was the predominantly Albanian (Shiptar) population of the Kosovo-Metohija region (henceforward Kosmet). Here the new rulers

---

[1] This had been the subject of bitter dispute from 1867 to 1914 between the Croats who claimed it and the Hungarians who made of it their principal link with the sea.

were faced with a solid block of foreigners, largely illiterate, living at a low level of development, and with a very high birth-rate. The first Yugoslav–Albanian settlement covering frontier and minority problems was not reached until 1926. It left Serbia with nearly 500,000 citizens of Albanian race, and the size of the minorities within Serbia, together with the continued presence of a large Serb minority in Croatia, made the new Government in Belgrade specially reluctant to abandon centralist rule.

Macedonia too had been acquired by Serbian conquest in 1912–13, confirmed in 1919. This was historically gratifying to those who remembered – and most Serbs did – the great days of Serbian power in the fourteenth century, but the incorporation of another economically poor province of mixed racial population faced Serbia and then Yugoslavia with acute problems. There was a large and belligerent Albanian minority – it was indeed the successful revolt of the Albanian population against the Turks which furnished the immediate occasion for the Balkan wars of 1912. There were also plenty of difficulties with Macedonia's Greek and Bulgarian neighbours, who claimed special interest. Since 1870 the Turks had encouraged a separate Church administration (by a Bulgarian exarchate) of much of Macedonia, and many Macedonians, including a Greek minority, had been brought up in Bulgarian-speaking schools and churches. More important, the Treaty of San Stefano, by which the Russians concluded their Balkan campaign against the Turks in 1878 made provisions for a Greater Bulgaria as large as the pre-medieval Bulgarian Empire, but designed to be a Russian satellite. The Bulgarians were resentful of the more restrictive international settlement imposed on them at the Treaty of Berlin later in 1878. After they had jointly with the Serbs defeated the Turks in 1912, they fought their allies for some of the territorial spoils of victory. The Serbs won convincingly, but the Bulgarians cherished their grudge and have been periodically encouraged down to the present day to make difficulties in Yugoslav Macedonia.

Finally the long-coveted lands of Bosnia and Hercegovina were, and long continued to be, an anomalous element in modern Yugoslavia. Croats and Serbs alike, as national feelings revived among them in the nineteenth century, regarded Bosnia as part of their natural or historical territory, but its social structure was foreign to both, for historical reasons. When the Turks took over the rule of Bosnia in 1460, a large proportion of the Bosnian nobility who had been 'Bogomils' – Christian heretics persecuted by Catholic and Orthodox alike – had no hesitation in embracing the Moslem faith, under which they were allowed to keep their estates. Thus Bosnia was governed for 400 years by a caste of nobles, Slav by race and Moslem by religion. Turkish overlordship was effectively exchanged for Austrian in 1878. The material conditions of Bosnia and Hercegovina were indeed much improved in the period 1878–1914, but the social status of the agricultural serfs was little changed. A very high proportion of these serfs were of Serb origin, and looked to independent Serbia for protection and improvement of their conditions. Thus the problem of social reform in Bosnia was linked with the tensions between 'Austrian' Croatia and independent Serbia, which from 1902 onwards relied on Russian support. It was 'not by chance', as Communist officials say, that the powder train which led to the First World War was ignited at Sarajevo, in June 1914. Nor is it 'by chance' that Bosnia-Hercegovina has provided the Republic of Yugoslavia with large problems of economic development and a field for some rivalry between Croat and Serb Communist parties.

3

Frontier and minority problems took a few years to crystallise. The political history of Yugoslavia between the two World Wars was however overshadowed from the first by the tensions between Serbs and Croats. The 'Kingdom of the Serbs, Croats and Slovenes' was from the first dominated by the Serbs. They had done much to win their own freedom in battle against the Turks, had been independent for nearly a century and practised a sort of parliamentary democracy before 1914. They had made a heroic contribution to the Allied cause in 1914–18. It was naturally the Serb dynasty of Karadjordje which provided a King for the new Yugoslavia. The Serbs regarded themselves as not only the largest constituent numerically of the new Yugoslavia, but also as the 'nation of government'. Their leaders behaved as if the new Yugoslavia was the Greater Serbia which had for long been the principal aim of their foreign policy. In the new administration most of the jobs went to Serbians.

Serb 'hegemonism' (to use the Yugoslav communist term) was acceptable or unacceptable to other nations of the new Yugoslavia in different degrees. It was welcome enough to the Montenegrins, who had indeed maintained their independence for centuries until the First World War, but had always considered themselves as closely akin to the Serbs. It was resented most by the Croats, who were acutely conscious of their thousand-year-old, largely Western and Catholic culture.

The resulting political strain was aggravated by economic and social tensions. The former Kingdom of Serbia had suffered the most obvious war-damage; but as the authority of Austria-Hungary faded in Croatia, there was acute shortage and inflation in the towns and in the countryside peasants took over many of the big estates. The new holdings were too often too small to be economic, and the large customs-free market of the Austro-Hungarian Empire was no longer available for Croat farmers. The Croat Peasant Party was formed under Stepan Radić in the hope of redressing their economic grievances. As early as November 1919, Radić was campaigning for a republican and federalist, or even confederate, Yugoslavia. However before the end of the year he withdrew his followers from the Constituent Assembly, where no party had a working majority. As a result it produced in the Vidovdan (St Vitus' day) constitution of 28 June 1921 a scheme which was far more centralist than the majority of Croats could accept. Radić and his Croat party at first refused to participate in parliamentary government. He visited Moscow and even temporarily affiliated his party to a Moscow-controlled Peasant International. The Croat Peasant Party was banned and Radić imprisoned. When he emerged, he re-formed his party under a new name (the 'Croat Peasant Club') and in the newly-formed Parliament of 1928 led the opposition against the 'Radicals', or party of Government. The experiment was short-lived. On 20 June 1928 'Democratic' insults were answered by 'Radical' bullets in Parliament. Radić's nephew was killed outright, and he himself was mortally wounded. The Croat representatives withdrew again from Parliament. Their new leader, Dr Maček, demanded a new federal constitution linking Croatia with Serbia no more closely than Hungary had been linked with Austria, the necessary revisions to be carried out by a non-parliamentary government responsible to King Alexander alone.

In fact the King dissolved Parliament himself in January 1929 and undertook the task of governing Yugoslavia himself under a highly centralised and repressive system – liberty of the press was stifled and all political parties of a regional or religious character were dissolved. The country was re-divided into nine large provinces, cutting across 'national' frontiers, and the 'Kingdom of the Serbs, Croats and Slovenes' was formally re-christened 'Yugoslavia'. Considerable efforts were made to rally Croatian opinion to the new régime and measures were taken to discourage the spirit of Serb chauvinism. But the new régime remained essentially a Serb one. By 1929 many Croatian leaders had left Yugoslavia, some to conduct separatist propaganda and organise terrorist activity, others to campaign with Western governments for Croatian autonomy within a Yugoslav framework.

A revised Constitution and a revived Parliament (September 1932) made little difference. Throughout Yugoslavia widespread opposition continued, which in Croatia was expressed by the Zagreb Manifesto of November 1932. This called for, among other things, the removal of Serbian hegemony and the re-organisation of the state in order to safeguard 'the Serbian nation, the Croat nation and the Slovene nation'. Soon afterwards claims for autonomy were made on behalf of the Slovenes, the inhabitants of the Vojvodina, and Bosnia-Hercegovina. The Government's answer was to intern not only Maček, but also Mgr Korošec and Dr Spaho, the Slovene and Moslem leaders. In April 1933 Maček was prosecuted for signing the Zagreb Manifesto and condemned to three years' imprisonment. Political discontent was everywhere reinforced by the effects – somewhat delayed in Yugoslavia – of the world economic depression.

Meanwhile the existence of Yugoslavia was threatened from beyond its frontiers. The Croatian terrorist exiles were given aid and comfort by Hungary; the Bulgarian Government encouraged dissidents in Macedonia, and Mussolini's Fascist régime exploited (to the extent of stimulating armed rebellion) the political unrest that resulted from desperate food shortages in the Dalmatian hill country. Anti-Yugoslav activity abroad reached its climax in the murder of King Alexander at Marseilles in October 1934, when he was on an official visit to France. The assassination was carried out by Croat terrorists trained in Hungary. The reaction in Yugoslavia was a temporary movement towards unity and the restoration of the civil liberties without which it could not be established. Maček was among those released from prison, the censorship was relaxed, and elections were held in spring 1935 for a new Parliament.

Again, as in 1932, it proved that there had been no real political change. The elections, which confirmed in power the parties of Government, were held under such plainly scandalous conditions that the Croat Ministers resigned and the opposition delegates formed a counter-Parliament in Zagreb. The Regent, Prince Paul, took the initiative in inviting Maček to special talks in Belgrade, in which the Croat leader accepted the Yugoslav idea and the continuance of monarchic rule, but insisted on the democratisation and federalisation of the state. A new government of national reconstruction was at last formed in August 1935 under Dr Milan Stojadinović, and by the end of 1936 some progress had been made towards federalisation, essentially on a 'trialist' basis, the dominant units being Slovenia, Serbia (including Macedonia and Montenegro), and Croatia (including Dalmatia and Slavonia). The provinces which fitted worst into this pattern were Bosnia-Hercegovina and the Vojvodina. In the former the eastern districts were almost entirely Serb, but the western districts had a Croat or pro-Croat majority and the Moslems, predominant in other districts, preferred autonomy. In the western districts of the Vojvodina too there were many Croats and Maček claimed that, if Macedonia and Montenegro were incorporated in Serbia, Croatia should inherit all the former Habsburg provinces except Slovenia.

Maček hoped that the issues of federalisation and democratisation would be solved either simultaneously or in close succession, and confidential negotiations between him and Prince Paul were held throughout the spring and summer of 1939. In August 1939 he accepted Prince Paul's view that some regulation of the Croat question was vital before the outbreak of a European war, and an Agreement ('Sporazum') was signed on 26 August. It gave some satisfaction to Croatian nationalists, without providing any wider solution for national or constitutional issues in Yugoslavia as a whole. The new province, or 'banovina', of Croatia was formed on a national basis out of two existing provinces – the remaining seven provinces remained unchanged, and cutting across 'national divisions'. The new Croat 'banovina' was to enjoy a special degree of autonomy, the Diet at Zagreb being revived to deal with matters other than those reserved for the central Government (defence, foreign affairs, commerce, transport and public security). The power of legislation was to be shared between the Diet and the Crown. The 'Sporazum' went some way to meet the demands which Croat politicians had long been pressing. If it had been concluded earlier, it might have prepared the way for a general federalisation of Yugoslavia, which would have strengthened both the Karadjordje dynasty and the country as a whole. But agreement was reached at the last possible moment before the outbreak of war. The extreme Croat separatists interpreted it as a sign of the weakness of the central Yugoslav government, and were encouraged to look to Hitler and his allies to secure for them complete independence.

4

The social and economic problems of Yugoslavia as a whole, and the economic disparities between its constituent nations, were enormous. Along with the East–West division (broadly speaking) between Serbs and Croats, Orthodox and Catholic, ex-Turks and ex-Austrians, there had long been a further historical division between north and south. The more northerly territories were economically the more highly developed, whether in the ex-Austrian or ex-Turkish sphere. Slovenia and the northern part of Croatia and Slavonia had close economic links with the Austro-Hungarian Empire, not always to the benefit of the inhabitants, as it appeared at the time, but much regretted when they became part of Yugoslavia in 1919. The southern parts of Croatia and Dalmatia, particularly the hinterland of the Dalmatian coast, were poor by any standard. Within the Turkish or Serb sphere the same division was noticeable. The most prosperous Serbs on the whole were the descendants of those who had made their way in the great migration of 1690 over the Sava and Danube into Austrian or Hungarian territory. Southern Serbia, Montenegro and Macedonia were miserably poor. In other circumstances a social reform or revolutionary party not tied to one of the nations of Yugoslavia might have emerged. As things were, the need for general social reform was long overshadowed by the national tension between Serbs and Croats, or found political expression within that tension. Radical movements arose soon after 1918 in Serbia, to parallel or out-trump the Croat Peasant Party. In 1919 the Serbian Social Democrats refused to take part in the 'Provisional National Representation' (preliminary to the Constituent Assembly), and succeeded in uniting centre and left-wing socialists in a 'Socialist Workers Party of Yugoslavia (Communist)' which then affiliated to the Comintern. The Communists polled over 12% of the votes cast in the elections and held 58 seats (the Serb Radicals and Democrats had 91 and 92 respectively, the Croat Peasant Party 50). At the end of November the Government took the threat of Communist-inspired strikes seriously enough to ban all Communist organisations, but did not interfere with the activities of any Communist deputies who attended sessions of the Constituent Assembly.

In June 1920 the 'Socialist Workers Party' assumed the name of the Communist Party of Yugoslavia (henceforward CPY); they had declared their aim to be the establishment by revolutionary means of a unified Yugoslav Soviet Republic,[2] and in December expelled those of their members who refused to accept the subordination of the new Party to the Comintern. The winter 1920–1 brought with it a fresh wave of strikes and the Government looked for the first opportunity of banning the Communist Party; it did not have long to wait. In

[2] They envisaged this as forming part of a Danubian federation, which would itself be federated with other Soviet Republics.

summer 1921 young Communists tried to murder the Prince Regent, and succeeded immediately afterwards in murdering the Minister of the Interior. In August a Law for the Defence of the State was passed, enabling the Government to take drastic action against terrorists; the Communist deputies were expelled from Parliament, and their party was declared illegal.

For twenty years and more the CPY had to operate underground. It was ineffective, not so much for this reason as because its leadership reflected in exaggerated form the debates on policy within the Soviet CP (for example between the Trotskyites and the Bukharinites), and because its line on the 'nationalities question' was not clear. By concentrating on the grievances of Yugoslavia's urban population, irrespective of 'national' borders, the CPY failed to exploit the grievances of the poor peasants throughout Yugoslavia, and particularly of the Croat peasantry, which thus tended to support the Croat Peasant Party. This led to the emergence of grave differences on the 'nationality question' within the leadership of the CPY. Sima Marković, the Secretary-General, was a Serb and a centralist; he would not countenance action which appeared to weaken the framework of the Yugoslav state. The left wing of the Party on the other hand favoured self-determination of the constituent provinces, up to and including the right of secession. In summer 1924 the Fourth Congress of the Comintern laid down the line to be followed, reproving the Yugoslav Party for persistent fractionalism and Marković personally for placing 'the whole question of national self-determination on a constitutional basis. . .This is bound to lead to a passive attitude on the part of the Communist Party in regard to one of the most burning questions at present agitating the nationalities.'

The Comintern proceeded to resolve that the Serbs, Croats, and Slovenes were three peoples, not one people. The nationalities question in Yugoslavia was a revolutionary not a constitutional one, and the CPY must fight for the 'separation from Yugoslavia of Croatia, Slovenia and Macedonia, and their establishment as independent republics.'

At the IVth Congress of the CPY, held at Dresden in October 1928, Togliatti (under the name of Comrade Ercoli) attended as representative of the Comintern, and read a further severe lesson to Sima Marković for relying too much on intellectuals and continuing to encourage 'fractionalism'.[3] Marković was replaced as Secretary-

[3] This although Marković had theoretically accepted the 'disruptive' Comintern line at the CPY's IIIrd Congress in 1926.

General by Djuro Djaković, and the Congress passed a resolution proclaiming its support for the independence of Montenegro (as well as of Croatia, Slovenia and Macedonia) and for the right of the German, Magyar and Albanian minorities to break away from the Yugoslav state.

All this was of theoretical interest only. The CPY was not effective in 1928 and from then until 1934 was subjected to very severe repression. Thereafter the Comintern line was reversed at its VIIth Congress, held in August 1935 in Moscow. The threat of Nazi Germany now overshadowed Europe as a whole, including Soviet Russia. 'New tactical orientations' were needed, and the period of the Popular Fronts was dawning. As far as Yugoslavia was concerned, this meant that the CPY should stop trying to disrupt the Yugoslav state, should seek alliance with any 'anti-fascist elements' that could be found, and 'while not departing from the principle of self-determination to the point of secession' should also 'take into account the present international situation'. So long as there was 'full equality of rights as between nationalities and the freedom and proper representation of the Croat and other nationalities' were fully guaranteed, the CPY should not support the secession of any nationality from the existing state of Yugoslavia.

5

With the help of the new policy line, the CPY succeeded in re-establishing to some extent the position which it had enjoyed before 1928. And from 1935 Josip Broz, who later acquired the cognomen of 'Tito', according to international communist custom, began to emerge as an important political figure. Tito's life has been recorded in full and admirable biographies for British readers, but something here must be said of the main outline of his career. Born in 1892 into a peasant family in Croatia, he had been trained as a locksmith, and called up to join the Austrian army in 1914. He was severely wounded and taken prisoner by the Russians in 1915. After two years of captivity he was released at the time of the Russian Revolution and spent three adventurous years, partly among the Kirghiz tribes, in the newly-formed Soviet Union. In 1920 he returned to Yugoslavia, a convinced Communist, and devoted himself to political organisation within Trade Unions (since the Communist Party was banned), becoming Secretary-General of the Metal-Workers' Union. In 1928 he was imprisoned with many other Communists for political activity, using his time in prison to supplement his practical experience as a leader and organiser by much reading in political theory (it was, he afterwards said, as good as a university). In 1934 he was released and was sent in 1935 to work for the Comintern in Moscow; in 1936 he returned to Yugoslavia and spent some months in Western Europe organising the flow of Communist volunteers from Yugoslavia to Spain. Then came another crucial summons to Moscow in 1937. This was the time of the Great Purges, and Tito might well have found himself due for 'liquidation'. Instead he was appointed Secretary-General of the notoriously difficult and 'fraction-prone' CPY.[4] From the Soviet point of view he was a man of impeccable working-class origin and industrial experience, Moscow-trained, with a gift for practical organisation and for leadership – one who in Communist phraseology had been 'tempered' for the job by much testing experience. Tito returned again from Moscow to Yugoslavia, and for the next three years was fully occupied in re-establishing the underground network of the Party and in constituting reliable cadres of underground workers. These included by 1939 a number who had had military experience fighting with the International Brigade in Spain (Koča Popović and Veljko Vlahović amongst their number).

Meanwhile throughout Yugoslavia there was widespread disillusion with the whole experiment of centralised parliamentary democracy. It was easy to ignore its economic successes – and in the mid-1920s and mid-1930s these had been considerable. The Croats opposed it on a national basis as a disguise for Serb imperialism. Liberals opposed it as a mask for autocracy and brutal tyranny. The young generation of student intellectuals[5] in particular could see nothing good in it. Many of them turned for a model, as young intellectuals were turning throughout Western Europe, to the Soviet Union, which had some economic achievements to its credit and had not compromised its ideals so obviously as the Nazis or the Western powers; it was comparatively easy to turn a blind eye to the horrors half-revealed by the Moscow trials of 1937. There were thus present many of the pre-conditions necessary for a social revolution in Yugoslavia. Bishop Strossmayer, the Croat statesman of the nineteenth century who had tried to gain equal status for Croatia with Hungary and to forge close links with Serbia, had foreseen that a European cataclysm would be necessary

---

[4] Tito's main troubles from 1937–9 were with the Croat communists, who formed a 'national' Party within the LCY, as did the Slovenes, and were unwilling to co-operate with non-communist opposition groups.

[5] Koča Popović, Milovan Djilas and Svetozar Vukmanović among them, to mention three who became famous after 1945.

if any Yugoslav state was to be established, and any prescient analyst of the 1930s could have said that a second cataclysm would be necessary if Yugoslavia was to be fundamentally reformed. The catastrophe of 1939 was easier to foretell than that of 1914.

3

War

In the five years preceding the Second World War, Yugoslav foreign policy had undergone considerable changes, and although Yugoslavia was one of the 'succession states' created in 1918, it could no longer be counted on to support the European system created by the Versailles Treaty. Economic factors had become an essential determinant of Yugoslav foreign policy. The world economic slump which started in 1929 did not hit Yugoslavia until 1932, but was then acutely felt. So far as foreign trade was concerned, it was Germany which was the main instrument of Yugoslav recovery. As a result of the German–Yugoslav Commercial Treaty of 1934, Germany became the main outlet for Yugoslav agricultural produce. In March 1936 the process was hastened by new preferential arrangements in favour of Yugoslav grain and livestock exports. This was followed within three months by the conclusion of a large-scale barter agreement – Yugoslav agricultural products for German machinery on a long-term basis. Relations with Italy were improved by a treaty of friendship signed in March 1937, in spite of the encouragement so recently given by Mussolini's régime to Croatian terrorists; and a similar friendship treaty was signed early in 1937 with Bulgaria. There was no official abrogation of the original post-war foreign policy based on alliance with France, and on the 'Little Entente' with Czechoslovakia and Romania. But Germany was nearer and could offer more; it was obviously becoming stronger and more dynamic, while the Western democracies' will to oppose it was very much in doubt. The German occupation of Austria in March 1938 – followed by declarations that the German–Yugoslav frontier was inviolable – did not arouse official anxiety in Belgrade. But the occupation of Prague in March 1939, was a different matter. By the beginning of 1940 it had become clear that the danger from Nazi Germany could easily threaten Yugoslavia.

Official Yugoslav reaction involved re-insurance wherever this was possible – friendly words from the Yugoslav Foreign Minister in Italy and Hungary (still neutrals), the improvement of relations with

Bulgaria, and the restoration of trade relations between Yugoslavia and the Soviet Union, followed by the despatch of a military mission to Moscow and the restoration of full diplomatic relations (the Royal Yugoslav Government had hitherto displayed total intransigence towards Soviet Russia). The pro-Axis Prime Minister, Stojadinović, was interned in a remote country village in 1940. By the end of 1940 indeed the current of Yugoslav public opinion had moved strongly against the Axis powers. Italy's defeats by the Greeks after her invasion of Albania and by the British in Cyrenaica (October and December 1940) gave some hope of resistance to the Axis, and the Turkish Government proposed to Prince Paul the conclusion of a Turco-Yugoslav military agreement to block further advance southward by the Bulgarians under German inspiration.

Early in 1941 however Prince Paul found himself up against new and very strong pressure from Germany, particularly as plans for British military aid to Greece developed. He was well aware of the military weight which the Germans could bring to bear immediately on Yugoslavia. In February Hitler suggested that Yugoslavia as well as Bulgaria and Turkey, should join the Tripartite Pact between Germany, Italy and Japan. Bulgaria did so, on 1 March; immediately German troops entered Sofia where they were available for use against Yugoslavia as well as against Greece. British diplomatic counter-pressure was not effective against such a threat. Moreover Prince Paul had always been obsessed with the threat of Communism and feared that, if he refused Hitler's suggestion, the whole basis of his dictatorial régime would have to be altered in order to gain popular support in a national emergency. He attempted to compromise. On 24 March the Yugoslav Prime Minister, Cvetković, and Foreign Minister, Cincar-Marković, travelled to Vienna under instructions to sign the Tripartite Pact. On 26 March they did so, subject to reservations which released them from its military obligations.

The immediate result in Yugoslavia was an overwhelming political reaction against Prince Paul and Cvetković. A coup d'état on 27 March resulted in the exile of Prince Paul and the formation of something near to an all-Party government under General Simović. The coup was received with wild enthusiasm in Belgrade at least. It was welcomed publicly in London and Washington and more indirectly, but unmistakably, in Moscow. The Germans countered with a massive air attack and invasion on 6 April. Yugoslavia might, in Churchill's words, have 'found her soul'. She soon appeared to have lost her body.

2

Within two weeks the Yugoslav army was totally smashed, and the country partitioned. The northern half of Slovenia went to Germany, the southern (including Ljubljana) to Italy, which also annexed most of the Dalmatian coast and offshore islands, including Split and Kotor, and assumed military control of Montenegro, nominally independent. Albania, already annexed by Italy in 1939, was enlarged to include Western Macedonia and the Kosovo region. Bulgaria, from which the German army had launched its main attack by land, took the rest of Macedonia and parts of southern Serbia. Hungary was given the richest part of the Vojvodina (the Bačka province) and two northern districts of Croatia, the Medjumurje and the Prekomurje. The local German minority (the *Volksdeutsche*) took over the administration of the Banat, the other main district of the Vojvodina.

All that was left of Yugoslavia was a truncated Serbia, directly administered until August 1941 by the German military authorities, and an 'Independent State of Croatia' (NDH), including Bosnia and Hercegovina. This was meant to become a Kingdom under the Italian Duke of Spoleto, with the title, intended to recall Croatia's pre-medieval glories, of Tomislav II. The new monarch in fact preferred to remain outside his Kingdom, and it was administered by the Croat 'rebels' (Ustaše), under their leader (Poglavnik) Ante Pavelić, who had left Croatia in 1929 and had organised terrorist activity since 1934 under the protection of the Hungarians and Italians.

The NDH soon proved to be an embarrassment to the Axis. Most patriotic Croatians were more outraged by the loss of Dalmatia to the Italians than pleased by receiving Bosnia and Hercegovina in compensation for it, or by enjoying a nominal independence as a gift from the Axis powers. Many of them, including the senior representative of the Catholic Church, Archbishop Stepinac of Zagreb, as well as the German military commander there, were uneasy about the conduct of the Ustaša régime, which launched a campaign of appalling and mindless terrorism against Jews, in deference to Nazi and Fascist anti-Semitism, and against Orthodox Serbs, in the name of the Catholic Church and in revenge for the 'Serb Imperialism' of the inter-war years. It was Pavelić who took racist doctrines to these horrible conclusions and in the long term paved the way for a leader who could rid himself of any racial or confessional labels.

In Serbia, though there was no active resistance for some weeks after the Yugoslav capitulation in April, various nuclei were being formed from among the officers and men who had preferred to make for the hills, according to an old Serbian tradition, rather than to surrender their arms and bow to the German authorities. Of these groups, known generally as 'Chetniks',[1] the most important was that established in May 1941 by Colonel Draža Mihailović, a young officer of the Royal Yugoslav Army, in Ravna Gora, a high plateau in Western Serbia. His immediate aims were to contact other and similar groups, to establish good relations with the local government authorities and local population, and to prepare for armed action in Serbia, to be co-ordinated if possible with the plans of the Western allies and of the Yugoslav Government in exile.

Plans were being prepared simultaneously by the CPY under Josip Broz Tito. The CPY had of course followed the Soviet line about the 'Imperialist war' between 1939 and 1941 and had officially shared Soviet hopes that the Axis powers and the Western allies would exhaust each other, leaving the Soviet Union as the most powerful force in Eastern and Central Europe.[2] From the beginning of 1941 however it must have been plain to Tito that Yugoslavia could well be involved in a war, whatever the intentions of Prince Paul. And from mid-April, even without definite fore-knowledge of the Nazi attack on Russia, he could see that there might soon be new opportunities for activities by a Communist Party which had not been discredited by the politics of the inter-war years and could thus acquire a popular basis. Tito could not follow the official Moscow line of collaboration with the Axis powers without appearing to acquiesce in the dismemberment of Yugoslavia. There is no reason to doubt his own later statements that before 21 June 1941 he was making emergency plans for action by the CPY.

The Nazi attack on the Soviet Union however forced his hand. The Comintern instructed the CPY along with all other European Communist Parties not to 'stand idly by while the precious blood of the heroic people of Soviet Russia is being shed. Mobilise all your strength to prevent your country being turned into a base to supply the Fascist hordes. . .'

This meant in effect trying to organise a people's war, by stimulating the enthusiasm of the many Serbs who thought that the German army was marching in Russia to a doom as sure and (more important) as

[1] Or 'member of a band' (cheta), particularly of the irregular military formations which had operated in the past (and as late as 1913) against the Turkish forces.
[2] Acceptance of the Soviet line caused some difficulties within the CPY. Some Serbs and Croats found it hard to give up the 'popular front' line, and there was left-revolutionary separatist activity in Macedonia and the Kosmet.

swift as that which had overtaken Napoleon. It also meant immediately entering into either competition or co-operation with Mihailović, whose hand was also being forced by popular enthusiasm for the Russian cause.

Mihailović was a Serb patriot, a professional soldier and a social conservative. Tito was a Croat, but not bound by Croat national patriotism; he was essentially a social revolutionary, a professional organiser, and still a profound believer in the identity of Soviet national interests with those of world revolution. The contrast has often been drawn, but has to be restated. In it is implicit the whole tragedy of the Yugoslav civil war which took place within the framework of the World War between 1941 and 1945. Mihailović's position was at first sensible and logical from a Serb viewpoint. He had perhaps no very consistent or inclusive political philosophy. He was however loyal to the Yugoslav crown. He saw Serbia as the only part of Yugoslavia which had retained any kind of independence, and as the foundation of the second kingdom of Yugoslavia, if this were to be reconstituted after an Allied victory (if not, Serbia, suitably re-enlarged, might again do well enough as a small independent power). The essential thing for him was that the Serbian land and people should not be exposed for the second time in thirty years to devastation and decimation. He did not expect a speedy defeat of the German forces in Russia. Given the probable length of German occupation of Serbia and the probable measure of German ruthlessness, premature military action against the occupier would in Mihailović's view probably lead to heavy and unnecessary losses. It would be time enough for the Chetniks to organise major military action when Germany had been defeated by her major enemies.[3] His problem therefore, after the German invasion of Russia, was not to be led too far by popular enthusiasm for the Russian cause, and at the same time not to surrender the leadership of the Serbian and Yugoslav resistance movement or movements to more activist leaders. His Serbian base and specifically Serbian connection were of course local advantages, but could easily become a disadvantage within the context of Yugoslavia as a whole. His professional military status was again an advantage in the short term, but did not qualify him for a guerilla war. Nor did he possess the personal ruthlessness

---

[3] Mihailović's position was consistent with at least one Serb historical tradition – that of Miloš Obrenović, who worked against the Ottoman authorities by a mixture of diplomacy, corruption of their local rule, and occasional use of armed force, but did not want to risk the enormous casualties likely to be involved in an armed uprising, at least until the Ottoman power had been steadily weakened by Russian military and diplomatic pressure.

and magnetism which a national leader should possess in such turbulent times. The Chetnik leaders were a turbulent and disorderly crowd, with narrow political horizons, much resembling the Serbian chieftains who rose against the Turks in 1814. And Mihailović was no Karad-jordje to discipline and control them.

On the other side, Tito had less obvious possibilities of local support in Serbia, the only possible area of political or military action for him in summer 1941 – for the Ustaše in the NDH were more active in suppressing underground opposition than the German authorities in occupied Serbia. Against this he and his small dedicated nucleus of Communists had many advantages from the first. They had no in-hibitions stemming from any fear of 'Bolshevism', and no hesitation in exploiting popular enthusiasm for the Russian cause. Nor did they hesitate to exploit the fear of reprisals in order to win recruits for the 'Partisan' army.[4] Outside Serbia Tito had an advantage in that the CPY was a nation-wide organisation, and was by this time committed to the concept of a single Yugoslav state. This enabled him to recruit from other parts of the country without any suspicion of serving the ends of a Greater Serbia. Moreover his commitment to social revo-lution inspired the loyalty of those under-privileged peasants who formed the greater part of his recruits.

Tito also had the advantage of Mihailović in the quality of his immediate subordinates. He himself had done much in the past three years to streamline the small CPY and to ensure that the main organis-ing posts were held by competent people who were completely bound to him by the discipline of the Party. He reaped the fruits too of the work undertaken by himself in 1936, when he organised the despatch of Yugoslav volunteers to fight with the International Brigade in Spain. Some of these were killed, but some returned with valuable military experience which was fully utilised in the next four years. Above all Tito himself, now in his fiftieth year, had the military, political and conspiratorial experience, and the power of managing men, which were necessary for a Partisan leader. And while his intellectual horizons were bounded by his own Marxist beliefs, he had travelled widely in Europe and was much more an international man than Mihailović and the Chetnik leaders. It was these qualities which enabled him to pursue from the first a line of his own in Yugoslavia, to profit from his

[4] Again there is a striking parallel with conditions at the time of the Serb revolt in 1804. Then too most people did not fight till they had no other choice, and fear of indiscriminate reprisals was the best recruiting officer. Karadjordje made sure that the uprising against the Turks would be a 'people's war' by killing a few Turks and letting the Turkish policy of reprisals do the rest.

opponents' mistakes in evolving a Yugoslav policy, and, when opportunity came, to deal most effectively with his allies on the international plane.

3

There are two aspects of the combined international and civil wars in Yugoslavia from 1941 to 1945 which must be seen clearly, if the post-war history of Tito's Yugoslavia is to be properly understood – the Partisan line on the 'nationalities problem', discussed in the previous chapter, and Tito's dealings with the Western Allies and the Soviet Union.

By the end of July 1941 something like a general revolt had broken out in Serbia, which was beyond the control of Mihailović and owed little to Communist activity. In late August Tito moved his own head-quarters from Belgrade to Užice, the centre of a sizeable bloc of liberated land, bordering on Eastern Bosnia, and attempted to establish a basis for military co-operation with Mihailović and his Chetniks. This was in accordance with Moscow directives for a common front of anti-Fascist forces, and by mid-autumn the local need had become urgent in face of the threat of German counter-attack. Political differences and suspicions were however too great on either side, and differences between the Chetnik leaders made even temporary co-operation with the Partisans difficult. By the end of November Tito had to evacuate Užice and to make his way westwards into Bosnia, leaving the people of Serbia to face hideous reprisals from the Germans. From this time till 1944, Tito had little influence in Serbia, and the Chetniks' main object was to preserve their military strength without provoking further mass reprisals. With this in mind they often either co-operated with the Serb 'collaborationist' troops under General Nedić, or reached *ad hoc* agreements with them, whereby the Chetniks moved unhindered in the countryside and left the towns to the Germans or to Serb forces under German licence. Mihailović intended to turn against the Germans in due course and was heartily mistrusted by them; but from this time on at least until 1944 his troops seldom attacked the Germans. This policy might have worked if Serbia, from which the Partisans had withdrawn, could have been isolated from the rest of Yugoslavia. Its dangers outside Serbia were however soon illustrated by events in Montenegro during the second half of 1941. There Partisans and Chetniks had combined at first in opposition to a half-hearted Italian attempt to establish a separate Montenegrin state. The insurgents nearly succeeded in driving the Italians into the sea. But, typically of their race, the Montenegrin communists pursued an extremist policy contrary to the general line laid down by Moscow. From 1942 on, Chetniks and Italians fought together against them, and civil war on a nation-wide basis had effectively begun.

Tito had meanwhile established himself in Bosnia and was able to recruit a considerable force on a national rather than an anti-Serb or non-Serb basis. He was helped very much in this process by the atrocities of the Ustaše. The wholesale persecution and slaughter of Serbs in Croatia and Bosnia led most of those who wished to survive to seek Partisan protection and join the Partisan troops. The Ustaše in fact forced upon Tito the doctrine which he would probably have adopted anyhow – that Serbs, Croats and Moslems must sink their racial and social differences in fighting the Germans and Italians, and their Ustaše and Chetnik allies.[5] It was particularly important for Tito, in view of his retreat from Serbia in autumn 1941 and Mihailović's reputation as a Serb leader, that the Partisan forces now included so many Serbs from Croatia and Montenegrins.

Moscow directives and common sense alike urged Tito to emphasise the representative national nature of his forces. In autumn 1942 he advanced from south-eastern Bosnia into the heart of the NDH. After capturing Bihać he re-organised his army as the 'National Army of Liberation and the Partisan Detachments of Yugoslavia'. He also held in Bihać on 26 November a conference of representatives from other liberated areas and from areas under enemy occupation, not least Macedonia and Slovenia. In the former the population had generally turned against the Bulgarian occupiers and the Comintern now backed the Yugoslav rather than the Bulgarian Communist resistance;[6] while in Slovenia Partisans had survived a strong joint offensive by Italian and Yugoslav anti-Partisan troops, who claimed to be acting for Mihailović. The assembly at Bihać was formally named the Anti-Fascist Council for the National Liberation of Yugoslavia (AVNOJ).

In summoning it, Tito had two ends in view. He wished to demonstrate that he was a national leader, not merely the opponent of a Serbian resistance movement, and that he could offer a viable alternative to the Royal Government in exile. He also wished to prove, in accordance with the 'popular front' line, that his movement rested on

[5] It was however difficult for Tito at first to restrain some of his units in Bosnia from pursuing private 'national' feuds.
[6] In February 1940 a temporary regional committee of the CP had been formed in Macedonia, with Šatorov-Šarlo as secretary. Djilas and Tempo tried to reassert the authority of the CPY, but in May 1941 Šarlo called for Macedonian independence and moved his headquarters to Sofia.

a broad political base and was not exclusively concerned with promoting a communist revolution. The choice of Dr Ivan Ribar as President of the Assembly was significant. He himself had been speaker of the former Yugoslav Constituent Assembly. His son, Lola Ribar, was a brilliant young student leader, who had been killed in action with the Partisans. In accordance with the policy implied by this choice, the new Assembly recognised the national rights of Serbs, Croats, Slovenes and Macedonians;[7] it further guaranteed the right of private property and individual initiative in industry, trade and agriculture. There was no intention, it proclaimed, of introducing any 'radical changes whatsoever in the social life and activities of the people except for the replacement of reactionary village authorities. . .all the most important questions of social life and state organisation would be settled by the people themselves through representatives. . .properly elected by the people after the war.'

For most of the year following the Bihać meeting Tito and the Partisans were more concerned with survival than with plans for the political future of Yugoslavia. In February they just managed to escape in face of the enemy's 'Fourth Offensive' from eastern Bosnia over the Neretva river into Montenegro, heavily defeating organised detachments of Chetnik troops on the way. In May the 'Fifth Offensive' exposed them to even more desperate dangers, as they forced their way out of enemy encirclement across the Sutjeska gorge and back into south-eastern Bosnia. But this was the lowest point of their fortunes. From late summer 1943, after the surrender of Italy, Tito's army became a substantial military force, with access to supplies from the Western Allies and the Soviet Union. His military and diplomatic dealings with both were a crucial prelude to his final assumption of power in Yugoslavia.

4

Meanwhile the Soviet Government and the Western Allies (particularly the British) had been heavily committed to Mihailović, who for more than a year and a half had represented King Peter's exiled government in Yugoslavia. In the late summer of 1941, as Hitler's armies drove into Russia and there were no military successes to show in the Middle East, the British Government welcomed with particular

---

[7] In an article of December 1942, Tito stated clearly the principle of self-determination for the nations of Yugoslavia, and mentioned the possibility of secession, with the caution that this would be denied to 'enemies of the people'.

warmth any sign of resistance in German-occupied Europe. Radio links were established with Mihailović in September, and a British liaison officer reached his headquarters at Ravna Gora. The British could give no more than moral encouragement and the hope of arms supplies in the future, and the obvious limitations of their support confirmed Mihailović in the general strategy of preserving his strength until the course of the war in Europe as a whole offered more scope for military action. He provided intelligence to the Allies and undertook acts of sabotage against German communications. However the publicity given to the Chetniks on the world broadcasting services of the B.B.C. built him up into a symbol of major military resistance, and his position was formalised in January 1942 when the Royal Yugoslav Government in London appointed him as their Minister for the Yugoslav armed forces.

Although the Soviet Government appealed through the Comintern for active help from Tito's Communists, and had radio contact with them, they were also anxious not to discourage any other possible allies. They had little or no certain knowledge of how much loyalty was commanded by King Peter, or of what general support Mihailović could attract within Yugoslavia. They were not ready to trust Tito's estimates on these points. Mihailović might prove to be the man who could weaken the Germans most. In spring 1942 he had made his way to Montenegro, and accepted nominal links with the Chetniks there and in Western Croatia, though he had little control of the local commanders, who were soon to be drawn into joint action with the Axis forces against the Partisans. In August however the Soviet Government, who had already extended diplomatic recognition to the Royal Yugoslav Government in London, raised their mission to the rank of an Embassy. Even after Tito had made his first conspicuous bid (in November 1942) to present himself as a Yugoslav national leader, Stalin was not ready to break relations with Mihailović. The Germans too regarded him as still dangerous, in view of the threat which loomed in 1943 of an Anglo-American landing on the Adriatic coast.

The complexity of the situation in Yugoslavia at the time is revealed by Djilas' account (confirming German official documents) of abortive negotiations between the Partisans and the Germans in March 1943. An exchange of prisoners was effected, but much wider possibilities were discussed or adumbrated, to the indignation of the Russians who were informed in advance. These involved a concentration of Partisan military effort against the Chetniks and, so far as necessary, the Italians, a cessation of hostilities between the Germans and the Partisans, and the promise of action by Partisans against any landing by the British and Americans who would, they thought, inevitably support Mihailović. The first step in this general direction was taken when the Slavonian Partisans ceased sabotage of communications between Zagreb and Belgrade, but Hitler vetoed any further steps on the German side, and soon the 'Fifth Offensive' was launched against Tito.

The crucial switch in Allied support from Mihailović to Tito took place gradually between spring and autumn 1943. For some months before doubts had been growing in Cairo and London, based on intercepted radio communications, about the relative value to the Allied cause of the two movements. British liaison officers were sent to Mihailović's headquarters. They found him still reluctant to act on a large scale against the Germans, and their own pressure for action was much resented, in the continued absence of military support and supplies. On the other side Captain Deakin,[8] who reached Tito's headquarters in Montenegro in late May 1943, saw plenty of fighting and was immediately involved in the 'Fifth Offensive' and the break-out over the Sutjeska.

Meanwhile the Yugoslav government in London commanded less and less confidence from the British. The Serb and Croat politicians in Professor Jovanović's cabinet were locked, it seemed, in perpetual disagreement. King Peter himself was determined on a marriage which his advisers regarded as untimely. By August 1943 the Yugoslav government consisted of civil servants only and, though Mihailović remained a cabinet minister, it appeared to have little connection or even concern with the main current events in Yugoslavia itself. The British Foreign Office was impatient and in summer 1943 the B.B.C. began to withdraw moral support from Mihailović. His position deteriorated rapidly. The Partisans profited far more than he from the Italian surrender, acquiring large amounts of equipment, and strengthening their position against the Chetniks in Slovenia and Montenegro. In September 1943 a full-scale military mission was sent to Tito's headquarters under Brigadier Maclean,[9] and military supplies for the Partisans were organised on an increasingly large scale.

In November 1943 Tito took some crucial steps towards establishing himself as the head of a national government for Yugoslavia. At the second AVNOJ Congress, held in Jajce, the Anti-Fascist Council was transformed into a Presidium of 67 members, representing the nations of Yugoslavia and some of the pre-war political groups. The Presidium

[8] Now Sir William Deakin.
[9] Now Sir Fitzroy Maclean.

assumed some legislative and administrative functions, while its Executive Committee, known as the Council of National Liberation, emerged as something like a provisional government, with Tito, promoted to the rank of Marshal of Yugoslavia, as Premier. It was announced that Yugoslavia would be reconstituted on a federal basis, and would include some of the territory held before the war by Italy.

The question of King and Monarchy will be settled by the people of its own will after the liberation of the whole country.

This was a declaration of independence, even if it was tempered by clauses designed to prove Tito's moderation. He had in fact already communicated to the Allied Foreign Ministers the 'determination of the Yugoslav people' never to let King Peter return, and the claim of AVNOJ to be the only legitimate authority in Yugoslavia. The Russians, anxious for their relations with the Western Allies, were angry with Tito for having gone so far at Jajce without formally consulting them. The British and Americans in fact took Tito's action fairly calmly, and at the Summit Meeting in Teheran early in December 1943 Churchill, Roosevelt and Stalin agreed to give Tito all possible help. In February 1944, the Russians eventually sent a military mission to his headquarters, but the execution of the Teheran decision was at first mainly in British hands. Military, technical and medical contacts between the British and the Partisans were close and often cordial. When in May 1944 German parachute troops descended on Tito's headquarters at Drvar, he based himself for a time on the island of Viš under British protection.

The Soviet Government remained in contact with the Yugoslav Government in exile, and Mihailović tried to counter the AVNOJ meeting at Jajce with a congress of Serbian, Croatian and Slovenian delegates at Ba in Western Serbia (January 1944). His star however was setting. In March Stanoje Simić, the Royal Yugoslav Ambassador in Moscow, declared his adherence to AVNOJ, and in spring 1944 the British Government brought pressure to bear on the Yugoslav Government in London to make their peace so far as possible with Tito. In June King Peter asked Dr Ivan Šubašić, a former Governor of Croatia, to form a new government which might co-operate and ultimately merge with Tito's National Liberation Committee. The King himself agreed not to return to Yugoslavia after the war until a plebiscite was held, and on 12 September urged the Yugoslav people in a broadcast to rally to the Partisan forces. Churchill felt a moral obligation to King Peter, but brought strong pressure to bear on him over the Šubašić appointment. It is hard to say how deeply Churchill and the British Cabinet believed in the possibilities of post-war co-operation between Tito and the King or his exiled representatives. Less evidence was available then than now about the extreme unlikelihood of a convinced Communist agreeing to such co-operation on an equal basis. But there was no illusion that Tito had been converted to liberal democracy. In the circumstances of summer 1944 the task for Churchill was to find an apparently decent way of reconciling former political loyalties with the military realities of the time.

Tito's allegiance to Communist doctrines was of course unswerving. By the summer of 1944 moreover Soviet Russia was well on the way to military dominance in Eastern Europe. Prudence alone would have made it necessary for Tito to reinforce his links with the Soviet Government, and in renewing his personal links with the Russians he was also obeying the dictates of his heart. The Soviet armies reached the eastern borders of Serbia on 7 September 1944. On 21 September Tito, without informing the British, flew to Moscow to conclude an agreement for joint Soviet–Yugoslav military action on Yugoslav territory. The entry of Soviet troops into Serbia on 28 September in overwhelming numbers was the beginning of the end of the war in Yugoslavia.

The same event showed up the fatal flaw in Mihailović's long-term calculations. He had rendered perhaps his most valuable services to the Western Allies as late as August/September 1944, when his Chetniks helped an American liaison team to evacuate hundreds of Allied – mainly American – airmen whose aircraft had been shot down during operations over South-Eastern Europe. Many of the American liaison officers for the area were less favourable than the British to Tito and the Partisans, and Mihailović hoped to the last that the Allies might still keep the ring clear for a final choice by the Serb people between Tito's and his own movement.

He had submitted plans to the Western Allies for keeping Chetnik and Partisan forces separate, and giving them specified military tasks under Allied command. Nothing came of these, and on 1 September Mihailović ordered a general mobilisation in Serbia, hoping that his forces would be able to co-operate militarily with the Russians before the main force of the Partisans arrived in Serbia. There was indeed occasional joint action by the Red Army and the Chetniks. But the Partisans soon made their presence felt and the general pattern in October was that Soviet troops joined with them in suppressing Chetnik organisations as well as in pursuing the retreating Germans, large numbers of whom withdrew in good order to form a new front against the Soviet army west of Belgrade and later on the Hungarian border. Tito's troops entered Belgrade on 20 October 1944. Neither the war against the Germans nor the Yugoslav civil war had ended. But this was the date on which it may be said that Tito's Yugoslavia was born.

4

In the Soviet camp

From the first Tito was careful to guard against the charge that he had only come to power as a result of the Soviet offensive and that his administration was dependent on the Red Army. Under agreements concluded between him and the Soviet Commander, Marshal Tolbukhin, the Partisan troops were the first to enter Belgrade, the Yugoslavs administered their own territory from the moment of its liberation, and Soviet troops stayed in Yugoslavia only for such time as was needed to pursue into Hungary and Austria their offensive against the retreating German armies. Such arrangements gave Tito and his lieutenants a sense of considerable superiority over, for example, the Romanians and Bulgarians, whose armies, as the Yugoslavs could say, had simply fought against the Germans on directive from Moscow.

It was thus from a position of great political strength that Tito concluded early in November a draft political agreement with Dr Šubašić, who had returned to Yugoslavia from England before the capture of Belgrade as a representative of the Royal Yugoslav Government to negotiate with the Communist authorities. It was agreed that the Anti-Fascist Council formed in 1943 should continue to be the nucleus of a provisional Parliament. Certain members of the Royal Yugoslav Government were to be included in the National Council which exercised executive authority. In due course elections should be held to a Constituent Assembly which would decide on the future form of the government in Yugoslavia, including the question whether the monarchy should or should not continue. This was in accordance with the lines of discussion held three months earlier between Tito and Churchill in Italy. The Soviet as well as the British Government approved the draft Tito–Šubašić agreement. King Peter proved more difficult to persuade, and negotiations between him and Tito dragged on until early in 1945. Then on 18 January Churchill made it clear in the House of Commons that

if we are so unfortunate as not to obtain the consent of King Peter, the matter [the Yugoslav constitutional agreement] will have to go ahead, his assent being presumed.

In February 1945 the 'Big Four' met at Yalta. They agreed on a declaration of democratic principles to be applied in Eastern Europe. They also urged Tito and Šubašić to conclude an agreement, along the lines of the November draft, as soon as possible. This recommendation was not at all welcome to many leading Yugoslav communists; but Tito himself was clearly aware that, whatever general principles and detailed interim agreements were laid down, he would be left with effective power. He knew that Stalin agreed with him on this.[1] The British and American governments may still have placed some hopes on the general principles agreed at Yalta, but had many more immediate and pressing concerns than the question how these would be applied. As Churchill had said in the speech quoted above:

We have no special interest in the political regime which prevails in Yugoslavia. Few people in Britain, I imagine, are going to be more cheerful or more downcast because of the future constitution of Yugoslavia.[2]

This confirmed Tito in the view that the whole constitutional process was little more than a convenient cloak, so far as the Western powers were concerned, for the Communist take-over. And so in March 1945 the last stage of the process was initiated. Three Regents were sworn in. Dr Šubašić's government resigned. Tito announced on 7 March that he had formed a new united Government, including Dr Šubašić as Minister of Foreign Affairs and six other members of the former Royal Government. The new Government was immediately recognised by the British, American and Soviet Governments; and power on the spot was exercised as before by the Politburo of the CC, CPY.

2

Meanwhile the war had continued. The Red Army had crossed the Hungarian border in November 1944. Their short passage through Yugoslavia had been militarily very valuable, politically much less so.

[1] Stalin had urged him in September 1944 to let King Peter return to Yugoslavia and knife him in due course.
[2] In *Eastern Approaches* (pp. 402–3) Sir Fitzroy Maclean recorded Churchill's more informal expression of this view in a conversation between them: ' "Do you intend", he asked, "to make Yugoslavia your home after the war?" "No, Sir," I replied. "Neither do I", he said. "And, that being so, the less you and I worry about the form of Government they set up, the better." ' Sir Fitzroy now has a house in Korčula, off the Dalmatian coast.

The Soviet troops had too often behaved as conquerors, not as allies. Stalin, it used to be said in 1945, had made two basic mistakes. He had let the Red Army see Europe; and he had let Europe see the Red Army. Left militarily to themselves, the Yugoslav forces at first made slow progress in set battles of a type new to them. Their offensive against the German and 'Quisling' forces in the Srem plain, Slavonia, and northern Bosnia were held up in bitter fighting. Indeed from January to March 1945 the Germans launched a number of counter-offensives to cover their general retreat. The last six months of the war alone cost the Partisan forces 30,000 dead and 70,000 wounded. To many Serbs the course of events served as a justification for Mihailović's policy of waiting and conserving the human substance of the nation. There was bitter feeling that the Serb people were being bled dry in operations which at such a late stage of the war seemed to them unnecessary and ill-organised.

Finally in April and May 1945 the Partisan forces broke through the enemy fronts in Bosnia, Croatia and Slovenia. The element of savage civil war remained to the end, and captives were ruthlessly executed (as no doubt the Communists would have been, had they been defeated). The Partisans captured Zagreb on 8 May and pursued the German and 'Quisling' forces over the Yugoslav borders, occupying Klagenfurt and Villach in Carinthia to the north[3] and entering Trieste to the south. Here they came up against Western forces in a confrontation which had important political consequences. Trieste had been ceded to Italy in 1919. The city itself and the villages along the coast on either side were largely inhabited by Italians. Slavs however formed a majority of the population of the mountainous hinterland, and there was a considerable minority of them in Trieste itself. Acquisition of the Italian-held coast, including Trieste, was a cardinal aim of Yugoslav policy as outlined at the AVNOJ Congress in November 1943. The Partisans gained control by May of most of the surrounding coastal district (the Primorje) and were fighting in Trieste itself when New Zealand troops entered it on 3 May to accept the German surrender. For over a month, Yugoslav troops occupied part of the city and set up a civilian administration. It was only in mid-June, under strong pressure from the British and Americans, which evoked insufficient counter-pressure from the Russians, that Tito consented to

---

[3] Up to 20,000 'Yugoslav Quisling' troops had surrendered to British and American troops, and were interned at this time in Austria. Some of these were repatriated by the Allies and executed by the Partisans, but such repatriations were soon halted.

withdraw his forces.[4] Under the arrangements then agreed the Anglo-American forces administered the city of Trieste and a small and narrow strip of territory to the north-west of it (Zone A), while the Yugoslavs retained possession of a large area (Zone B) to which they had laid claim south and east of the city. These arrangements were accepted by the Russians. They were nominally to remain in force until the inhabitants of both zones could make their views known in a plebiscite.

Immediately, the fact that Yugoslavia had been forced to acquiesce in a settlement of the Trieste issue falling far short of their hopes embittered the Yugoslav leaders against the Western powers, and reinforced their determination to back the Soviet Union whole-heartedly on major foreign policy issues. However they began to learn something at this time about the limits of Soviet diplomatic support. This would not extend to issues which to Stalin did not appear to justify a major quarrel with the Western powers. There was a second instance of this principle in summer 1945, when Soviet forces ordered the withdrawal of those Partisan units which had penetrated the Soviet zone of Austria, and did nothing to prevent the Western powers from taking similar action.

Even without active Soviet support, or perhaps precisely because they lacked it, the new Yugoslav government showed themselves extremely sensitive to what they regarded as provocations on their western borders. They were reluctant to accept the fact that large numbers of Yugoslavs who were outside their country at the end of the war (and not only those who had served with anti-Partisan forces) were unwilling to return. They suspected the Western powers of building up an anti-communist force from among them. U.S.–Yugoslav relations in particular reached their nadir when in August 1946 the Yugoslavs shot down two American aircraft which had overflown Yugoslav territory by mistake on their way between Italy and Austria.

Meanwhile they could at least assume that Soviet support would be forthcoming on points which did not involve the danger of confrontation with the Western powers. In Albania, the Yugoslav Communist Party had assumed a protective role over the Albanian party during

---

[4] General Alexander claimed that their presence in Trieste was contrary to an understanding previously reached between himself and Tito. The latter may however have been aware of the assurances given to the Royal Yugoslav Ambassador in London, after the Teheran Conference, that Yugoslavia's 'full territorial integrity' would be restored after the war, and her Western frontiers and claims against Italy settled 'bearing in mind the proposal put forward by President Wilson in 1919 on self-determination'.

the war, with full Comintern approval. After the war, the 'big brother' relationship was continued without much regard to Albanian pride. The Albanian army, economic administration and Party were controlled by men who were either nominated by the CPY or notoriously acceptable to it. Joint Yugoslav–Albanian companies for the development of Albania's resources were established in 1945–6, in accordance with Soviet practice, and in November 1946 a commercial treaty was signed which linked the Albanian economy very closely with that of Yugoslavia.

The case of Bulgaria was more delicate, involving as it did the debatable issue of Macedonian allegiance. The possibility of some kind of Yugoslav–Bulgarian federation had been discussed during the war between Tito and Dimitrov. Stalin had encouraged Kardelj to go ahead with federal plans in November 1944 and there were discussions about these early in 1945 between the Yugoslavs, the Bulgarians and the Russians. The Yugoslavs wanted to see the Bulgarian part of Macedonia (Pirin) joined to the existing Macedonian Republic, which was one of the six constituent parts of Yugoslavia. A Bulgarian Republic would then join the new Federation as a seventh unit, on the same footing as the other six. Most Bulgarians wished to retain Pirin Macedonia and to federate with Yugoslavia as a whole on equal terms. Stalin veered between the two views, and finally encouraged a non-committal policy. There was to be economic, military and political co-operation between Yugoslavia and Bulgaria. In July 1947 Tito and Dimitrov, for the Bulgarians, agreed to work by means of closer economic co-operation towards a customs union, probably as a step towards federation. The agreement was approved by the Russians and embodied in a Yugoslav–Bulgarian Treaty of Friendship, Co-operation and Assistance signed in November 1947, again without open reference to federation.[5]

The problem of the new Yugoslavia's relations with Greece was more closely linked with the development of the cold war in Europe, and thus even more liable to cause trouble between Yugoslavia and the Soviet Union. In late autumn 1944 the Greek Communists had tried and failed to seize power. They had enjoyed Yugoslav sympathy and attracted Yugoslav interest, but no more. Towards the end of 1945 Greek Communist leaders met with Yugoslav and Bulgarian representatives in Bulgaria. It was agreed that they should launch a new

[5] At the beginning of 1945 the Western powers were against any form of Balkan federation, and Stalin was not ready to encourage it openly; this was probably still the case. But at least until November 1947 the Yugoslavs were helping the Bulgarians to 'Macedonianise' Pirin, which the CP Bulgaria had agreed in August 1946 to be a necessary preliminary to federation.

rising and should enjoy substantial facilities from the Yugoslav side; a strong military mission was sent to northern Greece under an experienced general, Peko Dapčević, and substantial amounts of arms and ammunition were supplied.[6] Yugoslav aid was increased throughout 1946 and 1947, and was formalised in an agreement concluded at Bled in August 1947 between Yugoslav, Bulgarian and Albanian representatives, under which a Joint Balkan Staff was formed to help the Greek guerillas.

How far the Soviet Government was itself involved in the action of Greece's northern neighbours is uncertain. The safest conclusion is that Stalin preferred an indirect role in an area where the U.S. and British, to judge by the precedent of 1944, might react sharply. For a time he encouraged the maximum support to the Greek guerillas by the Yugoslavs, Bulgarians and Albanians; but after the formulation of the 'Truman doctrine' in March 1947, under which United States' support was pledged to Greece, he became more cautious. At the end of 1947 the Soviet Government was unwilling to recognise General Markos' newly-proclaimed 'Provisional Democratic Government of Greece'. The Yugoslav, Bulgarian and Albanian Governments were by this time equally prudent. However on general issues of foreign policy Tito had by then fully earned a reputation in the West for being an aggressively loyal supporter of the Soviet line. At the U.N. for example the Yugoslavs backed the Soviet representatives actively on disarmament issues, and in summer 1947 they denounced the Marshall Plan for the economic reconstruction of Europe as bitterly as Stalin could have wished.

3

In their domestic no less than in their foreign policy, the Yugoslav leaders were fully committed intellectually and emotionally to the communist cause and the Soviet model. Their immediate need of supplies for relief and reconstruction could indeed only be met by UNRRA (the United Nations Relief and Rehabilitation Administration), which was financed to a very large extent by American funds. It started operations in winter 1944–5 and there were initial difficulties about how far it should be allowed to work through its own staff. However it was soon agreed that it should operate only through the local 'People's Committees' which had been set up throughout Yugoslavia as the Partisans took over control. The extent of UNRRA aid,

[6] During 1946 the Yugoslavs were also pressing for the detachment of 'Aegean Macedonia' from Greece, but in summer 1947 they ceased to do so.

particularly in food, farm stock and seeds, medical supplies and transport equipment, was recognised and appreciated officially – it amounted
by the end of 1946 (when its operations ceased) to $425 million. But
this was regarded, in the words of Vlado Dedijer, 'not only as a
humanitarian gesture but also as a tribute by all nations who had
fought against Nazism, paid to the bravery and sufferings of Yugoslavia' – the payment of a blood debt rather than a claim in Yugoslav
gratitude – and there were bitter official complaints when the U.S.
brought the programme to an end.

Meanwhile the new Yugoslavia took shape as a highly centralised
one-party state. The centre of political power in 1945 was the Politburo
of the CPY. Its main instruments were the army and the CPY itself,
operating largely through the local 'people's committees'. A strong
central machine was in fact necessary to preserve order, to safeguard
supplies and to operate a rationing system. From April 1945 on the
effective government of Yugoslavia also took the measures necessary
to break the remaining strength of the former middle class. Currency
reform, confiscation of the property of former collaborators (a widely
extensible category), the nationalisation of most existing industry, and
the strict control of rents were all put into force. The implicit assumption behind this policy, probably held with deep conviction, was that
the Yugoslav civil war was not over. The 'bourgeoisie' would easily
revive, and would receive backing from the Western powers. 'The
most dangerous thing for us now', as Tito said to Dedijer, 'would be to
stop half-way'.

The Yugoslav revolution was not simply imposed from above.
Popular backing was necessary if Tito's ambitious plans were to be
accomplished, and there was plenty of genuine enthusiasm, particularly among the younger generation, for reconstruction and for a
new political and economic system. The main support for a general
reconstruction programme on communist lines was mobilised by the
People's Front, formed in August 1945, an 'umbrella organisation' in
which those non-communist parties which still existed would collabor-
ate with the Communists. It organised a single list of candidates for the
elections held on 11 November 1945 for a new Assembly, and made
sure that the elections achieved the right result. In fact there were no
effective non-communist candidates; in face of the constraints put
upon them, members of the pre-war political parties had resigned from
the Provisional Government and did not try to stand for election.
About 90% of the electorate voted for the official candidates. In
comparison with the total electoral mobilisation later achieved by

single-party Communist Governments the opposition figures were large,[7] particularly when it is remembered that the number of those disfranchised under the electoral law of summer 1945 was considerable. In Serbia especially there was widespread opposition to Tito and backing for King Peter; but elsewhere Tito was a genuinely popular national leader. He had fought his own war and won his own victories; he had attracted a large number of peasants, impoverished during the interwar years, to the Partisan movement; he had achieved a new relationship between the nationalities of Yugoslavia.

The body which first met on 29 November 1945 was primarily a Constituent Assembly but continued as a parliament after it had duly abolished the Yugoslav monarchy and discharged its constitutional tasks. The elections had been for a Federal Council, with members chosen for constituencies throughout the country on a population basis (one for every 40,000 voters) and a Council of Nationalities – a sort of Senate in which the constituent nations of Yugoslavia were evenly represented, with 25 members each for the Republics of Serbia, Croatia, Slovenia, Montenegro, Bosnia-Hercegovina and Macedonia, and fifteen each for the 'autonomous regions' of Vojvodina and the Kosmet. The new Yugoslavia thus took form as a Federal Republic, bound together by a unitary Communist Party.

The Federal system was confirmed by the new Constitution of 31 January 1946. This was based largely on the 1936 constitution of the Soviet Union and had an ill-omened resemblance to it in the general freedoms laid down (of religion, speech, association and assembly). It also provided for a highly centralised type of State Socialism, placing the means of production and foreign trade in the hands of the State and restricting both the ownership and the inheritance of private property, though the principle was laid down that land should belong to those who cultivated it. Powers were divided between the central government and those of the constituent Republics by specifying the responsibilities of the former – finance, economic planning, foreign policy, defence, communications and law. It seemed however that, in face of the Party activity, the federal principle in Yugoslavia would be no further operative than it had been in the Soviet Union. The Republican units had been equated in size by detaching from Serbia the new Macedonian Republic, and the two new 'autonomous regions' – the Kosmet, once the heart of medieval Serbia, and

[7] Not however in comparison with other East European states at the time, where other parties existed; in Hungary indeed the Communists in 1946 polled only 17% of the total vote.

the Vojvodina, the centre of the Serb population of the Austro-Hungarian Empire. Between the new units there was at first 'brotherhood and unity' in the sense that they were all equally powerless vis-à-vis an energetic and highly centralised Party leadership.[8] More positively (and this was important) there was some balance within the Politburo, where Tito's chief lieutenants were chosen roughly in accordance with the principle of nationality – Tito was himself a Croat, Kardelj a Slovene, Djilas a Montenegrin, and Ranković a Serb.

4

The principal aim of the new Government was no less than the total and rapid mobilisation and reconstruction of Yugoslavia, and it needed a completely secure political base. The Western powers were assumed to be bitterly hostile, and Tito's direct dealings with them were unlikely to make them less so. They, or King Peter in their name, could conceivably use against the new régime those 300,000 Yugoslavs who remained outside Yugoslavia in 1945–6. Tito regarded it as essential to ensure that there was no potential fifth column within his borders.

In the months following the Red Army's entry into Serbia the Chetnik forces had ceased to exist as an organised body. Some had joined the Partisans, some had attached themselves to the German forces or subsidiary formations retreating north and west; only a very few had accompanied Mihailović on his flight into Bosnia and back to a Serbian hide-out, near Višegrad. Early in 1946 he was a sick man, almost completely deserted by his followers. But while he remained at large he could still act as a focus for the opponents of Tito's régime in Serbia. Tito therefore judged it vital to capture him and to have him finally discredited and executed. In March 1946 Mihailović was captured. To blacken him by association, he was indicted along with members of the former Royal Yugoslav Government (tried *in absentia*) and with some notorious members of the collaborationist Serbian régime of General Nedić. The joint trial opened on 10 June and continued for over a month. Mihailović was sentenced to death on 15 July, and executed on 17 July.

The main effect of the trial was in *terrorem*. The Communist Party displayed the ruthlessness which would have been shown towards them if they had been defeated. It was a case, in Lenin's words of 'kto kovo?' – 'who comes out on top?' The verdict and execution were

[8] The Serb Republican CP was only created in 1945, and those of Montenegro and Bosnia-Hercegovina in 1948–9.

probably taken for granted in Yugoslavia as a whole. It is doubtful whether any Serbs who believed in Mihailović's cause were converted by the trial; his own bearing, his speech in his own defence, and the courageous fight put up by his counsel, Dr Joksimović, were all impressive. In Yugoslavia as elsewhere, Mihailović gave the appearance, not of a traitor, but of a man acting according to his lights and overwhelmed by events – 'carried away by the gale of the world', as he put it himself. Many of his former Serb followers regarded him as a martyr. In the West and particularly in Britain and the U.S.A., the conduct of the trial (however much free speech had been allowed at it) inspired a sense of bitterness and some guilt that we ourselves had helped to betray a brave man to unscrupulous enemies. The tribunal refused to admit evidence in Mihailović's favour from any of the British officers who had served with him, and Tito described the verdict as a victory over 'international reaction'. Other Yugoslav leaders dwelt in detail on the original support given to Mihailović by London (particularly the B.B.C.) without a word about subsequent British aid to the Partisans. Here was further evidence for the West that Tito was firmly attached to the 'Socialist camp', and paid no attention to the sensibilities of his former allies in the West.

The trial of Mihailović was followed at the end of September 1946 by a similar exemplary trial, that of Archbishop Stepinac of Zagreb, designed to settle accounts publicly between Tito's régime and the Catholic Church. The new constitution of 1946 guaranteed freedom of conscience and religion to all citizens, and allowed freedom for religious communities to engage in strictly religious activities, e.g. to run schools for the training of priests. But religion was not to be used as a cloak for political ends, and this was interpreted by the Communist Party as covering not only the formation of 'Christian' political parties but also the institution of Church schools with a general educational programme.

The majority of the population was Orthodox (nearly 50%, according to the 1948 census); but the Orthodox Church had accustomed itself during centuries of Turkish occupation to taking a very long view of its own interests and to living in peace or at least at truce with the political authorities,[9] and represented a less immediate threat. While only 36.7% of the total Yugoslav population were Roman Catholics, the concentration in Croatia and Slovenia was far higher. The

[9] Patriarch Gavrilo, who had been deported by the Germans to a concentration camp, used his authority on returning to Yugoslavia to enact a new Statute (June 1947) separating the Orthodox Church from the new Yugoslav State.

Catholic authorities were politically more active than the Orthodox hierarchy, and were responsible to an authority outside the country.

Tito was aware that the Roman Catholic Church could be a formidable opponent and in summer 1945 he offered a measure of conciliation to the Archbishop of Zagreb, Aloysius Stepinac. By autumn 1945 however Stepinac was speaking and writing freely against Communist electoral tactics and the programme of the People's Front, and Tito's régime had begun to take severe measures against the Catholic Church in Croatia. Under the Land Reform Act, Church lands totalling about 25,000 hectares in Croatia and Slovenia were nationalised. There were further protests from the Church and further Party propaganda and discrimination against the Church's educational activities and against individual church-goers. Archbishop Stepinac made his views about the Party's activities quite clear in sermons and pastoral lectures. Tito first tried through the Papal Nuncio in Belgrade to have him replaced. He met with a firm refusal from the Vatican and determined at this stage on a show-down. Stepinac was arrested on 30 September 1946 and charged with collaborating with the enemy during the war, and with resisting the Communist Government of Yugoslavia. There was no doubt that too many Catholic clergy, including Archbishop Šarić of Sarajevo, had shown far too much sympathy with the Ustaša régime during the war, and had condoned or turned a blind eye to their atrocities. Stepinac was tried jointly with an undoubted Ustaša criminal, to give added point to the charges against him.

There was a strong *prima facie* case for Stepinac to answer. But, as in the case of Mihailović, he made a powerful and obviously sincere defence of his conduct during and since the war, both in his own speeches and through his defence counsel.[10] Stepinac was moreover able to counter-attack effectively on the matter of Communist oppression of the Roman Catholic Church since the end of the war. He was of course found guilty and sentenced to sixteen years imprisonment. Again Tito had shown himself ready to deal firmly with a potential leader of opposition. But he had given Stepinac as well as Mihailović the chance of stating a full and powerful case. He had provided something like a martyr for Croat Catholics, and had shown total unconcern about governmental opinion in the West and about the views of that world-wide institution, the Roman Catholic Church.

For some time the CPY tried to avoid a similar clash with the

[10] This was the same man who in 1928 had made a courageous case at a Yugoslav royal tribunal for Tito, then Secretary of the Zagreb branch of the Yugoslav Communist Party.

Moslem religious community (IVZ), though many of its leaders could have been charged with collaboration during the war. By 1947 however anti-Communist feeling had grown among the IVZ. The CPY cut off state financial support and made it impossible for Moslems to keep their organisation going on a voluntary basis. In August 1947 the IVZ capitulated and exchanged any possibility of political autonomy for the renewal of state financial support.

Thus by autumn 1947 Tito had put an effective curb on the main religious organisations of Yugoslavia, and had taken, as it seemed, considerable long-term political risks in order to secure an immediate strengthening of his political authority.

5

At the same time Tito had embarked on agricultural policies which were fraught with the most serious economic and political consequences. Large-scale action was highly necessary in 1945. Even apart from the enormous devastation and loss of life caused by the war, there was great need for a new land policy in Yugoslavia. In 1941 nearly three-quarters of the approximately $2\frac{1}{2}$ million peasant holdings comprised less than 5 hectares. Agricultural machinery was at best primitive for the majority of land-holding peasants and often non-existent. Many of them were in debt and in effect worked for their creditors. There were about 3 million former peasants who had not found permanent employment away from the villages, and a large number of landless peasants, particularly in the Vojvodina. Emigration had been the main solution for their difficulties. It did not need a communist régime to determine on a transformation of Yugoslav agriculture.

The first steps in the Land Reform policy, as laid down in the Act of 23 August 1945, were welcome to a majority of the population. About 1.6 million hectares of land were expropriated from individuals or institutions or requisitioned from collaborators and *Volksdeutsche*. Roughly a quarter of this total consisted of forest, taken over by the State, and another quarter was also retained by the State for development, mainly as State farms. The remaining 800,000 hectares was redistributed, one half of it to over 250,000 families of peasants who were landless or farmed holdings below subsistence level, and the other half to families from the poorest regions of Yugoslavia (mainly Bosnia and Montenegro) who were resettled in the Vojvodina and the Sava valley.

So far so good. Nor was there widespread objection to the limitation of private holdings under the Land Reform Act of August 1945 to a minimum of 20 and a maximum of 35 hectares (most peasant holders had farmed less than the minimum). The further agricultural policies of the new Government however involved compulsory purchase of 80% of agricultural produce at fixed and low prices (the 'Otkup'). This was very unpopular particularly among the peasants of Serbia. So was the policy of collectivisation, even if this was initially on a small scale.[11] The pooling of doubtfully viable smallholdings into large co-operative farms could have been to the advantage of many peasants; but they resisted it as an attempt to deprive them of their property, even though at a time of general food shortage not even the most doctrinaire proponents of collectivisation were prepared to push it very fast or far.

Government policies were resisted from the first by the peasantry in spite of all the pressure which was exerted against them by withholding supplies, seizing property and arresting its owners. The strength of the peasants' position was that they were the only ones who could grow the food necessary for the country as a whole. For two years moreover the Serb peasants had a political spokesman, Dragoljub Jovanović, former leader of the Serb Peasant Party, who had been elected to the Presidium of the new National Assembly in 1945. From 1946 on-wards, in spite of attacks in the official press and the use of physical violence against his person, he continued courageously to criticise the Government's economic policies in the Assembly. In May 1947 he was arrested and put on trial in October. Here he defended himself vigorously, while the prosecution accused him of being a tool of the British Secret Service which was allegedly trying to organise a Serbian 'peasant bloc' in opposition to the régime. Tito's régime seemed to be following all too faithfully the Soviet pattern of sweeping and over-hasty solutions, the failure of which was blamed on sinister extreme forces who inspired sabotage within the country.

6

Tito's agricultural policy was one essential part of his general strategy for the economic reconstruction of Yugoslavia into a state which should also develop its own heavy industries, and thus not only become self-sufficient but also (a cardinal point of communist doctrine) acquire a

[11] It started with the establishment of 72 co-operatives covering about 50,000 hectares. By the end of 1946 there were 454 collective farms covering 121,000 hectares. Collectivisation took various forms, which are detailed in Chapter 6.

new caste of industrial and 'politically conscious' workers. The necessary labour force even for the limited number of factories working in 1945–6 could only be provided by mechanising agriculture and inducing a rapid flow of young men from the villages to the industrial centres. Agricultural overpopulation would eventually work to this end, but at a time of food shortage large numbers preferred to remain on the land. Hence the apparent necessity for collectivisation. Moreover the building of new factories required heavy State investment, and the resources necessary for this could most conveniently be acquired by a State monopoly in the sale of agricultural products. Hence the compulsory purchase of grain by the State, which was also the only way of guaranteeing supplies of bread to the urban population.

There was much to be said in 1945–6 for a centralised plan for the economic reconstruction of Yugoslavia. The devastation caused by the war had been almost total, and the economy had to be rebuilt from the foundations. UNRRA aid had done something to restore the basis of agriculture and communications, but much remained to be done especially in the latter field. Factories had been mostly put out of action and even the mines were no longer in working order. Nearly 1,700,000 out of a total population of 16 million had been killed. Wounds and disease gravely affected at least a million of the remainder. Labour was short everywhere and the supply of skilled labour had suffered particularly. An enormous effort was clearly necessary even to restore economic conditions to normal, and the new leaders of Yugoslavia were determined to do more. They believed profoundly in their own thesis – for which many facts spoke – that the resources of the old Yugoslavia had been exploited by foreign industrialists, mainly in their own interests, and that this situation must never recur. Massive and speedy industrialisation was therefore the order of the day, even if it involved years of rationing for the normal consumer and the imposition of strict economic and political discipline by the powerful organs of the new State, particularly the energetic and highly developed secret police apparatus of OZNA (later UDBA) under Ranković.

By spring 1946 the machinery for the new totalitarian economy was in being. Some 80% of industry was in State hands by the end of the war. So were transport and banking. The Basic Law on State Economic Enterprises created or legalised the structure of the Ministries and Directorates which were to control all activities of industry. New Trade Unions were set up to look after the general education of organised workers (a highly necessary task) and to see that they understood and carried out the economic policies laid down. In May 1946 further machinery was established for comprehensive economic planning, with a Federal Planning Commission totally controlling subordinate commissions at Republican and lower levels. The subordinate commissions might submit data on which plans were based, but once the plans were approved at the top they had only to carry out orders. The same applied with even greater force to directors of factories ('enterprises' in standard Yugoslav terminology).

Boris Kidrić, the first head of the Federal Planning Commission, spent the summer of 1946 in the Soviet Union, studying the Soviet model, and the first Yugoslav Five Year Plan for 1947–52 was published and put into effect early in 1947. This was the period of what was later known as 'administrative planning'. Whatever the nominal rights of enterprises, their managers were controlled in detail by Ministries which planned production in the utmost detail, allocated raw materials, and determined output, prices and investment policies. Products were sold largely to Ministries under elaborate supply contracts. Only trading enterprises could sell to consumers. Choice of job was strictly limited, as labour quotas were laid down for enterprises, and consumption of nearly all goods was strictly rationed. For the execution of this total plan, the Yugoslav leaders relied partly on their own ability to force the rate of investment by imposing tight discipline on the Yugoslav population and partly on the undoubted enthusiasm of the younger generation. The achievements of this Yugoslav 'Great Leap Forward' should not be underestimated. Industrial output was nearly doubled between 1946 and 1952, and communications much improved. Nearly a quarter of the Yugoslav national income was reinvested by the State; of this sum nearly half went to mining and manufacturing, about a sixth to transport. There was far too little (less than a tenth) for agriculture and virtually nothing for consumer goods. This alone was enough to ensure that the plan would break down in the long or medium run.

It was however brought to a stop by a different factor. Yugoslav reconstruction depended on the supply of capital equipment from abroad. The first principal supplier was defeated Germany. Yugoslavia was allotted 10% of the total reparations in capital equipment paid by Germany (particularly from the U.S. and British zones of occupation) and 6% of German assets abroad. This amounted to a considerable contribution. The next most important supplier of capital equipment was inevitably the Soviet Union. Under agreements reached in summer 1946 the Soviet Government promised loans and credits up to $300 million for the purchase of capital equipment from the USSR (the last substantial trade agreement of this period was concluded in July 1947, shortly after the publication of the Yugoslav Five Year Plan).

At this point the political disadvantages of 'facing East' began to become apparent. From the first the Soviet leaders showed a keen business sense in their dealings with the Yugoslavs, for all the talk of fraternal aid. By 1948 the faith even of the Yugoslav leaders who wanted to believe in the disinterested intentions of Stalin was beginning to be undermined. It began to dawn on them, according to their accounts written after 1948, that the true Soviet interests might be to exploit Yugoslav resources more directly even than Germany and the Western democracies had done in the past. Stalin did not want to help Yugoslavia to build up a balanced economy with flourishing manufacturing and processing industries. It suited him better to conclude long-term agreements under which the Yugoslavs bound themselves to sell raw materials, particularly mineral ores, at low prices, and ceased to process them at, for example, the Bor, Trepča and Zenica works which, in the official Yugoslav view, could be re-activated and modernised quite cheaply. Between 40 and 50% of Yugoslav exports to the Soviet Union in 1948 (and up to 25% of Yugoslav exports as a whole) took the form of ores and metals; and these were products which the Yugoslavs could have sold more profitably on the world market. In return they received only a small quantity of capital goods not of the latest design and expensive in relation to world prices. After 1948 at least Yugoslav political commentators saw this as part of a general Soviet plan for the economic union of Eastern Europe and the direction of production within this large area in the special interests of the Soviet Union alone.

By 1948 Yugoslavia had received Soviet equipment to the value of $1 million, or only 6% of the credits promised. The receipt of further substantial amounts of equipment seemed to depend on the formation of Soviet–Yugoslav joint stock companies, which could give the Soviet government a large say in the operation of the Yugoslav economy. The Yugoslavs agreed rather reluctantly to the formation of such companies in spring 1946, when they had decided to work out their first Five Year Plan. In August 1946 detailed joint discussions began about the formation of mixed companies and, according to Yugoslav sources, the sinister nature of Soviet economic strategy soon became clear. Vlado Dedijer in his biography of Tito gave an account of negotiations for the formation of a mixed company for the extraction of crude oil in Yugoslavia, which may be summarised to illustrate the clash of national interests. The Soviet representative first said that there were not sufficient oil reserves in Yugoslavia to justify any large-scale extraction. When the Yugoslavs had removed this objection, he put forward conditions for the formation of a joint company which were ludicrously favourable to the Soviet Union, claiming for example, that, according to Marxist doctrine the Yugoslav Government should not want the oil fields themselves as an investment on which they should receive any return from the profits of the company, since 'these were natural resources which had no social value'. Then he tried by all possible means to cut down on the revenue charges to be levied by the Yugoslav Government on production and export. Finally he demanded that the whole distributive network for the sale of petrol and oil products should be in the hands of the joint company. The Yugoslav negotiators were well aware of the terms of the recently-concluded agreement between the Soviet Union and Iran, and found it hard that much tougher conditions were proposed to them than those accepted for co-operation with what they regarded as a 'semi-feudal country'.

No doubt full understanding of Soviet intentions did not dawn quickly on the Yugoslav leaders whose faith in the Soviet Union as an example and an ally had long been absolute. No doubt there was some wisdom after the event in Dedijer's and other accounts of dealings with the Soviet Union from 1945 to 1948. Clearly however Yugoslav determination to follow the Soviet example of rapid industrialisation on a broad front was a principal, if indirect, cause of Yugoslav disputes with the Soviet Government.

5

The break with Stalin

The Soviet–Yugoslav dispute of 1948 is one of the most important and best-documented events of international history since 1945. It is easy now to see it as inevitable. It was far from appearing so at the time, even to comparatively well-informed observers in the West. Yugoslav foreign and domestic policies seemed to be firmly modelled on those of the Soviet Union. The Cominform (Communist Information Bureau), newly constituted to replace the Comintern, dissolved in May 1943, at its inaugural meeting in September 1947 had chosen Belgrade as the permanent seat of its Secretariat. This indicated appreciation of Yugoslav zeal, and the chief Yugoslav delegates, Kardelj and Djilas, were encouraged to play a very prominent part at the meeting. The CPY seemed at the time to rank second only to the CPSU.

After the event the Yugoslav Party leaders could trace a large number of historical lines which led to the break. None the less the letter signed by Molotov and Stalin on 27 March complaining of the shortcomings of the CPY came as a total shock to Tito: 'When I glanced over the first lines', he said afterwards, 'I was thunderstruck.' Until that date, although the Yugoslav leaders had plenty of evidence to show that the Soviet Union pursued a policy of ruthless self-interest even towards its allies, they had managed to accommodate that evidence within the general framework of the convictions which had for so long sustained them. There might be misunderstanding with the Soviet Party and with Stalin himself; but in the longer run, Soviet interests were those of the 'Socialist camp', the Soviet Union and Yugoslavia were on the same side in the vital struggle against 'capitalism' and 'imperialism', and the Soviet Union would recognise the very special position earned by the CPY as the result of its heroic struggles in the war. Djilas' *Conversations with Stalin* contains a most convincing portrait of the author as a young idealist, and in this respect he may be regarded as typical. In 1944, he saw in the Soviet Government 'something even greater than the leadership of my own Party and revolution – the leading power of Communism as a whole – nothing could have been further from my mind than the thought of denying the decisive role of the Soviet Party in World Communism, or of the Red Army in the war against Hitler.' However national pride in Yugoslav achievements was also strong in him, and even in 1944 he felt that 'externally and internally the Yugoslav revolution had transcended the needs and accommodations of Soviet foreign policy'. This feeling too was typical. It stemmed partly from the self-confidence which is a natural trait of the Yugoslavs. 'Znam' (I know) is a word frequently on their lips, and can easily mean 'No need to give me advice.'

The Soviet leaders had from the first mistrusted this self-confidence and, as they saw it, the narrow horizons of the Yugoslav Partisan and Party leadership. It was the Soviet Union which from summer 1941 onwards had borne the brunt of the German assault and had to shape its diplomacy to its political needs. In 1944 it was Stalin who was plotting the general course of communist policy for the post-war era. Understandably he had no intention of letting the needs and accommodations of Soviet foreign policy be postponed to the claims of a Yugoslav revolution. Stalin had a good memory. He did not forget Tito's apparent disregard for Soviet 'popular front' policies in 1942, nor certain exasperated war-time messages from him.[1] Nor indeed his speech at Ljubljana during the first post-war crisis over Trieste, a speech in which he seemed to be equating the Soviet Union with the Western powers as practitioners of Great Power bargains behind the backs of the nations particularly concerned. Stalin did not like the way in which the Yugoslavs had gone ahead with the construction of their own model of communism, without sufficiently consulting the numerous Soviet advisers, military, economic and political, on the spot in Yugoslavia. Soviet–Yugoslav economic negotiations had also been tough; in particular the chief Yugoslav negotiator, Vlatko Velebit, then Vice-Minister of Foreign Affairs, had fought for Yugoslav interests with a stubbornness to which the Soviet leaders had become disaccustomed.

It was a short step for Stalin from annoyance at such attitudes to more far-reaching suspicions. Tito had been close to the British during the war – might he not be maintaining or renewing his links with them?[2] Moreover he was pursuing a dangerously independent policy in the Balkans. Schemes for East European federation could result in an

[1] For instance: 'If you cannot help us at least don't hinder us by useless advice.'
[2] Stalin was not the only communist to have a deep respect for the British Intelligence Service. Djilas' account of his war-time journey to Moscow shows that he too was indoctrinated about its pervasive and dangerous activities.

undesirable increase in Tito's influence and possibly in undesirable repercussions on East–West relations in general.

This last point was of particular importance to Stalin at the end of 1947. Deadlock had just been reached on the future of Germany between the Foreign Ministers of the Soviet Union and U.S.A., Britain and France. The cold war was clearly about to be intensified. In March 1948 the coup in Prague brought a vital position in Central Europe under communist control, and consolidated what amounted to a Soviet Empire in Eastern Europe. The blockade of West Berlin, no doubt planned for some time, was instituted at the end of June 1948. Stalin recognised the risks of East–West confrontation involved in his new policies. He wanted to bring the Yugoslav régime into line with the other much more subservient governments and parties in Eastern Europe. Tito himself and his immediate subordinates must be replaced by more pliable characters. This was the essence of the matter.

Stalin's crucial misjudgement – and it had most important consequences for the future of Eastern Europe and of East–West relations – lay in thinking that it would not be difficult to find an alternative communist leadership in Yugoslavia. This misjudgement was probably based in part on hopeful detailed reports from Soviet Embassy officials, Party functionaries and liaison officers on the spot. A danger to which dictators are particularly liable (and even democratic Prime Ministers are exposed) is that their representatives will report only or mainly conclusions which are known to be welcome to them. Soviet officials however had some good reasons for misjudging the general situation in Yugoslavia. In the first place throughout the CPY there was an enormous fund of good will for the Soviet Union. Good Yugoslav communists were reluctant to deviate from Soviet lines, and only gradually came to realise that these could be determined entirely by narrow Soviet interests. It was the expression of a profound conviction, not merely a form of words, when Yugoslav leaders talked of the enormous value and unbreakable nature of the Soviet–Yugoslav alliance. Indeed they were expressing a double loyalty, from which the CPSU had long been able to derive very specific advantages. Djilas records something 'uncomfortably like a police interrogation' to which he was subjected in spring 1944, by an agent of the NKVD (Soviet secret police, later KGB). He gave this agent data about the CPY, reluctantly indeed – but he 'would not have hesitated' had he been asked by some of the Soviet Committee. He admitted that in 1945 'to give information to the Soviet Party was at that time not considered a deadly sin, for no Yugoslav Communist set his own Central Committee against the Soviet.' The Soviet liaison officers and their intelligence operatives thus had no difficulty in collecting information, and it was only in 1948 that the Yugoslav Government expressly forbade their officials to give economic information to Soviet representatives.

Soviet agents had no need of special sources to know that Tito's economic policies had aroused widespread opposition in Yugoslavia. They also knew almost certainly that there was opposition to them within the Politburo. The official Yugoslav story after the Soviet–Yugoslav break was that the CPSU had two willing informants from within the Politburo itself, and there is nothing improbable in this. One was Sretan Zujović, who had been trained in Moscow and was said to have kept the Soviet Ambassador, Lavrentiev, currently informed about the proceedings of the CC, CPY. Even more important to the Soviet leaders was the Croat Andrija Hebrang. His past was somewhat chequered, and the Russians may have been able to take advantage of this. During the war he had been imprisoned by Ustaša authorities, and doubts were expressed in 1948–9 about the circumstances under which they released him from captivity. Perhaps he had been acting as an agent for them at Partisan Headquarters. In September 1944 he was removed from the post of Party Secretary in Croatia, and was alleged in 1948 to have misused this position in order to discriminate against Serbs in Croatia. Be this as it may, he was back in favour by the end of the war. In 1946 he had opposed the policy of over-rapid industrialisation, and had been expelled from the CC, CPY; but he continued to act as chairman of the new Federal Planning Commission, and could give the Russians valuable information. At any rate when he headed a large Yugoslav delegation to Moscow in winter 1944–5, Djilas remarked on the fact that he submitted written reports to his Soviet counterparts. He may have informed and misled them later both about Yugoslav economic weaknesses and also about the extent of political opposition to Tito.

2

At the beginning of 1948 then the Soviet leaders had probably decided that it was time to get rid of Tito and that it would be possible to replace him by a more pliable Yugoslav leader. The pressure was put on gradually, and it was Tito who ultimately provoked a show-down. The last phase began when Djilas was invited to visit Moscow early in January 1948 to discuss Albanian affairs.[3] Immediately after

[3] Perhaps he was regarded as someone who out of personal ambition could be induced to intrigue against Tito within the Yugoslav Politburo.

his arrival, Stalin himself encouraged the Yugoslavs to 'swallow Albania' – or, in more polite terms, to proceed with plans for a federation, in which an Albania enlarged to include the large Shiptar population of the Kosmet, would become a constituent republic of Yugoslavia. Djilas was suspicious of this advice. He knew that the Russians in Albania had been doing their best to counter Yugoslav influence. They had periodically criticised in Belgrade aspects of Yugoslav policy – the formation of joint-stock companies and the provision of expert aid, at a time when the Yugoslavs themselves were so short of capital and skilled manpower. And, as Djilas did not know till February 1948, during his own visit to Moscow the Yugoslav Government in Belgrade was told flatly to discontinue its plans for reinforcing the Yugoslav military presence in Albania. Molotov complained sharply of the proposed Yugoslav action and of the lack of consultation with Moscow.

The next theme for a display of Soviet official displeasure was Balkan federation. Dimitrov had drawn the first Soviet fire by issuing a statement in Bucharest about the prospects of a Bulgarian–Romanian federation. This was sharply repudiated in *Pravda* and the Yugoslav and Bulgarian Governments were instructed to send high-level delegations immediately to Moscow for discussions of federal plans. Kardelj and Bakarić, Secretary of the Croat CP, set off to join Djilas and the members of Yugoslav military and economic missions who were already in Moscow (Tito had prudently refused to attend himself). On 10 February there was a meeting with Stalin and Molotov at which Dimitrov in particular was humiliated. Stalin told the Yugoslavs brusquely to proceed at once with plans for a federation with Bulgaria, and afterwards to annex Albania. Kardelj was rudely put down for venturing an optimistic forecast about the chances of the guerilla operations in Greece. Meanwhile the Yugoslav military delegation had not been able to arrange for any supplies of weapons or equipment for their own new industry and shipyards. The economic delegation could not secure any agreement to increase commercial exchanges under the Yugoslav Five Year Plan, or even a protocol in respect of trade for the current year. The only treaty signed was a Soviet text binding the Yugoslav Government to consult with the Soviet Government on all foreign policy issues. This was presented to Kardelj with no warning; he was ordered to sign, and reluctantly acquiesced.

Clearly there was already a grave crisis of confidence between the CPSU and the CPY. Djilas refused to believe that Stalin would proceed to logical conclusions. He reported diplomatically: 'There is no need to doubt for a moment the great love Comrade Stalin bears our entire Party, the Central Committee and particularly Comrade Tito.'

Tito himself knew better. On 1 March he called a meeting of the CC to consider the various Yugoslav delegations' reports. He made no attempt to conceal the very serious consequences of the attitudes now adopted by the Soviet authorities for the Yugoslav armaments industry and Five Year Plans. The CC had to discuss immediately Stalin's directive to proceed forthwith on federation with Bulgaria. This appeared to nearly all its members as a plot to dilute the Yugoslav leadership and weaken Yugoslav resolution in the pursuit of their own chosen path to Communism. The Bulgarians would be used as Soviet agents in Yugoslav councils. The Central Committee, unanimously except for Zujović, resolved to ignore Stalin's directive. They were well aware that they had taken a crucial decision.

Stalin did not immediately react to the challenge, and when he did so, it was in an indirect form. On 18 March the head of the Soviet Military Mission, General Barskov, informed the Yugoslav Chief of General Staff that Soviet military advisers and instructors in Yugoslavia were 'surrounded by hostility' and would therefore all be withdrawn immediately. On 19 March, the Soviet chargé d'affaires made a similar announcement in respect of Soviet civilian advisers. On 20 March Tito himself wrote to Molotov in pained surprise at the Soviet charges, contradicting them and suggesting that they must have been based on information which might not always have been 'objective, accurate, or given with good intentions'. The reasons adduced by the Soviet Government could not be, Tito wrote,

the cause of the measures taken..., and it is our desire that the U.S.S.R. openly inform us what the trouble is, that it point out everything which it feels is inconsistent with good relations between the two countries. We feel that this course of events is harmful to both countries and that sooner or later everything that is prejudicial to friendly relations between our countries must be eliminated.

Here was an invitation of which the Soviet Government was to take full advantage. The official battle was joined – still in complete secrecy so far as the West was concerned – with the Soviet note of 27 March 1948, signed by Stalin and Molotov on behalf of the Soviet Central Committee. They first justified in detail the withdrawal of their military and civilian advisers, citing evidence about the difficulty which the economic advisers experienced in getting information and the supervision to which they were subject from the Yugoslav security forces; also about direct or indirect insults to Soviet military advisers, including a reference back to an alleged statement by Djilas that 'Soviet officers were, from a moral standpoint, inferior to the officers of the British army.'[4]

Stalin proceeded to inform Tito of 'the other facts which led to Soviet dissatisfaction'. The Yugoslavs had, he said, alleged that great power chauvinism was rampant in the U.S.S.R., that the U.S.S.R. was trying to dominate Yugoslavia economically, and that the Cominform was merely a Soviet instrument; such allegations were normally covered by 'left phrases, such as "socialism in the U.S.S.R. has ceased to be revolutionary" and that Yugoslavia alone is the exponent of "revolutionary socialism"'. Trotsky was cited as an example of one who had accused the CPSU of degeneracy and 'We think that the career of Trotsky is quite instructive.'

Stalin then went over to the counter-attack. The CPY was in a poor state, still not completely legalised, and undemocratic in constitution. It did not practice self-criticism. It did not publish its decisions. There was insufficient 'initiative of the Party masses'. The spirit of class-struggle was lacking. No measures were being taken to check the growth of the capitalist elements in Yugoslav villages, and the CPY was effectively submerged in the People's Front, rather than acting as the chief leading force. This was a Menshevik heresy.

Finally there was the question of certain personalities, in particular Vlatko Velebit:

The Yugoslav comrades know that Velebit is an English spy. They also know that the representatives of the Soviet Government consider Velebit a spy...It is possible that the Yugoslav Government intends to use Velebit precisely as an English spy.

Djilas and Vukmanović–Tempo[5] were also specifically mentioned. According to Tempo, they both offered to resign in order to ease the situation for Tito, who refused to accept their gesture. Tito determined to discuss the reply to Stalin's thunderbolt at a plenary session of the CC on 12 April – the first called for nearly eight years. The previous day had been the third anniversary of the Soviet–Yugoslav Treaty of Friendship, Mutual Aid and Post-War Collaboration. It was important for Tito to preserve the appearance of friendship and in a message to Stalin he emphasised the 'unbreakable bonds' linking the Soviet Union and Yugoslavia. This however did not affect the general tenor of the draft reply, put to the CC by Tito and Kardelj, and again

[4] Djilas claimed to have said no more than that the 'assaults by Red Army soldiers' stimulated 'our opponents' to make this comparison.

[5] Henceforward Tempo.

opposed only by Zujović. In it Tito expressed surprise and indignation at the substance and tone of the Soviet allegations, which he assumed for the record to be based on false information supplied by Hebrang and Zujović. The main point of his defence was that 'no matter how much each of us loves the land of socialism, the U.S.S.R., he can in no case love his own country less'.

With shrewd instinct Tito chose to fight Stalin primarily on the issue of national independence, rather than on the questions of ideology raised in Stalin's letter. However these could not be left unanswered. The comparison with Trotsky was indignantly rejected and the charges against the CPY were denied. They had carried through drastic revolutionary changes but though these were derived from Soviet experience, 'we are developing socialism in our country in somewhat different forms'. The specific accusations about Yugoslav treatment of Soviet military advisers were denied. Djilas' remarks about Soviet officers had, it was said, been maliciously distorted. Velebit's past was still being investigated but so far nothing had been found to justify the charges against him. The Russian intelligence service was operating against the Yugoslav leaders and State, and trying to recruit agents among the Yugoslav people.

Tito then appealed to Stalin. His letter was evidence of

grave misunderstanding. . .which must be rapidly liquidated in the interest of the cause our parties serve. Our only desire is to eliminate every doubt and disbelief in the purity of the comradely and brotherly feeling of loyalty of our CC of the CPY to the CPSU. . .loyalty to the Soviet Union which has served us and will continue to serve us as a great example and whose assistance to our people we value so highly.

Finally Tito proposed that there should be a 'full mutual explanation between the two Central Committees' in Yugoslavia, and that the 'CC of the CPSU send one or more of its members, who will have every opportunity here of studying every question thoroughly'.

Tito cannot seriously have hoped that Stalin would retreat at this stage from the position which he had taken up in the letter of 27 March, particularly since Zujović had been accused at the CC meeting on 12 April of passing information to the Soviet Ambassador, Lavrentiev, and together with Hebrang put under investigation. However the Yugoslav leaders felt themselves bound to proceed cautiously and give the appearance of readiness to reach a dignified accommodation with the Soviet leaders; otherwise they might have been faced with trouble within the CPY. Stalin's next letter (of 4 May) proved that there was no chance of compromise; he was out for Tito's head. The Yugoslav defences against previous Soviet charges were brushed aside, and new accusations were added. Three members of the Yugoslav Embassy staff in London were British agents. The U.S. Ambassador in Belgrade 'behaved as if he owns the place' and his 'intelligence agents' moved about freely in Yugoslavia. The Yugoslav Government and Party treated the Soviet Ambassador in Belgrade as an 'ordinary bourgeois Ambassador' and the Yugoslavs 'put the foreign policy of the U.S.S.R. on a par with that of the English and Americans'. Tito's speech of 27 May 1945 on Trieste was cited as evidence of this, particularly the passage in which he expressed Yugoslav indignation at being used 'as a bribe in international bargaining' or at becoming 'involved in any policy of spheres of interest'.[6] The Soviet Union had done its best for the Yugoslavs over Trieste by diplomatic means. It was utterly wrong to equate Soviet with Western attitudes on the question. Did Tito expect the Soviet Union to go to war on his behalf? The explanations given at the time by Kardelj and Tito himself were inadequate (the Soviet Ambassador's account of his talks tête-à-tête with Kardelj was quoted, probably in the hope of embroiling him with Tito). Tito had an 'anti-Soviet attitude...towards the U.S.S.R.' If the Yugoslav leaders retained this attitude, this would mean 'renouncing all friendly relations with the Soviet Union, depriving themselves of the right to demand material and any other assistance from the Soviet Union'.

The threat and the attempt to split 'the Yugoslav leaders' from Tito were clear enough.

The further paragraphs about the inadequacies of the CPY's record in domestic policy drove this last point home. There had been virtually no social reform or collectivisation of land. The CPY had become a Menshevik party owing to the 'unbounded arrogance' of leaders whose heads had been turned by their own successes in wartime. These successes were in any case much exaggerated – the Partisan movement had nearly been destroyed by the German parachute attack on Tito's Headquarters at Drvar in spring 1944, and it was the Red Army who had rescued them. No CC representative would come from Moscow to Belgrade. Instead the Yugoslavs should submit the dispute to the Cominform.

[6] It appears from Djilas' *Wartime* that, when Kardelj was in Moscow in November 1944, to obtain Soviet consent to the formation of a coalition government, Stalin told him of the '50/50' division of influence in Yugoslavia agreed between himself and Churchill a month before. This was held against Stalin particularly after 1948, Djilas says, but 'no one in our leadership saw anything inappropriate or even unpleasant in that at the time. We understood it as the neutralising of British intervention...'

The further course of the exchanges can be covered more briefly. On 17 May Tito replied with dignity to the Soviet letter of 4 May. He would not submit the dispute to the Cominform; Stalin had circulated his letter of 27 March to the member governments, and the Czechs and Hungarians had already begun to slander Yugoslavia and its leaders. The case had in fact been prejudged. The Soviet leaders insisted (22 May) that the Cominform would in any case meet, whether or not Yugoslav members attended, to consider the serious consequences of Yugoslav actions. The meeting was however postponed until the end of June. Perhaps Stalin hoped that the evidence of a Communist front united behind him (including the French and Italian parties as well as the satellites) would persuade some Yugoslav Communists to turn against Tito. On 28 June[7] the Cominform met and agreed on a statement, repeating in detail the Soviet charges against the CPY's undemocratic nature and mistaken domestic policies. The last paragraphs expressed criticisms which must simultaneously have awakened agonising doubts among many good Yugoslav communists and a spirit of fierce patriotic pride in Tito's leadership, which was now to be shared by much wider circles of the Yugoslav people.

The Central Committee of the CPY had, it was said, 'placed itself and the Yugoslav Party outside the united Communist front and consequently outside the ranks of the Information Bureau'. They had 'broken with the international traditions of the CPY and taken the road to nationalism' under the influence of 'national elements' who had 'managed in the course of the past five or six months to reach a dominant position in the CPY leadership'. They seemed to think that they could 'maintain Yugoslavia's independence and build socialism without the support of the Communist Parties of other countries, without the support of the people's democracies, without the support of the Soviet Union'. By so doing they seemed to think that

they can curry favour with the Imperialist states. They think they will be able to bargain with them for Yugoslavia's independence and, gradually, to get the people of Yugoslavia orientated towards these states, that is, towards capitalism. [. . . .]

The Yugoslav leaders evidently do not understand or, probably, pretend they do not understand, that such a nationalist line can only lead to Yugoslavia's degeneration into an ordinary bourgeois republic, to the loss of its independence and to its transformation into a colony of the imperialist countries.

[7] The Cominform with great insensitivity chose for their announcement St Vitus' Day (Vidovdan) the anniversary, sacred to all Serbs, of the battle of Kosovo Polje in 1389.

The Information Bureau does not doubt that inside the CPY there are sufficient healthy elements, loyal to Marxism-Leninism, to the international traditions of the CPY and to the united socialist front.

Their task is to compel their present leaders to recognise their mistakes openly and honestly and to rectify them; to break with nationalism, return to internationalism; and in every way to consolidate the united socialist front against imperialism.

Should the present leaders of the Yugoslav Communist Party prove incapable of doing this, their job is to replace them and to advance a new internationalist leadership of the Party.

The Information Bureau does not doubt that the CPY will be able to fulfil this honourable task.

6

Evolution of the 'Yugoslav Way'

By the end of July 1948 it seemed unlikely that there could be any reconciliation between Stalin and Tito personally. In planning the next steps of Yugoslavia's domestic and foreign policy Tito had to bear in mind a number of uncertain factors. Was Stalin likely to be long in power? Was his health weak, and was there any likelihood of effective opposition to him over his treatment of Yugoslavia? More immediately important, how strong was Tito's own position? How well equipped was Yugoslavia to survive the economic pressure from the Soviet bloc, which had already commenced? And how much support was the Yugoslav economy likely to get from the West, given the strongly anti-Western line taken by Tito himself and other leaders since the end of the war?

The most urgent question concerned the solidarity of the CPY. How strong were the 'Cominformist' elements in it? In the eyes of the average Yugoslav communist, national pride was very important, but excommunication by Moscow was still a terrible blow. Tito had to prove to his own Party members that he remained a good communist and that Moscow had no excuse for excommunicating him.

The first steps were a CC resolution of 29 June, countering the Cominform resolution of the previous day, followed by a long historical justification of the CPY's record, made by Tito at the Vth Party Congress late on 21 July. The main themes of both were assiduously propagated in the CPY and the Army.

Tito also had to act speedily against any obvious 'Cominformists' in the CPY or elsewhere. After the arrest of Hebrang and Zujović in May, no leading political figures were removed from their position. The Soviet Government had probably counted too much on what these two could do to provide alternative leadership, and they may have even contemplated organising an operation to rescue them. If so, nothing came of it, and a later attempt to recruit some high-ranking officers to a sort of Yugoslav Communist Government in exile was also frustrated. The Yugoslav Ambassador in Bucharest was one of a few highly-placed temporary expatriates to declare himself in favour of the Cominform. A number of 'Cominformists' managed to cross the borders to Bulgaria, Romania or Hungary. But some important ones failed to make it. Arso Jovanović, Tito's war-time Chief of Staff, was reported shot in attempting to cross the Yugoslav–Romanian frontier on 13 August; General Petričević, Deputy Head (under Tempo) of the Political Administration of the Yugoslav Army, and Colonel Vlado Dapčević (brother of the famous Partisan General, Peko Dapčević) were also captured. A large number (probably thousands) of young Yugoslav students and technicians were studying or working in Russia at the time of the Cominform resolution, and were detained in the Soviet Union. Enough of them succumbed to Soviet pressure for the Soviet authorities to be able to run press and radio propaganda to Yugoslavia through a committee of 'Patriot-exiles'; but their number was not great. No doubt the Russians also hoped to exploit differences between the Yugoslav nationalities for the Cominform cause. As late as 1950 some Serbs from the Lika district, highly placed in the Croat party, were arrested for Cominformism and said to have been inflaming the national feelings of Serbs in Croatia. There was some trouble too in the Kosmet and Macedonia, and the Albanian and Bulgarian Governments violently attacked the Yugoslav official policy towards the minorities in these regions (the Yugoslav Government reacted by forming an Albanian League and a League of Bulgarian Emigrants, to carry the propaganda war into the enemies' camp).

The direct activity of the Russian Intelligence Service (RIS) within Yugoslavia was also dangerous to Tito's cause. The Russians tried to operate largely through former White Russians, who had taken refuge in Yugoslavia after 1918, and collaborated with the Germans during the Second World War; afterwards, to save themselves from punishment by the new Yugoslav Government, they received Soviet citizenship and worked in return on behalf of the RIS. It is hard to estimate the success achieved by the Russians. What is certain is that they were up against an effective counter-intelligence service, and Ranković later claimed that about 8,400 Cominform sympathisers were arrested.

More important than the immediate battle between Soviet subversion and Yugoslav counter-intelligence was the indirect effect of the Cominform's charges against Tito on the main lines of Yugoslav internal and foreign policy. He did not immediately strike out on a special Yugoslav 'road to Socialism'. Much of his long opening speech at the Vth Party Congress was devoted to proving that the Yugoslav

Party had always been good internationalists in a Communist sense and remained essentially loyal to the Soviet Union and the new 'People's Democracies', despite their legitimate pride in their own Yugoslav achievements. The end of Tito's speech was greeted by cries of 'Tito! Stalin!' Kardelj's speech at the same Congress on Yugoslav foreign policy explicitly recognised the division of the world into 'capitalist' and 'socialist' camps, and accused the Americans of pursuing a colonialist policy by trying to impose the Marshall Plan on Europe. At the meeting of the Danube Conference at Belgrade in August 1948, the Yugoslavs voted steadily with the other representatives of the 'Eastern bloc' to exclude the Western powers from the new Danube Navigation Commission which was to replace the pre-war International Commission.

On the internal front the Yugoslav leaders were even more determined to keep left. The Five Year Plan was to go forward. Boris Kidrić, head of the Federal Planning Commission, indicted Hebrang and Zujović in his speech to the Vth Party Congress for sabotaging 'the construction of Socialism'; they were accused of attempting to check over-ambitious planning and of insisting on the profitability of individual enterprises (a good instance of the risks of being right at the wrong time). The Yugoslav leaders were also highly sensitive to the charge made by the Soviet CC and by the Cominform that they had been remiss in collectivisation of agricultural land. Their new drive for collectivisation did not materialise until spring 1949, but the preconditions for it were established in the previous autumn.

This was a brave front, but by the end of 1948 the economic hardships involved in the policy of 'keeping left' and going it alone were widely apparent in Yugoslavia. Tito's own speech to the Congress of the Croatian CP at the end of November revealed something of the shortages even of the simplest consumer goods (e.g. matches) suffered in Yugoslav villages at the time, and hinted at the sort of hostility, unorganised no doubt and inarticulate for the most part, which was building up against the CPY.

In these circumstances Stalin probably assumed that further economic and political pressure on Tito's régime would be effective. By spring 1949 the Soviet-organised economic blockade was complete. A Yugoslav delegation was sent to Moscow in December 1948 to negotiate for an economic agreement. The best they could do was to fix a level of economic exchange at the level of one-eighth of that (already much reduced) which had obtained in 1948. When in February 1949 the other East European countries sent delegations to Moscow to form the

Council for Mutual Economic Assistance (COMECON), the Yugoslavs were not invited and were told in answer to their protest that the price of admission would be a renunciation of their existing policy. The Yugoslav Five Year Plan had been drawn up in 1947 on the assumption that the necessary credits, loans, raw materials and machinery would be supplied by the Soviet Union and (to a much lesser extent) the other East European countries, with which over half Yugoslavia's foreign trade was conducted. In 1948 57% of Yugoslavia's total imports and 52% of her exports resulted from trade with the Cominform countries. Admittedly foreign trade was not intended to be a major factor (less than 10% of the Yugoslav Gross National Product) in the fulfilment of the Five Year Plan. But it was still vital, and balanced bilateral exchanges with the Cominform countries were the essential element within it. The Cominform blockade was not total from summer 1948, but by March 1949 the pattern was becoming clear; by summer 1949 deliveries to Yugoslavia had been slowed down or stopped, and by the end of the year, trade with the Soviet bloc had come to a complete standstill.

At the same time Stalin was taking further political steps to complete the isolation of Yugoslavia. In July 1949 the Soviet delegation at the U.N. refused to continue support for Yugoslav claims to the areas of Carinthia where there was a substantial Slav-speaking population, and accused Kardelj in particular of having tried to embroil the Soviet Union with the West on an issue which they were unwilling to press for themselves. Early in 1949 Stalin effectively ceased to support the Greek Communist rebellion, by closing the Bulgarian and Albanian frontiers with Greece. When in late July 1949 the Yugoslavs took similar action on their own frontier, and thereby sealed General Markos' fate, they became involved in bitter polemics with the Soviet leaders about their alleged support of the 'Greek Fascist régime'.

At the end of the summer the signs became ominous in the extreme. From August 1949 onwards the Cominform countries and the Soviet Union successively denounced their treaties of friendship and mutual aid with Yugoslavia. Soviet divisions carried out manoeuvres on the Yugoslav–Hungarian and Yugoslav–Romanian frontiers, and the possibility of an invasion of Yugoslavia seemed by no means remote. A Russian note of 18 August, protesting against the arrest and mal-treatment of Soviet citizens in Yugoslavia, had ended with the threat that the Soviet Government 'will be compelled to resort to other, more effective means' and the Yugoslavs organised new plans for resistance in depth against aggression from the East.

This was followed at the end of September 1949 by a series of show trials in the Eastern European countries, featuring Tito as one of the main villains. The first of them took place in Budapest, with László Rajk as the principal victim. He 'confessed' to a conspiracy with the Americans and Tito, designed to transfer Hungary from the 'socialist' to the 'imperialist' camp (Tito, it was implied, had already effected the transfer of Yugoslavia). Trajko Kostov was put on trial in Sofia in December, and similar accusations were made against Tito. The invasion scare was temporarily past, but in face of Stalin's political and economic offensive it was clear throughout the CPY that there was no hope of working back to reasonable relations with the Soviet Union and the new model satellite Governments. The CPY as well as Tito had been finally excommunicated and outlawed. Tito therefore had nothing to lose and much to gain within the CPY by ideological counterattack. The beginning of 1950 may be taken as the time when a start was made on the evolution of the 'Yugoslav Way', which rested on the thesis that the CPY were the true Marxist–Leninists and that everyone else was out of step.[1]

2

At the Vth Party Congress the Yugoslav leaders had not claimed that theirs was a new model of Communism for imitation by all new Communist countries. In talking about Yugoslavia's economic development for example, Kidrič said that not all 'those forms which proved abundantly successful and positive with us...can be applied in all situations and all People's Democracies...' The main theoretical emphasis for a time was on the theme of equal rights in relations between small and big Socialist countries, and in late summer 1949 Djilas invoked the shade of Lenin to draw out some important implications of this theme.[2]

All peoples will arrive at Socialism – this is inevitable. But they will not all arrive there by exactly the same road. Each will introduce a modicum of specific characteristics...From the angle of theory, there is nothing more ridiculous than painting the future in this respect as uniformly grey, in the name of Historical Materialism...

Djilas went on to make a very important further point:

[1] A number of Yugoslav theoreticians however argue that a separate 'Yugoslav Way' would have evolved irrespective of Soviet pressure and that the beginnings of it are discernible in Yugoslav practice both during the war and in the 'administrative period' 1945–8.
[2] In an essay entitled *Lenin on Relations between Socialist States*.

The phase of history when a single Socialist State existed, encircled by Imperialist States in constant rivalry with each other, has ended. A new phase has begun – the phase of co-existence between a series of Socialist States which can no longer be encircled by the Imperialist States... By failing to comprehend the essential nature of the new conditions *and by revising Leninism*,[3] the leaders of the U.S.S.R. have reached extravagant conclusions in theory and practice. They have divided the world into two sectors – a capitalist sector led by the American Imperialists, and a Socialist sector led by the U.S.S.R. But *in fact there is a capitalist world where individual nations strive to liberate themselves from American domination, and the world of completely equal Socialist States,* completely equal workers' parties and democratic movements... *In Socialism there are no leading nations and States,* and there cannot be, unless they are to be converted into ruling nations and States – which in fact is happening to-day.

The show trials in Hungary and Bulgaria led to further analysis of Soviet 'revisionism', and inevitably evoked comparison with the Moscow trials of 1936–7. Perhaps Stalin had been wrong all the time, not merely badly advised since 1948. In autumn 1949 the relics of Stalin-worship in Yugoslavia were removed, and critical analysis of conditions in the Soviet Union was encouraged in the Yugoslav Party press.

The principal theme of Yugoslav theorists was now that, even if the Soviet Union remained a Socialist country in the sense of having abolished private capital, it had degenerated through the excessive growth of bureaucracy and State capitalism.[4] This was a dangerous doctrine, it might seem, at a time when the Yugoslav economy was still very highly planned and centralised, and when many of the senior members of the CPY enjoyed greater economic privileges than the average citizen. Probably indeed the purely theoretical analysis of 'Soviet revisionism' would eventually have led to the development of Yugoslav theories of decentralisation and self-management. This process however was very much hastened by developments in the international and the Yugoslav internal fields.

The attack by North Korean forces on South Korea took place at the end of June 1950. It was widely interpreted in the Western world as the beginning of a still more aggressive phase of Soviet foreign

---

[3] Author's italics.
[4] Kardelj in July 1949 pointed the way to detailed study of Marx's writings on the Paris Commune and Lenin's *State and Revolution,* in which the theory of workers' management is adumbrated; and in the autumn, Moša Pijade concluded that it was Soviet internal practice which was responsible for the errors of Soviet foreign policy.

policy. The Yugoslav leaders were not able at this stage to discount the possibility that this interpretation was correct – after all their own leaders had been under serious threat from the Soviet and satellite armies only nine months before. They made some attempts in July 1950 to distance themselves equally from both camps, and to blame the outbreak of war on the rivalry and intervention of the Great Powers. But the example of the U.N. intervention in favour of South Korea was not lost on them. Another U.N. intervention would be necessary in their own favour, if the Soviet and satellite armies crossed the Yugoslav borders. The Yugoslavs could not afford in the interests of their own defence to censure the U.N. action in Korea, even though this had clearly depended on American initiative. In September 1950 Kardelj as Yugoslav Foreign Minister pronounced North Korea guilty of aggression. Thereafter the Yugoslav delegation at the U.N. supported the U.N. intervention as far north as the 38th parallel.

Economic need also was forcing the Yugoslav leaders towards recognising that there was something to choose between the Great Powers and towards further accommodations with the West. By the summer of 1950 Yugoslavia was plunged into a severe economic crisis, resulting largely from self-inflicted wounds. After the Cominform resolution, the Yugoslav leaders felt bound to prove their political orthodoxy to the Party rank and file by maintaining and even increasing the tempo of industrialisation. This had to be done mainly from their own resources, and took the form largely of construction work – new roads, new apartment blocks, new factories, sometimes with little regard for the chances of maintaining their output. There was a massive propaganda campaign for quicker results and 'socialist competition', reminiscent of the days of the Stakhanovite movement in the U.S.S.R., or of the 'Great Leap Forward' in China (1958). Most of the German prisoners-of-war who had made a substantial contribution to the Yugoslav labour force until 1948 had been repatriated. A good deal of forced Yugoslav labour was available, largely the so-called 'administrative prisoners', who had been detained without trial by local police forces, usually for failing to fulfil agricultural delivery quotas.[5]

There was however bound to be a large time-gap between all this activity and corresponding results in terms of improved communications, new machinery, and even more of consumer goods. The shortages caused by the Five Year Plan's concentration on industrial 'objectives'

[5] Ranković himself later revealed, when the 'administrative' system of detention was abolished, that 'arrests' were often made simply to fill up the required labour quota.

were increased by the Cominform blockade and could not immediately be made good. Wages and prices were nominally frozen, but money was of decreasing use in providing for the necessities of life, and the black market in second-hand consumer goods, or goods brought in from abroad by privileged officials, became all-important for city-dwellers at least. Far more valuable than the official currency were coupons, or 'bons', issued in return for foreign currency and entitling the holder to purchase at specially stocked shops.[6] 'Bons', commission-shops at which goods provided by private citizens were sold by the State for a handsome commission, and food parcels sent from abroad, particularly by American citizens of Yugoslav origin, were the principal means by which the more fortunate city-dwellers maintained their standard of life.

The countryside was a different matter. Compulsory purchase of agricultural products became increasingly important and attempts were made in the circumstances prevalent after 1948 to enforce it rigorously. This led in the direction of collectivisation, which had become more desirable for political reasons too. The Yugoslav leaders wished to rebut the Cominform allegations that they were unwilling to dispossess peasant proprietors. But for some months after the Cominform resolution their official policy was to proceed gradually, and if possible to persuade the peasants into collectives. When by the beginning of 1949 it became clear that persuasion was not proving successful, the Central Committee determined on a more forceful policy, partly to advertise their orthodoxy, partly to strengthen their control of agricultural production, and partly to ensure a more regular labour-supply for their enlarged industrialisation programme.

After the harvest of 1949 (a comparatively good one) a massive drive for collectivisation was initiated, and there was a sort of 'socialist competition' between local authorities to record the highest degree of collectivisation in districts. At the end of 1948, there were 932 collective farms, at the end of 1949 4,263, and at the high tide of collectivisation in 1950 6,626, covering some 2,500,000 hectares or about 17% of Yugoslavia's cultivable land. The collectives, or in the normal Yugoslav phraseology, 'peasant working co-operatives', were of two main

---

[6] This point was brought home to me when I first arrived in Belgrade as an Embassy official in August 1951 (when the worst of the economic crisis was past), and found myself unexpectedly alone at Belgrade railway station. I had acquired some dinars at the official (and quite unrealistic) rate against sterling. I offered a tip, handsome by my innocent reckoning, to the porter. This was scornfully rejected. Both he and my taxi driver were exclusively interested in the 'bons' which I had acquired, along with dinar-notes, for my sterling.

types (each with two sub-divisions), according to whether the peasant received payment only for work done, or an annual rent on the land which he had contributed (in either case he could retain up to a hectare of land as a private plot). Taking collective and State farms together, nearly a quarter of Yugoslav cultivable land was under 'Socialist' ownership. This was a figure which compared well, in Communist political terms, with what had been achieved in other 'People's Democracies' of Eastern Europe.

Immediately however the results of the new collectivisation drive were disastrous. In spring 1950 the Yugoslav Government was faced with peasant opposition, and the enforcement of compulsory deliveries and collectivisation led to resistance and riots over an extensive area, if not on a fully organised scale. The trouble was particularly severe on the borders of Croatia with Serbia and Bosnia, in the old military frontier district, from which so many Partisans had been recruited in 1941–4. In clashes between peasants and special armed detachments of the Ministry of Interior there were a number of fatal casualties and hundreds of arrests. The Croatian Party leaders alleged that the discontent had been fostered by Party representatives of the Serb population in Croatia, so that an undesirable 'national' element was added to an already dangerous economic situation. Partly as a result of disruption in the countryside and largely because of weather conditions the harvest of 1950 was extremely bad.

It was in these circumstances that Tito felt bound to turn to the West for more economic aid, as well as some political protection. In late summer 1949 the Yugoslavs had applied to the World Bank and the U.S. Export-Import Bank for credits of $250 million. They received much less than they asked for,[7] but the ice had been broken. Western aid began to flow by the end of 1950, and meanwhile there had been important developments in the 'working style' of Yugoslav Communism, which had the incidental effect of making it more acceptable to non-Communists in the West.

3

In the circumstances the Yugoslav leaders had to adapt their system of government in order to prevent economic breakdown. There was no question of renouncing their 'socialist' convictions, but a new 'socialist' system had to be evolved which would enable the economy to work,

---

[7] $29 million from the Banks concerned, and about the same amount in commercial loans from Britain and Holland.

would clearly differentiate Yugoslavia from the bureaucratic State socialism of the Soviet Union, and would thus incidentally open the way for support from the West, which seemed increasingly necessary from summer 1950 on.

In his speech to the Yugoslav National Assembly on 26 June 1950,[8] Tito of course did not admit the impending collapse of the Yugoslav centralised system of administration. He started from a continuation of Djilas' thesis that the Soviet Union had developed State socialism and bureaucracy to an inadmissible degree. He then drew the contrast between Soviet actualities, and Lenin's doctrine about the role of the State, as expounded in *State and Revolution* (which was written just before the October Revolution and was therefore pure theory, untainted by the experience of power). Its main argument was that:

(i) after a successful revolution, the 'dictatorship of the proletariat' would have to continue for a time, but could be enforced (since *ex hypothesi* the people backed it) by a comparatively small apparatus of force.

(ii) As a socialist society developed and the class struggle diminished, even this small apparatus could be cut down.

(iii) At the final stage of communism, class differences would have disappeared entirely, and the 'State' itself, together with any repressive apparatus, could wither away.

Stalin in 1939 had explained the obvious discrepancy between Lenin's forecast and the large repressive resources of the Soviet State. The 'army, punitive organs and intelligence service' were directed against the State's external enemies, while the main task of the State within the Soviet Union was 'peaceful economic-organisational and cultural-educational work'. This doctrine still held in 1950 both for the Soviet Union and for Soviet-dominated Eastern Europe. It was now explicitly rejected by Tito. The Soviet Union could hardly be described as encircled by enemies, particularly since China was now under a communist régime:

To maintain that the functions of the State as an armed power...are purely directed against the outside, is to speak without the slightest knowledge of the actual situation inside the Soviet Union. After all, what is that gigantic, bureaucratic, centralised apparatus doing?...What are the NKVD and the militia doing?...Who is deporting millions of citizens ...to Siberia and the far north? Can anyone pretend that these are measures against the class enemy?...who is obstructing the free exchange

[8] Tito's exposition took place two days after the outbreak of the Korean war, when the concept of two 'world camps' did not look entirely mistaken.

of opinion in the Soviet Union? Isn't all this done by the most centralised and bureaucratic State apparatus, one that shows not the slightest trace of withering away?

Yugoslavia on the contrary would faithfully follow Leninist principles and allow the State to wither away, in accordance with the social conditions of the time. The process had already started:

First, the decentralisation of State administration, particularly in economic matters. Second, the transfer of factories and economic undertakings in general to self-administration through workers' collectives. The decentralisation of the economic, political, cultural and other sectors of social life is not only profoundly democratic, it also contains the germ of the withering-away process – the withering away of centralism, and also of the State in general, of the State as an instrument of repression.

State property in the means of production was the lowest form of Socialist property. From now on in Yugoslavia it would

gradually merge into higher forms of Socialist property. This is our road to Socialism, and as far as the withering away of the economic functions of the State is concerned, it is the only right road.

Tito's speech of 26 June was to some small extent a justification of steps already taken by the Yugoslav leaders. The law of May 1949 on People's Committees (the successors of the war-time National Liberation Committees) had given greater political and economic powers to the District, as opposed to Republican or Federal, levels of government. Administrative decentralisation was carried further at the turn of the year 1949–50, when many economic functions had been transferred from Federal to Republican or even District level. Many of the Federal Ministries responsible for the direct management of the economy were abolished; but the economy continued to be managed from above. This was devolution only from one type of bureaucracy to another, often less experienced and efficient.

However the Basic Law on Workers' Self-Management, introduced by Tito, was designed to introduce sweeping changes. The first experiments in 'workers' self-management' had indeed begun at the end of 1949, with the establishment by over 200 firms of advisory bodies on which the workers were specially represented; but their functions were purely consultative and were not intended to diminish the responsibility of the Managing Directors, who were still appointed by the State. The governing principle of the new Law on the other hand was that

Factories, mines, transport, trade, agricultural, forest, public utility and other state economic enterprises, as the general people's property, shall be managed by working collectives on behalf of the social community, within the framework of the state economic plan. . .The working collectives shall exercise this right of management through workers' councils. . .

The Workers' Council of each enterprise was to be elected for a one year term by all workers of the enterprise in a secret ballot. The councils would vary in size, according to the scale of the enterprise, from 15 to 120 members.[9] They were responsible, under a chairman elected by themselves, for supervising the overall management and operation of the enterprise, and for approving the periodical accounts and production plans.

The relation of the Workers' Councils to management was of course crucial. They were responsible for electing the boards of management, of up to eleven members, three-quarters of whom had to be workers engaged directly in production; only one-third of the board members could serve a second successive term, and a third term was impermissible. Here was one safeguard against creating a new bureaucracy. The director, who would be *ex officio* a member of the management board, was to be appointed by a higher economic association, or the relevant organ of government. His duties were defined in detail by the Basic Law. He was to organise the process of production, and enforce the orders and instructions of the appropriate higher bodies, as well as those of the managing board. He had to conclude contracts and allocate the assets of the firm 'within the economic plan and conformably to the conclusions of the managing board'. He had powers of hiring and firing workers, of assigning them to jobs and of ensuring discipline, subject to consultation with the Workers' Council when major changes of policy were involved, and to the decisions of the managing board when workers appealed against changes of job or termination of employment.

Djilas in *The Unperfect Society* (1969) gave an account of how the new Law was evolved. He himself wanted in spring 1950 to make a start in creating the 'free association of producers', foreshadowed by Marx, but was hesitant about transferring responsibility to the workers at such a difficult time for the economy. Kardelj and Kidrič felt no such reserves, but both thought that a long time would be needed. Kidrič then said that some scheme should be worked out immediately, and Kardelj proposed the Workers' Councils as the main instrument of self-management. Tito had heard of the detailed proposals probably

---

[9] The list of candidates for election to councils was to be drawn up by the Trade Union branch of the enterprise, but a given number of workers or employees could present an alternative list.

some weeks before the Federal Assembly met in June, but had not been concerned with working them out. According to Djilas, Kardelj and he himself had to press Tito hard to adopt their scheme which would represent a new type of democracy:

Tito paced up and down, as though completely wrapped in his own thoughts. Suddenly he stopped and exclaimed:
  'Factories belonging to the workers – something that has never yet been achieved!'

The Basic Law on Workers' Self-Management derived from the anarcho-syndicalist line of the European workers' movement. Anarchic tendencies however seemed likely to be under firm control. Central planning continued. The director had large powers. A 'monolithic' Communist Party was in the near background. But it is also true that the idea of 'self-management' soon acquired some substance in Yugoslavia, and that the Basic Law of June 1950 has been the foundation of a very distinct and individual Yugoslav 'road to socialism'.

4

Throughout the remainder of the years 1950 and 1951 various other laws and decrees were passed which distanced Yugoslavia increasingly from the Soviet pattern of Communism. On the economic side, the limits within which the Workers' Councils should operate were more strictly defined. On the one hand a new law of January 1951 allowed for free price formation for non-rationed goods; it was supplemented by further derestrictions in September 1951, and by the end of the year consumer rationing was largely eliminated (though not of course widespread shortages). On the other hand, it was decided at the end of 1950 to extend the Five Year Plan (due to expire in 1951) to the end of 1952, and then to proceed on the basis of annual plans only. In preparation for the new pattern of decentralised planning, three laws were passed in December 1951. Under the first and most important of these, the Law on the Management of the National Economy, the scope of detailed central planning was restricted and the Federal Government was responsible only for fixing 'basic proportions' in the Federal social plan.[10] Within the limits imposed by these 'basic pro-

[10] The 'basic proportions' included minimum rates of capacity utilisation for various branches of the economy; an overall figure for investment in the development of production; figures for the basic wages to be paid within each Republic for each branch of the national economy; and average rates of 'accumulation and funds', i.e. the contributions to be paid by all enterprises into the 'social funds' (wages, social security and capital amortisation); and similar rates for contribution to government administrative funds.

portions', which seemed to be highly restrictive, and by supplementary 'social plans' at Republican level, enterprises had to work out their own production plans, which would form the foundation for future estimates of production, taxation, etc. at the higher levels.

Under the second new Law (that on Budgets), the scope of the Federal Budget was heavily restricted – to state-owned property, and necessary state expenditure, particularly on defence. The third new Law – on Social Contributions and Taxation – laid down that in principle enterprises should contribute to the 'social community' according to the size of their payroll, and then defined types of enterprises which, because of any exceptionally favourable conditions for their operations, should pay supplementary contributions. The Law further fixed categories of those who had to pay income tax (private farmers, private professional men, etc.), and designated the turnover tax as the instrument for manipulating the distribution of the national income. The assessment and levying of taxes was to be carried out principally by District and other local People's Committees (in practice the local Committees below District level had no say in the assessment).

By the end of 1951 too there had been drastic changes in the tempo and method of collectivisation. Peasant resistance to the big drive for collectivisation in 1950 and 1951 convinced the Yugoslav leaders that they would have to rely much more on local interest and much less on centralised direction in their conduct of economic affairs. Towards the end of 1951 there had been massive withdrawals from co-operatives, in Macedonia especially. In November 1951 it was announced officially that the policy was changed, and that 'the consolidation and gradual enlargement of collective ownership...in the hands of the general agricultural co-operatives[11]...becomes the basic method of further socialist transformation of the village'.

Thus Yugoslav leaders were evolving a new system, stimulated by the economic experience of the period since 1948, and their own political needs (whether so much decentralisation was likely to produce the economic results best suited to their condition is another matter). They were also introducing in 1950 and 1951 certain political and social modifications of communism as they had hitherto practised it. The primary aim was to secure more general support for their own régime, but at a time of economic crisis they probably took account of the political effect abroad. Some degree of 'liberalisation' might improve their prospects of securing aid from the Western powers. In

[11] General agricultural co-operatives were in essence voluntary associations of peasants for mutual help.

autumn 1950 it was announced that a new criminal code would be drafted. This was adopted in February 1951 and was based on the principle that there could be no crime or punishment unless this was specified by law. Arbitrary action by the police (and, shortly afterwards, by administrative officials), was much reduced and the previous extent of it was revealed by Ranković, the Minister of Interior, in a startling report of June 1951 to the Central Committee. This was the beginning of a series of judicial reforms.[12]

A further and more immediately popular step towards the rule of law was taken in autumn 1950 by Tito when he abolished many of the special privileges, especially with regard to food and housing, that Party and Government officials had enjoyed. Finally came action more directly aimed at Western public opinion. Important properties were returned to the Serbian Orthodox Church (September 1951) and Tito published his offer to release Archbishop Stepinac from captivity, if he would leave the country or retire to a monastery (the offer was refused).

The Western powers, and particularly the U.S. administration, may not have paid much attention at the time to the evolution of the 'Yugoslav Way', nor have been greatly impressed by Tito's more liberal gestures on the Yugoslav domestic front. However, as Tito's need for economic help from the West grew, the Western leaders were faced, as they thought, with the increased possibility of renewed confrontation with the Russians, and were correspondingly anxious to build up Yugoslavia as a possible bastion against Soviet or Soviet-inspired aggression. Thus the interests of Yugoslavia and the West were beginning to coincide. In autumn 1950 Tito gave a clear signal by declaring that, even if Yugoslavia could not accept Marshall aid, its effect in France and Italy had not been disastrous. The first formal request by the Yugoslav Government for American foodstuffs was made in October 1950. A favourable answer and other forms of Western aid were soon forthcoming. On 14 November the British Government announced a gift to the value of £3 million. On 16 November the U.S. administration promised grain worth $10 million from their stocks in Germany, with $20 million worth more to follow. On 18 November President Truman recommended to Congress a large-scale scheme of aid to Yugoslavia, and on 29 November, an American–Yugoslav Aid Agree-

---

[12] The series was completed in 1954, with the provision that judges must have legal qualifications and could only be removed for causes specified by statute, and that public prosecutors would also have to be legally qualified and placed under the jurisdiction of the Courts.

ment was concluded in Belgrade. In return for what they were about to receive, the Yugoslavs promised to give priority to the U.S.A. in the purchase of some strategically important raw materials, and to give facilities to U.S. observers to supervise the distribution of aid to all in need, regardless of their political sympathies.

By the end of January 1951, the sum of American aid had reached $17 million, with a further $35 million promised, and a further £2 million from the British. A conference was held in London during summer 1951 to determine the form and modalities of the further and continuous economic aid which would clearly be required, if the Yugoslav economy was to be put on its feet after the excesses of total planning and the effects of the 1950 harvest. The Governments of Britain, France and the U.S.A. agreed to pay the Yugoslav Government an annual grant, with no strings attached, the amount to be fixed annually by mutual discussion. The U.S. Government was to bear 66.6% of the burden, the British 25%, and the French 8.4%.

The London agreement of summer 1951 was supplemented by a U.S.–Yugoslav agreement of 14 November on the re-equipment of the Yugoslav Army, reached after prolonged negotiations. The main crux had been whether or not a large U.S. military mission was needed to supervise the training of the Yugoslav army in the use of the new weapons. In the end the Americans contented themselves with the training of Yugoslav officers in American army camps, and with the establishment of a small group of 30 Americans as a Military Aid section within their Embassy in Yugoslavia.[13]

First steps towards the re-shaping of the Yugoslav internal system were thus paralleled by first steps towards the Western orientation – or 'occidentation' – of Yugoslav foreign policy; but Tito at least was determined that these first steps should not lead either to liberal democracy or to a Western alliance.

[13] This was appropriately headed by a General Harmony. [!]

7

Wither away?

The 'Yugoslav way' evolved rapidly, and to the foreign observer it had distanced Yugoslavia greatly from other communist countries by spring 1952. One simple measure of the difference between Yugoslavia and other Communist régimes was to compare the newspapers. The Belgrade daily *Politika* was no longer entirely taken up with success stories about production in Yugoslavia, and reports of strikes and slumps in the Western world. It had begun to carry again informative surveys of international politics, advertisements from the main Belgrade stores, serials imported from abroad,[1] and a Walt Disney comic strip. The 'self-managing' paper began to be concerned with securing the maximum revenue for itself. The same principle made enterprises pay more attention to the quality of goods produced for the home market; and as the trade agreements made with Western countries also committed the Yugoslav authorities to the import of some consumer goods, the net result was a considerable improvement in the variety and quality of the goods available in Yugoslav shops.

It was not only managers who were concerned with the profit motive. The wage system adopted in 1952 was a compromise between centralised control and freedom for enterprises. There were limits imposed by the Federal Government, the Republican or local social plans (in the form of taxes), and the Trade Unions (in the shape of wage norms). But the enterprises would also pay from profits a variable incentive wage to workers.[2] The restrictive side of this system appeared more obvious than the freedom which it permitted, but the permissive side had its effects in the political as well as the economic sphere.

[1] I remember in particular a vaguely progressive novel by J. B. Priestley and Alex Weissberg's horrific account of Soviet concentration camps, *The Conspiracy of Silence*.

[2] The Republican or local social plans fixed the total amount of the wages fund at the disposal of each enterprise. Within this total, the fund was divided into a basic wage fixed by law (payment of 80% of this was guaranteed by the Federal Government, if an enterprise could not meet its obligations), and a supplementary bonus wage, for work above the norm fixed by Trade Unions, paid at a rate fluctuating within limits also set by the Federal Government.

The system was also applied to agricultural co-operatives, which began to apply strict profit-and-loss accounting, and to take more seriously the warnings against waste which had been constantly issued, by Tito himself amongst others, from 1949 onwards. More agricultural produce became available; and not only from the co-operatives. Private peasants, who had hoarded their produce under the system of compulsory purchase at low prices, could now get a fair price for it and could buy rather more with their money.[3]

So far as the new system worked, it also involved hardship for the numerous workers who were dismissed from enterprises which needed to look to their payrolls (for a time it was usually the women who were sacked first). Some price control continued, but wages too often failed to cover the uncontrolled prices for some of the necessities of life. Hence the continuance of a considerable 'parallel economy' in the form of leisure-time work away from the factory, which could be expensive to the community in the expenditure of personal energy (and of materials belonging to the enterprises).[4]

In general however the quality of life in Yugoslavia was improving, and not only as the result of the new economic system. The legal reforms of 1951 also began to have their effect. By 1952 much less was heard about arbitrary action by the UDBA, and those members of the former middle-classes (particularly in the cities) who had formerly been particularly subject to their attention began to gain in confidence. There was a considerable degree of freedom of speech and movement and of contact with foreigners.[5] Members of the former bourgeoisie were still exposed to various forms of indirect discrimination, for example in the allocation of jobs. But generally in 1952–3 the spread of self-management went together with a marked increase in civic and political freedom.

The tensions engendered by this process within the political structure of the new Yugoslavia were considerable. There was the tension between the 'principle of profitability' – the need to set market forces

[3] I was told by a highly intelligent Yugoslav Vice-Minister in 1952 that the Yugoslav peasant had once again proved his native talents by immediately grasping the 'principle of profitability', one of the current slogans of the time.

[4] There was a story current at this time about the gypsy who applied for admission to the local Party organisation. His political education was tested by a simple question: Why did Marshal Tito hold so many high offices of state? The answer came pat: 'Of course none of us can make do with just one job.'

[5] My wife and I for example were able to travel widely without previous notice, to stay, often with non-official Yugoslav friends, in hotels or small mountain huts, or to camp at will by the roadside – this was before the days of highly organised tourist traffic and camping sites – where passing peasants would converse with frank and dignified curiosity.

free and to provide some stimulus for the worker – and the almost equal need to keep the economy under some kind of control. The framework of 'basic proportions', apparently rigid enough, did not always prove sufficient to keep original economic sin under control and to prevent the enterprise benefiting its workers unduly at the expense of the community. There was tension too between the new 'self-managing' class, which comprised not only the managers of enterprises but also those in charge of social security and educational institutions, and on the other hand the officials of Federal, Republican and local Governments. If the former became fully independent in their ways, how much business was left for the latter to do? There was tension above all between the new 'self-managers' and the activists of the Communist Party who had for six years run Yugoslav affairs down to the smallest detail.

Western analysts of the Yugoslav scene in the early fifties tended to discount the possibility of such tensions, and to conclude that, behind the facade of self-management, the Communist Party exercised a control firm enough for all the practical purposes of a dictatorship. The new managing boards of enterprises as well as the Workers' Councils, tended after all to be packed with members of the Party, moving to new positions from their factory cells. The activists on District and other Councils, as well as in the Republican and Federal Governments, were also members of the Party. All would act, it was thought, on the same central directives, and life would go on much as before. Such analysis underrated the deep need felt by many Yugoslav leaders right down the line for the profit motive and economic incentives, if they were to increase production. The managing directors of big enterprises were often to all appearance good communists; but when the directive was to conduct economic operations at a profit and benefit their own working force thereby, local loyalty was apt to prevail over any social conscience towards the community as a whole, and over any previous conviction that profit was sinful.

2

Various constitutional steps were taken from January 1952 to the end of March 1953 in order to formalise the 'Yugoslav way'. The General Law of 1 April 1952 on People's Committees reorganised local government to bring it into line and into closer co-operation with economic and social self-management.[6] People's Committees were established for

6 A previous law of 1949 had gone some way in this direction.

groups of villages, or small towns, for towns large enough to rate a separate committee; and for subordinate districts of big cities.[7] They were empowered to draw up their own budgets and social plans, within the limits established by Federal and Republican Laws, especially the Law of December 1951. The Executive Committees of the former People's Committees were abolished (on the ground that they could too easily be turned into the permanent instruments of a centralised bureaucracy) and their functions transferred to the People's Committees as a whole, or to subordinate committees.

Another change under the Law was the creation of 'Producers' Councils' as further chambers of the District, town and city Committees. These were to be elected every two years from various general branches of production, in direct proportion to the percentage contribution of each branch to the 'total social product' (gross product) of the district concerned. They were subordinate to the main Committees at each level but had equal responsibility for all problems involving local economic affairs. In particular the creation of the Producers' Councils put workers' representatives in a position to have some say in determining the total size of their enterprises' wage funds, as well as in allocating its distribution within the enterprise.

The Producers' Councils could be regarded as a legacy of syndicalist theory. An apparent step towards direct democracy was taken by the institution, also under the 1952 Law, of 'voters' meetings'. These were intended to enable the maximum number of citizens to keep some control over their local People's Committees. On the other side they provided a forum at which citizens could be enlightened about local and higher government policy, and perhaps be mobilised by the CPY to represent the general 'social conscience' against bureaucratic or 'particularist' tendencies on the part of the People's Committees.

The CPY too had to adapt its 'working style' to the existence of self-managing enterprises and institutions. It made a formal effort to do so at its VIth Congress, held at Zagreb in November 1952. This proved to be a very important turning-point in the political evolution of Tito's Yugoslavia. The general object of the Congress was to demonstrate that there could be many ways to communism, according to the specific circumstances of each country, that the Yugoslavs themselves adhered to the doctrines of Marx and Lenin, and that Stalin and his fellow-leaders were the true heretics. The transfer of the factories to self-management was described by Tito as an 'epoch-making act'. The

---

[7] At a higher level they were also created for districts, including a varying number of small towns or villages, and for large groups.

Politburo of the CC, CPY, was renamed the Executive Committee (the name Politburo smelt unpleasantly of Stalin) and was enlarged to take account of Republican national susceptibilities. The Party was told emphatically that it had a new role – not to administer government but to inspire social and political action within the new framework of industrial and local self-management. Members of Party organisations at each enterprise or institution must continue to act as good communists, but individually, in virtue of their local position as citizens and producers. Administrative (i.e. dictatorial or forcible) methods must be abandoned, and the Party was now to rely entirely on persuasion. Tito did not quote Milton's *Areopagitica*, but might have claimed the following as the motif of his exposition: 'Let Truth and Falsehood grapple; who ever knew Truth put to the worse, in a free and open encounter?'

Kardelj, in introducing the Law on People's Committees to the Yugoslav National Assembly on 1 April, had spoken bold words about the future, or non-future, of the Party: '...the alternative between the Marxist teaching of the withering away of the State *and, with it, of any Party system*,[8] and the Stalinist theory of the strengthening of the State, furnish the touchstone of real Socialism today.'

Tito, in speaking at the Party Congress in November, was a good deal more cautious about withering away. The role of the Party, he said, would be even more responsible and important than before, now that its main task was that of socialist education. The Party must remain cohesive, must not turn into a mass organisation and must not adopt Western liberal-democratic ideas.

Nevertheless it was allowed that other and more progressive political tendencies existed in the West. The Social Democrats of Western Europe should be cultivated, and this task was entrusted particularly to Milovan Djilas. It was he who explained to Western journalists on the spot the significance of the transformation of Yugoslav Communism, symbolised by the change of name from Communist Party of Yugoslavia to the League of Communists of Yugoslavia (henceforward LCY). It would welcome increasing contact with other 'progressive forces', not least the British Labour Party and Trade Union movement.

The VIth Party Congress did something to convince public opinion in the West at least that the Yugoslavs had found a new and independent way to Communism which might in fact lead them to something near to Social Democracy in the Western sense of the words. This

[8] Author's italics.

impression was strengthened by the subsequent Congress (February 1953) of the People's Front, which also changed its name to the 'Socialist Alliance of the Working People of Yugoslavia' (henceforward SAWYP), in virtue of the change in the nature of its principal activities. These were now to be mainly educational – the transmission to the people on a very broad front of the ideas formulated by the LCY, together with the supervision of elections and of the functioning of the People's Committees and social organisations. It was hard indeed to tell where the educational functions of the LCY were to end, and where those of SAWPY were to begin. At the least it was intended to provide some additional means of bringing the 'social conscience' of the Yugoslav people as a whole to bear on any narrowly selfish deviations of self-managing enterprises or institutions. It was significant, for example, that the daily Belgrade newspaper *Politika* was put under the nominal control of SAWPY, and that the other main daily, *Borba*, formerly the organ of the CPY, became in 1954 SAWPY's own newspaper. This made little difference to its content, but enabled the LCY to claim that it was not engaged in 'administrative' activity even in the educational field.

The conclusions of the Law on People's Committees and the VIth Congress of the LCY were formally embodied in the new Constitutional Law of January 1953, which partly replaced that of 1946. Article 3 pronounced the People's Committees of municipalities and Districts to be 'the basic organs of state authority', and limited the powers of Federal and Republican Governments to the rights (admittedly still considerable) specified by the Federal and Republican Constitutions. The links between deputies to the National Assembly and their constituents were strengthened by a provision that the deputies should be *ex officio* members of the People's Committees of their constituencies, and that they should be subject to recall by their constituents.

The emphasis of the new Constitution was on direct democracy, with the People's Committees (which were in close touch with their local Workers' Councils) as the basis. It was naturally assumed that this sort of direct democracy would counter any tendencies to bureaucratic centralism of the Soviet type, which was still regarded as the main political danger. More optimistically, it was assumed that it would also alleviate the old national tensions, between Serb and Croat particularly, and that the industrial workers would be more conscious of their class than of their nationality. This assumption was given concrete form by the abolition of the Council of Nationalities as a separate unit of the

Federal Assembly.[9] Instead ten deputies for each Republic (together
with six for the Vojvodina and four for the Kosmet) were empowered
to meet separately on occasion, to debate certain kinds of bills which
particularly affected the interests of Republics. The original Council of
Nationalities was replaced by a separate Council of Producers (smaller
by about a third than the Federal Assembly); its members, like those of
the Councils at lower level, represented the main categories of economic activity and met separately, or together with the main Federal
Chamber, to discuss economic questions.

Another new body, the Federal Executive Council (henceforward
FEC) was established under the Constitutional Law of 1953. It could
initiate and enforce legislation, but its members were to be elected by
the Federal Assembly, and were meant to have no direct administrative
responsibilities. The theory behind this was that there should be a
distinction between the policy-forming side of the executive function
and the purely 'administrative' organs. In Yugoslavia, as elsewhere,
this distinction soon became blurred. The responsible Secretaries of
State for the most important Government departments were before
long made *ex officio* members of the FEC, or were appointed from
within its ranks.

The office of President of the Republic was also instituted, as the
highest executive function, with the main duties of representing the
State, presiding over the FEC, and acting as supreme commander of
the armed forces. The President was to be elected by the Assembly for
four-year terms (like members of the FEC and of the Assembly itself),
and was to be responsible to it. Inevitably Tito was the first occupant
of the office.

Such in broad outline was the constitutional machinery by which
the Yugoslav way to socialism was to be realised.[10] It was evolved by a
political decision, mainly as the result of compelling economic circumstances. Another aspect of the same circumstances led the LCY to take
decisions about Yugoslavia's agricultural organisation which were of
more immediate importance to the country than any clause of the new
Constitution. By 1952 official policy was to consolidate and enlarge
gradually the system of socialist co-operatives. For most of 1952 this
line was maintained and the movement for withdrawal from the co-

----

9 It had in fact never met separately except, as constitutionally bound, to debate
the social plan and constitutional amendments.
10 The passage of the Constitutional Law was followed by elections to the Federal
Assembly in March 1953. These were held under a new voting system, which led
to the emergence in some Macedonian Districts of unofficial candidates, afterwards eliminated from the ballot.

operatives was held in check. Party agents continued to deny the necessary legal aid to peasants who wanted to withdraw after three years in accordance with their legal rights; indeed they and their lawyers, if they had found any, were sometimes prosecuted for hostile agitation against the co-operative system. On the other side, the system of compulsory deliveries became increasingly difficult to enforce and was officially relaxed by degrees throughout 1952. This benefited the private sector in agriculture and made the co-operative sector even more unattractive. From the state point of view, the co-operatives were proving very inefficient. It was admitted by spring 1952 that only a third of them operated at any profit, and that an equal number were working at a loss – often a serious loss. Moreover the summer of 1952 brought a drought, though not so serious as that of 1950.

The VIth Party Congress in November 1952 did not produce any indication of major changes to come in the agricultural system, though the Croatian Party leader, Bakarić, was known to consider it impracticable. The 1953 Constitution continued effectively to discriminate against the peasantry by giving extra political weight to the industrial workers through the new Producers' Councils. But a major swing in policy was announced by Kardelj to the congress of the People's Front in March 1953. Kardelj introduced this by an attack on the Soviet agrarian policy of driving independent peasants into *kolkhozes*. In the U.S.S.R., he said, the productivity of agricultural labour had remained low, and the machinery available to the collective farms was inefficiently used. Bureaucracy again was the enemy which stood in the way of higher agricultural production. Most of Kardelj's points of course applied to the Yugoslav efforts at collectivisation. He implied that only a few members of the Party still pursued 'administrative methods' (i.e. used pressure little, if at all, short of force), and that only a few peasants went slow at sowing time, hoarded their produce, or sold it privately. Nevertheless he concluded that in Yugoslavia too it was necessary to eliminate as soon as possible 'those administrative and other artificial elements in our agriculture which today make the economic evolution of the villages more difficult and have a negative political effect as well'.

Marx had said that 'higher' systems of production developed only as material conditions for their existence were created. The Yugoslav peasants would decide for themselves in favour of co-operative agriculture when they could see, as they would come to do, that it had become economically necessary for them. The process could not be hastened by administrative pressure or political propaganda.

On 20 March 1953 a decree on the Reorganisation of Peasant Co-operatives was announced, permitting the dissolution or re-organisation of all peasant co-operatives. Peasants were free to leave them and take back all the land, buildings, inventory and livestock which they had originally contributed, though they were still subject to some financial obligations to their co-operatives. The re-organisation of these was left in essence to the local People's Committee, and a large choice of pattern was allowed. By the end of 1953, only about 1,250 working co-operatives remained out of the nearly 7,000 that had existed three years earlier. The decision was made in effect to jettison the co-operative system, at least for some time, in order to achieve increased agricultural production and to reconcile the peasants with the newly evolving political and social system.

3

The Yugoslav leaders did not evolve their way to socialism in order to please any foreign government. They were under strong internal compulsions to do so. Nevertheless the international situation of their country was bound to be an important factor in their calculations. For the years 1952–5 inclusive Western aid was an essential factor in the revival of the Yugoslav economy. The foundations of the Western aid programme had been laid before the end of 1951. In summer 1952 the U.S. administration made a further $30 million credit available to counter the effects of the drought, and by the end of the year Yugoslav foreign trade had again reached its total level of 1948, with the main Western powers taking the place of the Soviet bloc. It was not only economic needs that dictated some 'occidentation' of Yugoslav policy. In 1952 the 'cold war' was very much on, and there was some further rapprochement with the West over defence policy. From the Western point of view some assurance of Yugoslav co-operation, at least to the extent of friendly neutrality, was important, both to protect the right flank of the NATO forces in Austria, and to provide a land connection between Greece and Turkey (which became members of the NATO alliance in October 1951) and NATO forces in Central Europe. For these purposes closer links were desirable between Yugoslavia, Greece and Turkey on the one hand and Yugoslavia and Italy on the other. The latter proved harder to forge than the former.

The Yugoslavs were still alarmed at the evidence provided by incidents on their own eastern borders about the Soviet propensity for indirect aggression. At the end of 1950 they dropped the issue of the

Macedonian minority in Greece which had served them as one excuse in the preceding years to help the cause of the Greek rebels. Ambassadors were exchanged in December 1950. Throughout the next two years trade and other relations with Greece steadily improved, and finally a Yugoslav military delegation visited Athens. Similar steps were taken to improve Yugoslav–Turkish relations and in March 1953 a tripartite Treaty was signed at Ankara, providing for diplomatic and military consultations as necessary between Yugoslavia, Greece and Turkey, as well as for economic, technical and cultural co-operation.

On Yugoslavia's north-western borders, it had become clear to the Yugoslavs in 1949 that their claims to the Slovene-speaking areas of Carinthia around Villach and Klagenfurt were unrealistic, and they had gradually mended their fences with the Austrian Government. Relations with Italy were much more difficult since the Yugoslavs were unwilling even to appear to drop their claims to Trieste. At the Paris Peace negotiations of 1946, the Yugoslavs, backed up to a point by the Russians, had demanded the port and hinterland of Trieste. Under the Paris Peace Treaty in 1946, a Free Territory of Trieste (FTT) was constituted, to be administered by a Governor appointed by the Security Council of the U.N. The Russian and Yugoslav strategy had been first to reduce the size of the FTT to a minimum, and then to block the appointment of a Governor, in the hope of making the whole experiment unworkable. In practice the city of Trieste itself and the Western Zone A of the FTT continued, as in 1945, under the administration of an Anglo-American military occupation force, with increasing participation of the Italians, while Yugoslav forces occupied and administered the Eastern Zone B.

Such was the situation in the early months of 1948, when the cold war seemed to be approaching a crisis. On 20 March, in order to help the Italian Christian Democrat party in a crucial election, the U.S., British and French Governments addressed a declaration to the Soviet and Yugoslav Governments proposing that the whole FTT, including Zone B should be given back to Italy. The authors of the Tripartite Declaration regarded it as a tactical move only, and had no idea that the text reached Belgrade precisely when Stalin had decided to put the severest pressure on Tito.

The Yugoslav leaders were in a very difficult situation. After the break with Stalin, with no prospect of diplomatic support from the Soviet Government, it looked to them as if the Tripartite Declaration might turn into a serious policy commitment for the West. Their tactics were to maintain the boldest possible front during the years 1950–3, when the Western powers might have tried to bargain economic and military aid to Yugoslavia for concessions to the Italians over Trieste. Tito maintained his claim to Trieste itself, but admitted publicly that it was useless to press it. He declared himself ready to renounce Zone B only on condition that the Italians renounced Zone A. He refused the offer (April 1950) of the Italian Foreign Minister, Count Sforza, to partition Zone B along ethnic lines (which would have resulted in transferring the coastal region to Italy).

By spring 1952 the Western powers too found themselves in a difficult diplomatic position. They did not want to delay the formation of something like a South-East European front against possible attack by the Soviet Union. Equally they did not want to alienate Italy, an original member of NATO, by making any concessions to Yugoslavia, which until so recently had been virtually in the enemy camp. On 20 March 1952, the anniversary of the Tripartite Declaration of 1948, there were violent anti-Western demonstrations by the Italian population in Trieste. With elections looming in Italy, the British and Americans decided to give something more to the Italians. After British–U.S.–Italian talks in London, it was announced in May that the Italian authorities would take over the greater part of the administration of Zone A. The Yugoslavs protested,[11] but by now had too much at stake on good relations with the West to do more.

Yugoslav links with the West at this time appeared all the more important in the light of what was happening in Moscow and the Soviet bloc during the last phase of Stalin's life. In November 1952 another of the great show-trials was staged – that of Rudolf Slansky in Czechoslovakia. The new villains of Muscovite mythology were no longer 'Titoists', but 'cosmopolitan' and 'Zionist' conspirators (recruited of course by the Americans) against the peoples of the Soviet Union and its satellite states. The implications of the Slansky trial were not so immediately dangerous to Yugoslavia as those of the Rajk and Kostov trials in 1948. However they were more alarming to the West; the new charges seemed to indicate that Stalin was set on promoting a further round of the cold war, and on whipping up nationalist sentiments for this end. This impression was enhanced by the announcement of the 'Doctors' plot', made by Tass in January 1953. It was alleged that a terrorist group of doctors had been discovered who 'had set themselves the objective of shortening the lives of leading personages

---

11 The historian will not have to wait long before official documents reveal a typical battle of despatches on the whole subject between the British Embassies in Rome and Belgrade, headed by the cousins Sir Victor and Sir Ivor Mallet.

of the Soviet Union by using harmful methods of treatment'. The 'terrorist group', it was alleged, were linked with the 'Joint', 'the international bourgeois-nationalist organisation which had been created by the American espionage service allegedly to provide material aid to Jews in other countries, but in reality to conduct a comprehensive campaign of espionage and terrorist and subversive activity in a series of countries, among them the Soviet Union'. Tito could interpret these signs of the times better than most; he probably feared the initiation of a paranoiac foreign policy by Stalin, and became the more willing to enter into some limited partnership with the Western powers. Already in September 1952, the British Foreign Secretary, Anthony Eden, had visited Belgrade. No important agreements were reached between him and Tito, but much was made of the occasion officially.[12] In March 1953, Tito himself paid an official visit to England, not without some apprehension on either side about the popular reaction to his arrival.[13] He returned without any formal treaty, or decisive step towards an alliance (neither would have been acceptable to him, particularly as Stalin was by then dead) but with strong personal assurances from Churchill about British and Western interest in the integrity of Yugoslavia. He was able to quote Churchill's assurance that 'should our ally, Yugoslavia, be attacked, we would fight and die with you'. This, Tito said, was a 'sacred vow and it is enough for us. We need no written treaties.'

4

Tito's visit to London marked the high tide of the first phase of 'occidentation' in Yugoslavia's foreign and domestic policy. At the beginning of March, Stalin had died. The Yugoslav leaders were very cautious about developments in Moscow, but it became possible for them to hope again, after nearly five years, that the Cominform's anti-Yugoslav policy might be radically revised. In May 1953 Molotov received the Yugoslav chargé d'affaires in Moscow for the first time since 1948, and on 4 June Tito announced that Yugoslavia was ready

[12] Tito lunched, together with Kardelj, Ranković and Djilas, at the British Embassy – a marked sign of favour at this time. At Tito's own reception, the newly-married Jovanka Broz, his third wife, appeared for the first time quite unexpectedly as Yugoslavia's leading lady; Eden, who could also have brought a newly-wedded wife to Belgrade, was not best pleased by the surprise.

[13] There was strong opposition to the visit in advance from British Catholics in particular. It fell to me personally to reassure Tito that H.M.G.'s attitude was unchanged. I also had the opportunity, while the visit was in progress, of seeing the relief and delight of some junior Communist functionaries that it was going well.

to accept the Soviet proposal for an exchange of Ambassadors. This
did not necessarily imply, he said, the normalisation of relations, and if
relations were normalised,[14] this would not affect Yugoslav relations
with the West. For some time Yugoslav polemics against Soviet policies
remained very sharp. The general line however left some room for
hope, and was authoritatively expressed by Kardelj in a statement
about the release and rehabilitation of the Kremlin doctors, early in
April:

The future will show whether the bureaucratic and despotic system of the
Soviet Union will be consolidated again, or whether it will gradually
decompose from below as a result of the pressure of the working masses. In
any case, internal developments have already gone further than had been
expected. Even if bureaucratic tyranny rallies again for a time, it will be
far from retaining its former inner and outer strength.

Kardelj developed his analysis further in an article in *Borba* of
28 June 1953, the fifth anniversary of the Cominform resolution, in
which he commented on the workers' riots which had broken out that
month in Czechoslovakia and East Germany.

There are various alternatives for the further development in the Soviet
Union, but none of them can be Stalinist. The changes in Soviet policy
are by no means sweeping, and in themselves do not alter the situation.
But they are of greater importance as symptoms of the process that caused
them. They show that the internal social processes in the Soviet Union
have by now gone so far that the new men. . .who wish to strengthen their
positions can. . .earn. . .support only by means of a political line virtually
directed against Stalin.

This was the analysis on which Yugoslav officials based their discussions with Western diplomats. The implication, particularly after the
'liquidation' of Beria in July, was that new 'social processes' were at
work, which would result in the adoption of a new and more moderate
foreign policy.

This conclusion was particularly welcome to some of the LCY
leaders and to many of the rank and file. They had not been adequately
prepared for the westward swing of 1951–3. To many Western
observers the new Yugoslav system may have looked like an elaborate
façade behind which the LCY could operate as before. To the average
local LCY functionary things looked very different. Bourgeois individuals and 'capitalist' aid were becoming at least semi-respectable.

---

[14] In autumn 1953 Yugoslav officials took the line that relations with the Soviet
Union were now 'normally bad', as opposed to 'abnormally bad'.

The process of operating indirectly through the Workers' Councils and People's Committees might be more effective in the end, but what exactly was involved in the transition from 'administrative methods' to 'persuasion'?

Many of the LCY functionaries were not sophisticated people. Some found it best to rest on their laurels after the VIth Congress and virtually to give up their function as 'transmission belt' to people outside the LCY (most of them in any case had other primary jobs). Others continued to issue orders as before. The result of the latter tendency was painfully apparent in the crisis of collectivisation, but to many of the LCY the decrees of 31 March 1953 virtually dissolving co-operatives came as a most disagreeable surprise and was regarded as a defeat. Less than two months later a new decree was issued to placate the conservative communists, who thought that the way had been left open for the return of capitalism and a new *kulak* class to the countryside. The permitted size of private holdings was reduced from twenty to ten hectares (about 24 acres), and the land acquired by the state as a result of this reduction was used, not to settle more private peasants in the countryside, but to enlarge the state farms or co-operatives.

At the end of June the Central Committee of the LCY was convened at Tito's island home, Brioni, to review progress over the first half of 1953. Tito found that the decisions of the VIth Congress had led to excessive passivity in the LCY. Some of the Workers' Councils, in spite of all the restrictions on their freedom, had succeeded in raising wages to what appeared a socially undesirable level. The instructions sent to all LCY officials in the so-called Brioni Letter of the CC were nominally directed against all forms of deviation, to left and right alike. It was however the liberal wing of the LCY which had to bear the brunt of the criticism. The same tendency was apparent in the autumn elections to the new-style Assemblies. The vast majority of candidates at national level were nominated at voters' meetings, by 'conscious socialist forces', organised by the LCY and SAWPY, whose 'persuasive' efforts bordered on the 'administrative'.[15]

Events in Trieste meanwhile allowed Tito to make a show, at little cost to himself, of standing up to the West and satisfying his conservative communists on an issue of foreign policy where the people of Yugoslavia as a whole were behind him. The U.S., British and French Governments were anxious to consolidate relations on the military as well as on other levels between NATO and the Balkan Pact, concluded

[15] At Republican level a considerable number were nominated by petition of at least two hundred voters, and certain 'non-official' candidates were elected.

in March 1953. Italy was reluctant to do so, unless her position in Trieste was improved. With Giuseppe Pella as the head of a weak minority Government in Rome, which needed some conspicuous success, it was decided in summer 1953 to bring about a *fait accompli*. The Anglo-American troops would withdraw from Trieste; the Italians would enter the city and take over the administration. There would be no formal renunciation by the Italians of their claims to Zone B, and Pella might regard the entry into Trieste as merely a first step. The Western Allies however made no commitment on this; they rather assumed that the Yugoslavs would first consolidate their grip on Zone B, and that a final *de facto* division of the Free Territory would thus be reached.

This was not far off what happened; but events were spread over a full year. On 8 October 1953 the British and Americans announced that their troops would shortly be withdrawn from Zone A and the city of Trieste. Tito appeared to take the news quietly when it was announced to him, but soon street demonstrations were initiated in Belgrade and Zagreb, with hostile slogans and damage to the Allied 'reading rooms' there. There was genuine popular feeling behind all this,[16] even if the LCY played a leading part. A partial mobilisation was ordered, Yugoslav troops moved to positions along the Yugoslav–Italian frontier, and Tito announced that, if Italian troops moved into Trieste, Yugoslav troops would move against them. The Yugoslav reaction was tougher than had been expected in London and Washington. An assurance was given that Anglo-American troops would not move out before the details of the newly proposed division were settled by talks in which Yugoslav representatives would participate. The Italians in turn organised rioting in Trieste, but the revised arrangements stuck. Within a month troops were withdrawn from the borders on either side. In 1954 secret talks took place in London between British, American, Italian and Yugoslav officials. Agreement on the *de facto* division of the FTT was finally announced in October 1954.

Tito had done well enough out of these proceedings. He had demonstrated to his conservative communist supporters that he was ready, as occasion demanded, to stand up to his Western protectors. He had

---

16 Typified by the slogan *Život damo, Trst ne damo* ('We give our lives, but not Trieste') unofficially translated by Western diplomats as 'Trst or brst'. Demonstrations were strictly limited. It is illustrative of Yugoslav–Western relations at the time that on 9 October my American counterpart gave a small dinner party at which he and I discussed the crisis calmly and informally with the head of the appropriate department of the Secretariat of Foreign Affairs.

safeguarded Yugoslavia against any further effective claim by the Italians to Zone B, although the Trieste agreement of October 1954 was in form only provisional. He had admittedly renounced the Yugoslav claim to Trieste itself, but could claim that he had done so as part of a satisfactory bargain. The terms of the agreement of October 1954 were in fact considerably more satisfactory to him than those of the Anglo-American declaration of October 1953. Perhaps the most important long-term aspect of the whole arrangement was that it had been reached without Soviet participation or objection. This suited Tito and the Western powers alike. The latter had by now to bear in mind the possibility of a Soviet–Yugoslav rapprochement, and of dealing with a Yugoslav Government strengthened, particularly at the U.N., by Soviet diplomatic support. This was therefore a good time at which to get the Trieste issue out of the way. Tito himself on the other hand could remember how ineffective Soviet support over Trieste had been in 1945–8. If any Yugoslav–Soviet rapprochement took place (and he surely had the possibility in mind himself) before there was some settlement, a new phase of the East–West 'cold war' might spread to the Trieste area, and Italian claims to Zone B might be kept very much alive. Thus Tito also had his reasons for reaching a settlement of the Trieste problem at this stage.

5

By October 1954, when the Trieste settlement was achieved, internal events in Yugoslavia had rendered Soviet–Yugoslav reconciliation more likely. These centred round the case of Milovan Djilas. In 1952 he was recognised as one of Yugoslavia's three outstanding political theorists – much younger and more a man of action than Moša Pijade, more brilliant and less of a schoolmaster than Kardelj. As a student of Belgrade University before the war, he had become an ardent communist and suffered in Royalist prisons. He had been a gallant fighter with the Partisans, and has left an unforgettable picture of himself as a young idealist in his *Conversations with Stalin*, recording his experiences in Moscow on official missions in 1944 and 1948. After the break with the Cominform he had emerged as one of the main theoreticians of the 'Yugoslav way'. His 'image' was that of the perpetual student, the *enfant terrible* of the original Yugoslav Politburo. His informal manner and the breadth of his intellectual interests had not always endeared him to his conservative communist colleagues, but had made him in the early fifties the ideal liaison officer with the Labour and

Social Democrat parties of the West;[17] his personal links with Aneurin Bevan and Jennie Lee were particularly strong.

Djilas had led the attacks on Soviet bureaucracy after 1948, and had helped Kardelj and Kidrić to evolve the Law of 1950 on Workers' Councils. Over the next years he became convinced that democracy could be and was being hampered almost as much in Yugoslavia as in the Soviet Union by centralised planning and administration, and by the detailed intervention at all points in the process by the Party. The de-centralisation of the administrative machine was not enough. The Party had to be separated in fact as well as in theory from day-to-day administration. So far Djilas was only keeping pace with Kardelj, who had publicly talked about the 'withering away' of the Party to the Federal Assembly in 1952. And although Djilas was the most persuasive exponent (particularly to the foreign press) of the LCY's new 'non-administrative' role at the VIth Congress in November 1952, he did not at this point go beyond the other leaders. It was the swing-back to conservative communism and the Central Committee's Brioni Letter of June 1953 that set him to think seriously whether the LCY's style of work was going to differ at all fundamentally from that of the CPY before 1950.

In a pamphlet about political developments in the Soviet Union, published in October 1953, Djilas expressed criticisms of Stalinist bureaucracy which could easily be applied to the LCY apparatus in Yugoslavia. He spoke with obvious inner knowledge about the conditions of life in a totalitarian party once it had attained power – the 'intrigues, mutual scheming and trap-laying, pursuit of posts, careerism, favouritism, the advancement of one's own followers, relatives, 'old fighters' – all under the mask of high morality and ideology'.

Obviously tight discipline and a dedicated caste of professional politicians were required during a period of revolution. But once this was over, society should be able to function with the minimum of professional politicians and without a centralised leadership. Then 'the system of professional politicians and the centralist role of the Party turn into sources of bureaucratic hindrance to social development'.

Power, for Djilas as for Acton, corrupted. But Djilas at this stage avoided anarchist conclusions. 'To renounce power is possible, progressive and socialist, but only if the power. . .does not fall into other hands,

---

[17] It is perhaps worth mentioning a short conversation in 1953, between him and Donald McLachlan, then Foreign Editor of the *Economist*, about Karl Popper's *The Open Society and Its Enemies*.

if there is. . .no other social class and no other party with access to power.'

In his next writings, a series of theoretical articles published in *Borba* during the months of November and December 1953, Djilas went a good deal further. In a genuine democracy there must be no ideological monopoly and complete freedom of expression; this applied to the existing political monopoly of the LCY – there was 'socialist consciousness' by now in Yugoslavia outside the ranks of the LCY and it must be allowed to express itself freely, if socialism was to be furthered. Party discipline must be relaxed: 'The unity of the socialist forces under the. . .changed objective conditions is only possible as a "disunity", as free utterance of the different socialist opinions on different internal problems.'

The customary communist practice of regular political meetings must be discontinued and 'in the given circumstances, professional officers of the Party, Youth League and so forth are. . .superfluous. . . They "control" activities, "cultivate" consciousness, and are "active". And since they have no real functions, they invent some, and thus revive the "revolutionary" forces of bureaucracy which were about to disappear.'

Djilas' immediate point was that the LCY must start to 'wither away' much faster, if the programme of the VIth Party Congress was to be adequately fulfilled. More subversive was the implication of his argument that Stalinism was not an unnatural deviation, but a likely or even inevitable development of the totalitarian one-party state, whether in the Soviet Union or elsewhere.

Djilas' exposition continued at intervals over two months without any intervention from Tito – the only man in a position to intervene effectively. Tito, whether or not he had read Djilas' articles in detail, had approved the idea of the series in advance; perhaps he wanted Djilas to stick his neck out and to render himself liable to discipline.[18] It was however widely assumed that, if the articles continued to appear, they must reflect Tito's own line on matters of such significance; and they began to earn some approval within as well as outside the LCY. Not however among the conservative communists, who were outraged by Djilas' heresies and would lose their jobs if his philosophy were put into practice. At the end of December, the Slovenian leaders protested to Tito, and he decisively disavowed Djilas' ideas. But Djilas was not

---

[18] There would be some parallel here to the action of Mao Tse-tung who in spring 1957 encouraged the 'Hundred Flowers' campaign, only to cut the blooms later that summer.

prepared simply to drop them. In the January number of the LCY monthly *Nova Misao* (New Thought) he published his famous critique of the communist leaders' life-style. His point – that the enjoyment of power had corrupted both the doctrines and the old puritan morality of the revolution – was illustrated by examples to which names could be readily given by those in the know. The women of the 'new class' suffered even more than the men from Djilas' scathing comments. It seemed more likely at this stage that he would suffer for his heresy than that he would be supported by any overwhelming ground-swell of public opinion. And so it proved.

A plenary session of the Central Committee was called in mid-January 1954 to discuss the Djilas case. The result was never in any doubt. Only Vladimir Dedijer, biographer of Tito and head of the international department of SAWPY, had the courage to stand up openly for his friend. After two days of listening to abuse and accusations from his former friends and colleagues, Djilas performed the ritual acts of self-criticism that were expected of him:

I collaborated in the campaign against the Soviet Union...in the course of which I went on to criticise several matters in Yugoslavia...which reminded me of the Russian conditions – some remnants, some externals. I...did not comprehend the process as a whole. Because I saw these things I became frightened of bureaucracy, and carried my criticism further, step by step. As a result of my isolation I conceived this abstract democratic theory, which, if applied concretely, would mean exactly what the comrades have underlined here – a mobilisation of the petty bourgeoisie, of the bourgeoisie of Social Democratism of the Western stamp...

Djilas was expelled from the Central Committee and suspended from all offices in the LCY. A few months later he left the LCY altogether. The first phase of the long-drawn-out Djilas affair was vital for the Yugoslav leaders and for Tito himself. Djilas had exposed himself, apparently without effective preparation within the LCY or among the public at large, to grave charges of 'revisionism'. The verdict of his peers upon him was a further step back towards communist orthodoxy of the old type, and very important for Tito's next reconciliation with the Soviet Union.

8

Yugoslavia and the Soviet Union, 1954–7

The years 1954–7 inclusive were dominated in Yugoslavia by the theme of Soviet–Yugoslav relations. The Yugoslavs recognised that normalisation was likely to be a slow process even after the fall of Djilas. The Cominform journal for January 1954 interpreted this as the result of popular pressure on the Yugoslav régime, and continued to insult Tito. This was hardly a step forward, and indicated that progress towards a new type of relationship between Yugoslavia and the 'Socialist camp' would be complicated by the in-fighting between Malenkov and Khrushchev in Moscow, of which the occasion (if not the deeper cause) was the problem of priorities for industrial investment. The fact that Malenkov met with strong opposition in pursuing a non-Stalinist economic policy (in favour of more consumer goods) temporarily strengthened the position of the conservative communist leaders in other East European countries, who had been most deeply involved in the anti-Yugoslav campaign following Yugoslavia's expulsion from the Cominform. This in turn strengthened the scepticism of the Yugoslav leaders about the likelihood of fundamental changes in Soviet policy.

Meanwhile in Moscow the restoration of Soviet–Yugoslav relations was becoming a key issue between Malenkov, Khrushchev, Molotov and other leaders engaged in a struggle for supreme power. The proponents of reconciliation with Yugoslavia held that it would help the Soviet Union to restore the unity of the 'Socialist camp' in Eastern Europe on a new and more flexible basis, which could ultimately be stronger than a master and servant relationship. Such a move would improve the Soviet image in the non-Communist world and would facilitate both negotiations with the Western powers and the growth of Soviet prestige in Africa and Asia. In Moscow a special committee was set up under Shepilov to examine the problem of relations with Yugoslavia, and concluded that ideologically the Yugoslavs could still be considered as 'socialists'.

In early autumn 1954 Khrushchev suggested confidentially to the Yugoslav CC a new Soviet–Yugoslav understanding, based on the facts that the CPSU had settled with Beria and the LCY with Djilas. The implied bargain was unacceptable to the Yugoslavs, but they noted the fact that it was Khrushchev alone who had signed the letter, and that a new tone was evident in it. In mid-October the Soviet Government made a public and more acceptable gesture, by announcing their approval of the agreement reached between Yugoslavia, Italy, Britain and the U.S.A. over Trieste, thereby renouncing their right to have any further say in the question.

From this time on, Soviet–Yugoslav relations improved rapidly. Essentially the initiative came from the Soviet side, though the Yugoslavs were probably not entirely passive. At the celebration of the October Revolution in Moscow, 7 November 1954, the Soviet spokesman referred publicly to the desirability of removing obstacles to normalisation, resuming trade and organising cultural and other contacts with Yugoslavia. Tito replied before the end of the year (21 December 1954), still in fairly cautious terms. The Soviet Government, he said, had taken the initiative and admitted that:

Yugoslavia was wrongly dealt with and condemned in 1948. These statements – and others which will some day see the light of day[1] helped us to accept normalisation. . .Normalisation is greatly facilitated by the Soviet leaders' statement that they respect relations based on equality of rights and non-interference in the internal affairs of our country, and in addition the fact that they accept our viewpoint that this normalisation should not be detrimental to our relations with the Western countries.

So far, so good; but no major change in Soviet policy towards Yugoslavia could be finally determined before Khrushchev had strengthened his own internal position. Malenkov was banished to a distant power station in February 1955; more important for Soviet foreign policy, the position of Molotov, who with Stalin had signed the letters to Tito of 27 March and 4 May 1948, was being undermined. This became clear in March 1955, after Tito had publicly taken issue with a speech by Molotov to the Supreme Soviet, in which he implicitly accused the Yugoslavs of not having done enough towards normalisation. On 11 March *Pravda* issued a conciliatory statement:

. . .the Soviet Union adheres firmly to the position that every state has the right to pursue any line it wishes in domestic and foreign policy. No one in the Soviet Union would think of 'explaining' the successes achieved in

[1] Including no doubt Khrushchev's suggestion of October 1954 to the LCY (mentioned in Tempo's memoirs).

normalising Soviet–Yugoslav relations by saying that the Yugoslav leaders have now 'realised their mistakes' or are trying to 'mend their ways'.

To those who read between the lines it was plain that Molotov had tried to sabotage the policy of reconciliation with Yugoslavia, and had been firmly slapped down.

On 14 May, a joint communiqué was issued announcing a meeting between top level representatives of the Soviet and Yugoslav Governments at the end of the month. On 15 May, Tito made it clear in a public statement that this represented a bold and welcome decision of the Soviet leaders and that

in the course of preparations for this meeting, we let the Soviet leaders know...that we want to talk on an equal footing and as an independent country...and that we shall let no one...meddle in our domestic affairs... The East and the West...will know what we talked about and on what we reached agreement, for we have no intention...of doing anything at the expense of someone else. It is not our fault if those in the West who had certain illusions about Yugoslavia becoming something other than what she was are disappointed...I think that relations should be the same between all countries. We shall not adhere to any bloc...

A Soviet official commentary in *Pravda* (18 May) similarly denied any Soviet intention to isolate Yugoslavia from the Western world.

And so 'East and West' enjoyed on 26 May the remarkable spectacle of Khrushchev, Bulganin, and other members of the Soviet delegation landing at Belgrade airport and making a public apology to Tito:

We sincerely regret...and resolutely sweep aside all the bitterness of that [post-1948] period...We have thoroughly investigated the materials upon which the grave accusations against and insults to the leaders of Yugoslavia were based at that time...these materials were fabricated by the enemies of the people Beria and Abakumov, the contemptible agents of imperialism who had fraudulently wormed their way into the ranks of our Party.

The apology may have been incomplete, but the principles enunciated in the joint Belgrade Declaration of 2 June 1955 seemed to be completely in accordance with Yugoslav ideas about independence and equality. The main point was agreement on:

The indivisibility of peace...Respect for sovereignty, independence, territorial integrity, and for equality between the states...Recognition and development of peaceful coexistence between nations, irrespective of ideological differences and differences of social systems...Mutual respect and non-interference in internal affairs for any reason – whether of an economic, political or ideological nature – since questions of the internal structure, differences of social systems and differences of concrete forms in developing socialism are exclusively a matter for the peoples of the different countries...Development of bilateral and international economic co-operation...

The declaration also contained statements of agreed policy on more concrete issues:

The undesirability of military blocs.
The admission of Communist China to the United Nations, and the satisfaction of China's rights to Taiwan.
The reduction and limitation of armaments, and the prohibition of atomic weapons.
A system of collective security for Europe, based on a treaty.
An agreed settlement of the German question on a democratic basis.
Support for the efforts of Asian and African peoples to strengthen their political and economic independence.

Western observers could regard all this as a bargain – tolerance of the Yugoslav way to socialism in return for Yugoslav support for the Soviet line on the main world issues of foreign policy. They suspected also, reasonably, since the two delegations were headed by Khrushchev and Tito, that the 'expanding co-operation' envisaged between the two countries would spread from the government to the Party level, whatever Yugoslav spokesmen said at the time. However, few outside observers grudged Tito his hour of triumph. At a time when East–West summit meetings were very much in the air, the Soviet–Yugoslav reconciliation was a concrete sign of a new look in Soviet foreign policy which might be more favourable to the West.

2

For Tito, trained in the Soviet Union and brought up politically to seek light from the East, reconciliation with Khrushchev on Yugoslav terms was an enormous emotional as well as political prize. There were however good reasons for proceeding carefully. At least until new economic agreements were concluded with the Soviet Union, the Yugoslavs were reluctant to endanger those relations with the Western powers, and in particular the U.S.A., which had been so profitable to them in the recent past (not least in 1954, when another disastrous harvest had forced them to ask once more for American grain shipments).

In 1955–6 it looked as if Soviet–Yugoslav economic relations were rapidly improving. In August 1955 an agreement had been signed on economic relations and co-operation, which envisaged an increase of trade to $40 million in 1955, rising to $70 million in 1957. Credits were granted of $30 million in gold to cover Yugoslav short-term debts, and $120 million in roubles for the construction of artificial-fertiliser factories. This was supplemented by remission of Yugoslav debts incurred in respect of arms purchases, and in February 1956 by a further credit of $110 million. By the end of June 1956 credits granted to Yugoslavia amounted to nearly $300 million, at an interest rate of 2% only. American aid meanwhile diminished but still continued.

In general however the improvement of Soviet–Yugoslav relations depended on the political fortunes of Khrushchev, his position in relation to his political opponents and his success in undermining the Stalinist traditions in Soviet policy. When in May 1955, Khrushchev blamed the break in 1948 entirely on Beria and Abakumov, the impulsive Tempo put the crucial question to him bluntly: What is to prevent the emergence of another Beria or another Stalin under your system? The only satisfactory answer to this question would be for the Soviet leaders to allow far more fundamental changes in the system than had (or have) ever taken place. Tito knew that Khrushchev was working for some changes and that other members of the Soviet Politburo were opposing him. It is now known, and Tito may have learned of it at the time, that after the Belgrade Declaration the whole question of Soviet–Yugoslav relations was discussed again at the Plenum of the CPSU Central Committee in July 1955. Again Molotov expressed strong support for Stalin's policy in 1948, on the grounds that if Tito had gone unpunished then, his example of National Communism might have infected Poland in particular. Molotov was out-argued and the Central Committee was publicly stated to have approved the results of the talks at Belgrade – and also to have expressed the desire for an ideological rapprochement between the CPSU and the LCY 'on the basis of Marxist-Leninist principles'. Molotov however retained his position, and clearly the XXth Congress of the CPSU, due to meet in February 1956, was likely to be the scene of an interesting confrontation between Soviet 'liberal' and 'conservative' communists.

Tito must have awaited with intense interest its conclusions. According to Tempo, he was not surprised by Khrushchev's 'secret' speech, and may have been prepared for it by his private talks with Khrushchev the previous summer.[2] In this speech Khrushchev went a long way

---

[2] Tempo wrote in his Memoirs about his own conversations with Khrushchev early in March 1956, when Khrushchev spoke at large about plans for reviving Lenin's ideas for co-operative councils of workers, peasants and soldiers, and for converting the Red Army under cover of its nuclear umbrella into 'territorial units of the people under arms'.

towards accepting the Yugoslav theses most important for international relations between the 'socialist' countries of Eastern Europe and between East and West – the need to repudiate Stalin's method of rule, and the possibilities of different ways to socialism, of transition to socialism without armed revolution, and of peaceful co-existence between East and West. *Borba* published a condensed version of the speech on 25 March, and described it as heralding an 'entirely new orientation by the CPSU'.

The fact that Khrushchev had advanced his new ideas in the face of opposition within the Soviet leadership had very important implications for the Yugoslavs. It showed that a 'progressive' line in Soviet internal and external policies was in the ascendant. Moreover by his repudiation of Stalin at the XXth Congress Khrushchev had also committed himself *de facto* to a change of the leadership in the other countries of Eastern Europe. While the old Stalinist leaders were still in power there, the Yugoslavs were bound to assume that they had powerful backing from 'conservative communists' in Moscow.[3] Conversely, if Khrushchev's policies were adopted in the Soviet Union, the star of 'conservative communists' in Eastern Europe was bound to decline. Khrushchev's original hope was perhaps foreshadowed in an article published by the CPSU theoretical magazine *Kommunist* in September 1955; it was to preserve the primacy of the Soviet Union (justified by its advanced state of development) within a 'commonwealth' of socialist states, which would be united by common long-term interests, economic and ideological, rather than by a command structure and identical institutions. This was a theory very welcome to the Yugoslavs, though by March 1956 there was a good deal of scepticism about its application. Tito's newly-appointed Ambassador to Moscow, Veljko Mičunović, confided to his diary on 12 March:

We regard the Belgrade declaration as a sort of socialist 'Magna Charta' which ought to apply to Yugoslavia's relations with the Soviet Union and other socialist countries as well...All in all the Russians seem to regard it as just another temporary agreement about current relations between the two countries, with no special lasting significance.

None the less after the XXth Congress of the CPSU Khrushchev took some steps to conciliate the Yugoslavs. In April 1956 the Comin-

---

[3] During 1954 a former supporter of Kostov re-appeared in Bulgarian public life, and in Hungary Gábor Peter, who had staged the Rajk trial, was condemned. But in Romania conservative communists seemed to have the upper hand (trials of Patrescanu and Luca), while in Czechoslovakia the purge of friends of the former Foreign Minister Clementis (including Dr Husák) continued.

form was abolished. It had long ceased to function, so this was a gesture of little substance; but it was symbolically important for Tito. He was now ready to enter into Party as well as governmental relations with the Soviet Union – a step which was formally taken during his triumphant visit to Moscow in June 1956. This resulted in a further joint affirmation by Khrushchev and Tito of an essentially Titoist line: 'that the. . .conditions of socialist development are different in different countries, that the wealth of the forms of socialist development contributes to their strengthening, and. . .that any tendency to impose one's own views in determining the roads and forms of socialist development are alien to both sides'.

No other aspect of Yugoslavia's reconciliation with the Soviet Union could give Tito greater satisfaction than this part of the Moscow declaration. Mićunović's diary (already quoted) for the second half of June strongly suggests that the crucial phrases cited from the Moscow declaration represented essentially a Yugoslav draft. Khrushchev wanted the Yugoslavs to sign a statement about ideological unity and to draw them much closer to the 'Socialist camp'. Immediately after Tito's visit, the satellite Party leaders were summoned to Moscow to be informed about it by Khrushchev. He said not a word about the Moscow declaration. To quote Mićunović again: 'Thus to ignore the Moscow declaration the day after its signature can only indicate Soviet discontent with this document. In any case the Russians in this way gave the leaders of the "camp" clearly to understand that what they had signed with Tito was not valid for Soviet policy towards the governments and parties of the "camp".'

It soon looked as if Khrushchev wanted at the least to go slow on reconciliation with Yugoslavia, if only to placate his conservative communist rivals. Negotiations for Soviet credit to finance a large aluminium plant in Yugoslavia – always a good barometer of Soviet–Yugoslav relations – were again slowed down in July.[4] The Tito–Khrushchev honeymoon had proved to be almost literally a nine-days wonder.

3

The basic reason for Khrushchev blowing hot and cold on Yugoslavia lay in the difficulties which faced him in Eastern Europe. The CPs of Yugoslavia's neighbour states had been in no hurry to act decisively on

---

[4] Veljko Mićunović's diary, *Moskovske godine 1956–8* (My years in Moscow), is particularly revealing. It was published in 1977, in Zagreb, but no translation is yet available.

the new situation created by Khrushchev's visit to Belgrade. Until the end of 1955 they were concerned merely to normalise relations with Yugoslavia in the sense of concluding new agreements about trade (even this for some time proved to be impossible for the Hungarian Government), cultural exchanges, etc., all without making any major changes in the personnel of their Party leadership and institutions. After March 1956 however things were bound to change more rapidly. From Khrushchev's point of view the two countries in which action had become most urgently necessary were Poland and Hungary; here the Stalinist leaders had the least popular backing and had to cope with major economic problems. In Poland a succession of comparatively minor crises was sparked off by the death in mid-March 1957 of the Stalinist General Secretary of the CP, Bierut. The powers of the secret police and of the Government in general began to be curtailed, and open complaints were made against the economic policies which had led to a decline in the Polish standard of living. This led in June 1956 to a workers' revolt in Poznań, which could only be suppressed by military action. Here was a serious warning to the Soviet leaders and to Tito of the possibly disruptive effects in Eastern Europe of Khrushchev's policy. Tito praised the firm line taken by the Polish Government, and the Soviet delegations to the Seventh Plenum of the Polish Central Committee, held late in July, carried a firm message to the Poles: 'Every country should go its own way to socialism, but we cannot permit this...to break up the solidarity of the peace camp... certainly not under the pretext of respecting national peculiarities or extending democracy.'

The Polish pro-Stalinist 'Natolin' faction began to take heart, and by mid-October threatened to take over power. They were however forestalled by moderate Communists who favoured Gomułka.[5] The 'October Revolution' which brought Gomułka to power did not of itself clearly demand Soviet counter-action. It was the culmination of a fairly gradual process of de-Stalinisation, but the Polish Communist Party had remained on the whole in control of this; Gomułka himself wanted to execute the necessary programme of domestic reform through the Communist Party and without leaving the Soviet bloc. The greatest danger of Soviet intervention arose after he had assumed power, when anti-Soviet demonstrations began to spread through Poland.

[5] Gomułka had been imprisoned in 1949 for taking a 'nationalist' line against the Stalinist leadership, and was not released till spring 1956. Many of his supporters at this time were by no means anti-Soviet.

At this stage however the Soviet leaders were almost exclusively preoccupied by the situation in Hungary, which was also of more direct concern to Tito. There Rákosi, the key Party and Government figure in spring and early summer 1956, had assumed power just before Khrushchev's 1955 visit to Belgrade in succession to Imre Nagy, who as a prematurely 'liberal' communist had tried from July 1953 to April 1955 to put into effect non-Stalinist economic policies (not least increased investment in agriculture and light industry) within a framework of orthodox communist institutions. In spring 1955 he was expelled from the Hungarian Politburo. From the first there was strong opposition to Rákosi and support for Nagy from the influential intellectuals of Hungary, and the Belgrade declaration of June 1955 intensified it. However in January 1956 Nagy had formulated a thesis about Hungary's position which went further than anything proposed by Yugoslav theorists and accepted by Khrushchev. He recommended, as the best way of preserving Hungarian interests: 'the active co-existence of progressive democratic socialist or similar countries with those other countries having a different system, through a co-ordinated foreign policy and through co-operation against the policies of power groups, through neutrality or active co-existence'.

After the XXth Congress of the CPSU Rákosi first tried to adapt his own policies to the new facts of life in the 'Socialist camp'. In particular Rajk (executed in 1949 for alleged links with Tito) and his associates were rehabilitated. At the end of June however Rákosi went into reverse, and decided to interpret the Soviet–Yugoslav Moscow declaration as allowing him freedom to pursue a Stalinist way to Socialism. He attacked the discussion clubs which spread Nagy's views and on 12 July announced the Central Committee's decision to 'liquidate the Nagy conspiracy' by arresting him and hundreds of his associates. The Soviet Government decided that they could not risk a Hungarian Poznań. Mikoyan, their main trouble-shooter, was sent to Budapest and Rákosi announced his own resignation on 18 July.

At this point Tito became closely involved with the Hungarian situation. Mikoyan flew from Budapest to Brioni to consult with Tito, Kardelj and Ranković and tried to recommend to them Gerö, a close associate of Rákosi, as the latter's successor. Tito, though no supporter of Nagy, was far from satisfied with the Soviet choice, but finally agreed to it. As he suspected, Gerö had little support outside the Hungarian army and secret police. Tito did what he could for him, receiving him in Belgrade on 15 October, and announcing on 23 October (after the Polish news had broken) that a Yugoslav delegation would visit Budapest. However the Rákosi régime had left a fatal legacy of popular ill-will. Gomułka's unhindered succession to power in Poland was interpreted in Hungary as meaning that the Soviet army would not intervene to defend Stalinist leaders against other more nationally-minded Communists. The Hungarian people started to demonstrate against their government and the shots fired against them by Gerö's secret police only increased their determination. During the night of 23–4 October, Nagy was recalled to be premier, but Gerö was retained as First Secretary of the Party, and a member of the Politburo, Marosan, appealed on its behalf for Soviet military aid against the emergence of armed 'rightist' forces. The first Soviet intervention in Hungary began, apparently in aid of the Nagy government which had been set up by Hungarian anti-Stalinists. On 28 October Nagy negotiated a cease-fire and on 29 October Mikoyan, who had flown with Suslev to Budapest, promised that all Soviet troops would soon be withdrawn. On 30 October the Yugoslavs appealed to the Nagy Government to stop the fighting and not to let a situation persist which could be exploited by 'international reaction'.

At the same time, the Soviet Government issued a declaration on *Friendship and Co-operation between the Soviet Union and other Socialist states*, designed to contain the Hungarian situation and to constitute a charter for a new-style Soviet 'commonwealth of socialist nations'. This was an adaptation for Eastern Europe of the main general points of Khrushchev's secret speech at the XXth Congress, and of the Soviet–Yugoslav declaration of June 1956. The 'principles of full equality, respect for territorial integrity, state independence and sovereignty, and non-interference in each other's domestic affairs' must obtain between members of the 'great commonwealth of Socialist nations'. These principles, it was admitted, had been violated, economic relations between the Soviet Union and other 'socialist' states must be re-examined, and Soviet economic and military advisers should be recalled. Most immediately important 'the stationing of troops of one member state of the Warsaw Treaty on the territory of another. . .takes place on the basis of an agreement between all its participants and not only with the agreement of that state, on the territory of which, at its request, these troops are to be stationed or are planned to be stationed'.

This last clause was probably not entirely reassuring to the Hungarians. In any case Nagy was being steadily pushed towards an extreme National Communist position. On 31 October he revealed that he wished to negotiate Hungarian withdrawal from the Warsaw

Pact, and on 1 November he officially proclaimed Hungary's neutrality.

It is doubtful whether Khrushchev or any other Soviet leader would have observed meticulously the terms of the declaration of 30 October. However it was not until the beginning of November, when world attention had been partially distracted by the Anglo-French intervention in Egypt, that the Soviet leaders finally decided to suppress the Nagy régime by force and to demonstrate unmistakably that for them Yugoslavia was a special case. They might conclude a special arrangement with communist leaders who had never adhered to the Warsaw Treaty, but they would not tolerate a breakaway by one of the signatories.

Events in Poland and Hungary had in a sense confirmed the Yugoslav analysis of Stalinist forces and their incompatibility with conditions obtaining in East Europe in 1956. But the Hungarian insurrection against Communism and the Soviet interventions faced Tito with a very awkward problem. Whatever his estimate of Nagy and his ability to contain the anti-Communist forces in Hungary, Tito had to reckon that if he came out against all forms of Soviet intervention, he could not effectively help Nagy, and would lose the possibility of further influencing either Gomułka in Poland or Kádár, Nagy's successor in Hungary, whom Tito counted as a 'progressive force', far preferable to Gerö. He would also forfeit his special position with Khrushchev, whom he still reckoned as fundamentally anti-Stalinist. At the end of October Khrushchev flew to Brioni to consult with Tito, who gave his advance consent, with much less difficulty than anticipated, to the second Soviet intervention in Hungary, and all that it entailed. Khrushchev may therefore have been all the more irritated by the full analysis of the Hungarian events made by Tito in a major speech at Pula on 11 November. Here Tito condemned the first Soviet intervention in Hungary, and said that the situation in which it seemed necessary should never have been allowed to arise. On the other hand he reckoned that the second Soviet intervention was the 'lesser evil', and that it probably prevented the triumph of 'reaction' in Hungary and Hungary's withdrawal from the 'Socialist camp'. The implications of Tito's speech were that the existence of the 'Socialist camp' was necessary and a good thing; and that within it the Soviet leaders ought to have applied the principles which governed Soviet–Yugoslav relations.

The Pula speech was a compromise which satisfied no one. A large number of Yugoslavs were uneasy about the endorsement of any Soviet intervention, particularly when this was followed (on 21 November) by the surrender of Nagy from his asylum at the Yugoslav Embassy in

Budapest to Kádár and (two years later) a Russian firing squad. In Western eyes Tito seemed to be applying a double standard – one for Suez and quite another for Hungary. Other potential National Communist leaders in Eastern Europe realised that, if things came to a crunch between the Soviet Union and themselves, they would get no effective support from Tito. The Soviet leaders published their official reply to Tito in *Pravda* of 23 November. It was fairly restrained, but they rejected Tito's implication that Yugoslavia could serve as any kind of model to the Warsaw Treaty States; they were indignant about his propensity to criticise remnants of Stalinism in the Soviet Union and about the way in which he seemed to lay down the law about other Communist Parties in Eastern Europe. For some time Khrushchev was as willing as other Soviet leaders to see him cut down to size.

The essential moral of November 1956 was however that in the last resort Tito supported the existence of a 'Socialist camp' even if he could not join it. His reaction to the Hungarian events was as important in defining the limits of Yugoslav external policy as was his treatment of Djilas in defining the limits of Yugoslav internal policy. It was not by chance, as communist editorial writers say, that in January 1957 Djilas was imprisoned for publishing in an American newspaper bitter criticisms of both Soviet and Yugoslav policy towards Hungary.

9

Problems of self-management

The main importance of the Yugoslav example to Eastern Europe, even at the time of Tito's greatest influence on Khrushchev, has lain in the facts of national independence and equal dealings with the Soviet Union rather than in the constitutional, economic or ideological specifics of the Yugoslav model. These however have had some indirect significance for the world outside, and the four years between spring 1954 and spring 1958 witnessed developments, particularly in the Yugoslav economy, which influenced Yugoslav political ideas and foreign relations.

The framework ('basic proportions') for the first Yugoslav approach to the operations of what has been called a market economy had been fixed by the laws of December 1951.[1] The Republican and District Assemblies had the main responsibility for assessing tax rates, and the wage system established in 1952 left only a small proportion of gross profits to be distributed by the enterprise itself in the form of 'variable wages'. The wage system in its original form did not survive the experiences of 1953, when large 'variable wage' payments were made and threatened to produce inflation. From early 1954 a system was introduced of compulsory loans to the government from surplus profits. From December 1954 enterprises could dispose of their net income only with the consent of the local People's Committees, which thus assumed large social and economic responsibilities. The main instrument however for redistributing the country's financial resources was the General Investment Fund (GIF), constituted in 1954, and fed by a general sales tax and taxes on the fixed assets and working capital of enterprises.

By 1955 therefore economic 'self-management' seemed to be very

[1] The proportions were to be fixed annually in the Federal Social Plan. From 1953 onwards this was drawn up by the Federal Institute of Economic Planning, which replaced the Federal Planning Commission – a minor step away from the Stalinist model.

narrowly limited, along with any opportunities for the misuse of freedom of economic action. However original sin persisted in various
forms. In particular the 'social consciousness' of many People's Committees proved to be inadequate. Their main source of investment
funds was taxation levied on local enterprises, and their interest was
that the maximum number of such enterprises should exist. Already in
1954 tax revenue for Republics, Districts and lower levels combined
was 85% over the 1953 level, and about twice that which had been
anticipated in the Federal Social Plan. Production was indeed greatly
increased, but often in the wrong direction. Re-investment by well-
established enterprises was too often discouraged. The local committee
tended to encourage new investment for investment's sake. Hence
unnecessary duplication, the creation of uneconomic units of production, increased demand for raw materials, and raising of prices.[2]

Inflationary pressures were increased by the policies of the Yugoslav
National Bank. This had become a very powerful organisation. It was
responsible for collecting all contributions and taxes laid down in the
Federal, Republican and local social plans, and for banking all the
funds of enterprises. In 1954 it was given the further duty of compiling
statistics about prices, savings, key investments and the balance sheets
of the enterprises. In the same year it was decided to entrust Republican and other branches of the National Bank with 45% of the newly
formed GIF for their free disposal, subject to supervision of branches
at each level by those at the next level upwards. The local branches
also received quotas of short-term credit funds from the state, subject
nominally to strict conditions about the type of project for which they
should be used and the rate of interest which they should charge for
various types of use. In fact the local branches were very ready to yield
to local pressure and grant credits for new enterprises.

These unforeseen developments naturally affected price policy. The
intention in 1952 had been that the government should determine the
prices of basic raw materials and other materials which had to be
imported for scarce foreign exchange; finished goods would however
find their own price level on a free market.[3] Again the planners had not
allowed for original sin. Partly owing to previous government policy,
there were too many firms which had acquired something like a mono-

---

[2] At the same time the committees, in helping to determine the 'variable wages' paid
by enterprises, often encouraged them to save on their wage bills, and to stifle
incentive by insufficient differentiation between skilled and unskilled workers'
wages.

[3] At the end of 1953 Kardelj talked of internal trade which would function as a
social service, satisfying the needs of the market but not working for profit.

poly position, and could increase their profits simply by fixing higher prices rather than by increasing productivity. The problem of inflationary prices was also temporarily increased by the introduction of a comparatively free market in foreign exchange. At the beginning of 1953 the Government's control over foreign trade was decentralised, and a Foreign Exchange Settlement Centre was established where enterprises (which were allowed to retain a share of the foreign exchange holdings earned by exporting) could buy and sell fairly freely. The result was a short period of wild fluctuation in the foreign exchange market, and in prices of goods imported, or dependent on the import of raw materials.

While the problems of Yugoslav industry were piling up, at least the vital agricultural sector had not been subject to further experiments, in spite of a drought in 1954. A sensible 'cadastral' taxation system, based on estimates of the size and quality of peasant holdings and the crops to be grown, replaced the old system based on the attempt to assess the peasants' yearly earnings after the harvest. The 1954 plan further provided for easier short-term credits for peasants and long-term contracts between them and purchasers. A law of June 1954 even allowed for the free purchase of agricultural land within a two-hectare limit. The Yugoslav Government's agricultural policy owed much to the wisdom of the Croat Prime Minister, Vladimir Bakarić, who initiated the drive for 'intensified agriculture', designed to increase productivity in the private as well as in the collective sector. Collectivisation remained the goal, but it was now realised that this could best be encouraged by creating market conditions which would make clear the advantages of voluntary co-operation, and ultimately collectivisation. This moderate policy had an incidental and temporary advantage. It slowed down the influx of peasants from the country to the town, which had come to exceed the capacity of Yugoslav industry to absorb untrained peasant labour. The only snag for the Yugoslav Communist leaders was that the peasant's standard of living tended to remain in real, if not in monetary, terms above that of the poorer urban workers, and that the peasants tended to spend their earnings in increasing their own personal comforts rather than on the productivity of their farms.

2

A number of specific steps were taken in 1955 to cope with the problems of the Yugoslav economy. The most important of these was a marked change of investment policy, designed to prevent the waste of

resources by competitive local investment, to produce more consumer
goods which would mop up increased purchasing power, and to prevent
inflationary price-increases by 'speculators' – whether private peasants
or firms in the position of monopoly suppliers. Tito summed up the
essence of the new line in a speech to the Fourth Plenum of SAWPY
in November 1955. He would not admit outright that any radical
changes of policy should be made, but his criticisms of existing practice
signified an important change of course. His own summary ran as
follows:

...it is wrong to put the question whether we shall complete enterprises
and objects which are essential to our economy and do not demand too
much hard currency and other resources. Things should be put in this
way: first, we shall not begin on any important new construction this year
[1956]; secondly, we should put off the further building of factories which
have only just begun, and are not crucial for the present phase of our
development, but preserve what has been built; thirdly, we should lengthen
the building time allowed for enterprises which are very expensive;
fourthly, in the case of factories which are nearly completed, we should
adapt them as soon as possible for production, not waiting until everything
is one hundred per cent completed but leaving further completion and
expansion to the enterprise itself. In particular we should pay the greatest
attention to the fullest possible use of capacity already created, and...to
the maximum use of possibilities of co-operation between industries,
including the defence industry...

All this, he repeated, was not to involve any basic change in the
policy of developing heavy industry, it was to be only a 'limited
breathing-space' in which Yugoslav producers could collect their
strength for a further but easier step forward in economic development. In pressing for a more even rate of progress over the whole
industrial field, and a better deal for the Yugoslav consumer, Tito was
aligning Yugoslav economic policy with that being pursued in 1955–6
by most other East European governments, including that of the Soviet
Union.

If the change in the general direction of investment was to be implemented, the banking system had to be put under tighter control. In
March 1955 the FEC decreed that enterprises would have to deposit
with the lending bank a fixed percentage of collateral for each loan.
Plans were made to replace the local branches of the National Bank
and to replace them by independent and more specialist banks (for
agriculture, commerce, etc.). These were to be linked with the National
Bank, which would prescribe financial conditions, such as the amounts
of reserves to be held, or the rates of interest to be charged for various

kinds of loan. The new banks were also to be linked closely with the local communities, drawing the greater part of their funds from them rather than from the General Investment Fund, and supervised mainly by the People's Committee which would have a much closer responsibility than before for their financial viability.

The changes in investment policy were accompanied or closely followed by certain institutional and administrative changes designed to stabilise the economy. A new Price Control Bureau was established in March 1955 to put an end to disturbances in the economy due to the 'insufficient sensitivity of enterprises to shifts in prices of production and investment materials' (which resulted in over-charging the customer). The National Bank resumed its control of foreign exchange dealings.[4] Some efforts were also made to co-ordinate industry vertically. In 1954 a Federal Industrial Chamber had been created, to bring under one roof the small number of industrial associations which had been formed under the 1950 Law on Workers' Councils.[5] In 1955 membership of this Chamber was made compulsory and it was given powers of supervision which enabled it to perform 'the role of social co-ordinator, harmonising the relations between the individual branches of the economy and between economic organisations and society'. The Yugoslav leaders hoped that vertically organised industrial associations could help in checking the 'localist' excesses of People's Committees and enterprises within their areas,[6] and could act as a transmission belt for agreed Federal policy. In an article of spring 1956 Kardelj said that the associations should be entrusted with broad responsibilities, provided that the FEC and other Federal administrative organs could effectively supervise all decisions 'with a wider social significance'.

The same principle of organisation was extended from the economic to the social field, not least to the education and the social services. Each profession, as well as each enterprise, would have its own elected 'self-managing' organisation, starting at the local level and linked vertically with organisations at Republican and Federal levels. These could again serve as transmission belts for Federal or Republican policy,

[4] Until the end of 1955 the Bank operated through the Foreign Exchange Centres, where bidding continued to be wild. In 1956 it resumed direct control and limited to 10% the quota of foreign exchange which could be retained by enterprises on export deals.
[5] This provided for co-ordination of economic policy by 'higher economic associations in each branch of industry'. In parallel with the Federal Industrial Chamber, a Federal Chamber of Foreign Commerce was formed in 1954 to encourage more uniformity and co-ordination in the foreign trade field.
[6] For example by informal integration of enterprise plans to avoid duplication, and by informal rationing of scarce raw materials.

and could act to some extent as substitutes for the 'administrative methods' of the pre-1953 CPY. Co-ordination was particularly important in the field of social security. The abolition of the Federal Social Security system in 1950 and its replacement by a number of local units with widely different economic strength and little co-ordination had the effect of increasing differences in the standard of life between the more and less developed regions of Yugoslavia. By the end of 1955 these had been mitigated by the creation of emergency funds at Republican level, and by the re-establishment of a Federal Social Security Institute with co-ordinating powers.

A further administrative re-organisation was initiated in June 1955 – commended by Kardelj, Yugoslavia's main political theorist, on largely ideological grounds, but designed also to help in the co-ordination of 'localist' policies. This was the Law on the Formation of Communes. Its ultimate object was to replace the original district organisation by a system of less numerous local units, self-sufficient in agricultural and industrial strength, and hence able to generate the funds for their own administration. Here was a Yugoslav tribute to Marx's theories of the ideal state, built around the example of the Paris Commune of 1871, and in some ways anticipating the Chinese Communes of 1958. Kardelj explained that ultimately the number of districts would be reduced from 4,121 (the figure for 1955) to 1,438. The process of forming Communes however proceeded slowly – less than 500 were formed by 1957 and of these only 95 had Councils of Producers to co-ordinate economic policy. Existing People's Committees were reluctant to relinquish powers to the new units and could not be compelled to join them, while the division of function between the remaining Districts and the new Communes was by no means precise.

3

Thus extensive attempts were made to adapt economic and administrative machinery in order to meet the problems arising from the system of self-management. This however could not be made to work by organisational changes alone. It had to be operated in the right social spirit, and the question arose for the Yugoslav leaders by the end of 1955 whether this was being adequately inspired by their chosen ideological instruments – the League of Communists and the Trade Unions.

The Yugoslav social historian, Dušan Bilandžić, writing from a near-official point of view, has described the period 1954–6 as one of ideological stagnation. The decision of the VIth Party Congress in November 1952, the Brioni Letter of June 1953, and Djilas' fall from grace in January 1954 had left LCY members at the lower levels puzzled about their duties. Especially in the remote country districts many of them were not well suited for the sophisticated role foreseen for them by the VIth Congress. Speaking at the Montenegrin Congress in October 1954, Blažo Jovanović, the Republican general secretary, mentioned the 'considerable number of Communists who are either semi-literate or illiterate, who can hardly read the newspapers...and if they can... can hardly understand what they write about. It is their prime task... to learn how to read.'

The figures had of course improved since the end of the war. In Bosnia-Hercegovina for example in 1948 less than 22% of the Party members had had more than a primary education, whereas by 1954 over 63% had attended a secondary school for at least some years. But still the LCY was too large and unsophisticated for its new tasks. In the two and a half years from January 1954 to June 1956 it was reduced considerably in total numbers, from 700,000 to 636,000.

The LCY was meant to act on Yugoslav society through other bodies, some of which were not so obviously political. There was SAWPY, which included other 'transmission belt' organisations, such as the Youth Organisation and the Federation of Veterans. There was the Yugoslav Army, particularly important for educational work, which has remained one of the main unifying factors in the Yugoslav Federation.[7] However the LCY's most important ally in its campaign against economic localism, the most urgent task of the mid-1950s, was the Union of Syndicates (or Confederation of Trade Unions) of Yugoslavia, henceforward CTY. Until 1950 the main task of the Trade Unions in Yugoslavia, as in other Communist countries, had been to stimulate campaigns for higher production in fulfilment of the extravagant Five Year Plan. They had also assumed responsibility for the industrial education of large numbers of workers recruited to factories direct from the countryside. As the new system of self-management came into operation at factory level, and the LCY itself resigned direct responsibility for administering the economy, the role of the CTY as a means of policy co-ordination became more important. The most

[7] The Political Department of the Army was initially strengthened in the years following 1948, as a defence against Soviet subversion, and put under the charge of Tempo, one of the most energetic of the Yugoslav leaders. After the danger from the Cominform was past, it was one of the chief areas for political lecturers, who found audiences of an impressionable age mobilised for them.

prominent CTY representatives in CTY factory branches were Party members and could theoretically do much of the LCY's work for them. There were however disadvantages in the fact that virtually all members of Workers' Councils were Trade Union members; there was little that they could do in the second capacity which they should not be doing in the first. The lesser fry thus tended to become good 'localists', while some of the leaders tended to become over-active and to develop a 'command psychology'.

In summer 1954 Tito had to remind the Trade Unions of the limits and of the importance of their proper task – not formal political education, nor production campaigns, but industrial education and inculcating a sense of social responsibility to the community as a whole. Again at the IIIrd Congress of CTY in May 1955, it was decided to cut down the size and importance of the higher levels of the vertical CTY organisation, and to ensure that members at the lower levels busied themselves with practical measures for improving the health, housing and cultural welfare of the workers. The last phrase could still cover a good deal of activity, in that 'socialist culture' could be regarded as including political education. Again Tito, in his opening message to the Congress, had explained clearly what were the essential problems that they had to solve:

I realise that...you will still have to master various obstacles and difficulties in your work of educating the constantly renewed intake of workers who flood every day into our factories. Many of these bring with them a negative ballast, resulting from our unhappy past and often have ideas foreign to socialism which influence other more politically minded workers ...I have to say that the community as a whole is liable to particular danger from those tendencies which embody a narrow view, confined to the interests of the single enterprise or commune, and not embracing the interests of our community as a whole.

4

From 1956 to spring 1958, when the VIIth Party Congress was held at Ljubljana, Yugoslav industry was flourishing, to judge by overall production figures, and the state of agriculture improved in spite of a further drought in 1956. A good part of this improvement could be ascribed to skilful economic diplomacy and to Yugoslavia's improved commercial and financial relations with East and West alike. On the Western front some cancellation and some rescheduling of Yugoslavia's debts, especially to the U.S.A. and Western Germany, had been achieved before Tito's reconciliation with Khrushchev in 1955–6, at a time when it seemed worth while to Western Governments to pay a certain economic price in order to preserve the independence of Yugoslavia.[8] Western credits were used particularly to finance the construction of new factories for consumer goods, initially to import raw materials for them, and also to import greater quantities of consumer goods direct. In summer 1956 negotiations with Western Germany[9] were proceeding for credits to finance the construction of factories in Yugoslavia (especially in the field of bauxite processing) to be repaid by the products of the factories. At the same time the markets of Eastern Europe were being opened to Yugoslavia, as more liberal economic trends developed within the 'Socialist Commonwealth'. Here was an area in which Yugoslav exports could perform comparatively well, even if they could not earn the hard currency needed for the imports most essential to the economy.[10]

Meanwhile the Yugoslav leaders did not attribute the general economic growth of the years 1953–7 to external factors. They reckoned that it was mainly due to the changes in their own economic system. So far as the new system had given rise to new economic problems, these were sometimes ascribed to lack of central control but more often to an insufficiency of self-management. From 1949 onwards, when the analysis of the defects of Stalinism was completed, 'bureaucracy' had become official enemy no. 1. To it were ascribed most of the faults that became apparent in the Yugoslav system, even if to the eyes of the ordinary observer these resulted quite clearly from excessive local independence. The argument was that, in so far as local enterprises and committees did not take a broad social view of their duties to the community as a whole, they were pursuing narrow and thus bureaucratic interests. Conversely the voice of the workers, uncorrupted by bureaucratic intermediaries and representatives, would always be in favour of the broad social view and the interest of the wider community. This was a large act of faith, but one should not underestimate the intensity with which it was performed. There was a further important fact. Large assemblies of workers could be more easily influenced by persuasive spokesmen of the LCY than could management boards or Workers' Councils who had acquired detailed technical knowledge

[8] Tempo's Memoirs for this period (when he had general responsibility in the FEC for the direction of the economy) give a vividly egocentric account of Yugoslavia's successful attempts to get aid from the U.S.A. in particular with minimum conditions, and without over-scrupulous attention to observing even these.

[9] These became more important as Soviet credits were delayed – see Chapter 8 above, p. 101.

[10] A continuing problem for Yugoslavia has been to identify imports from E. Europe which their economy really needs.

of their job. The paradoxical conclusion was that the Yugoslav leaders tended to regard the extension of self-management as facilitating social control by the LCY.

In 1956–7 there were two crucial economic debates in which this argument featured prominently. As regards the general scope and the particular direction of investment, the principal question was how much should be devoted to heavy industry, energy and communications, and how much to consumer goods. This question was one which on the face of it had little to do with more or less self-management. Tito had laid down a general directive in 1955, and the social plans for 1955 and 1956 had called for more production of consumer goods. In 1956–7 however it seemed that, in spite of tighter control of credit, there was still too much investment in new projects *tout court* or in projects which would be profitable only in the long term. Some effort was made to lay down more effective long-term directives for investment, and in 1957 the first of a new series of five-year 'perspective plans' was published to supplement and generally guide the Federal Planning Institute's annual social plans. Broadly the alternative policies were to re-institute more control at Federal and Republican level, or to leave more money with the enterprises to invest as they saw fit, on the assumption that the man on the spot would act more rationally than the man in Belgrade. The proponents of the second alternative could argue their case more openly (the centralist solution would clearly give rise to 'bureaucratism'), and it was generally regarded as a step forward that by the end of 1957 40% of the 'social product' was disposed of by Workers' Councils, as opposed to 22% by local committees, and 11% by self-managing institutes of social insurance. It was however clear in 1958 that no satisfactory solution of the investment problem had been reached.

The disposal of the wage fund was the second main theme of dispute between the Yugoslav leaders at this period. From 1955 till 1957 basic wages were still determined on the basis of tariff provisions laid down by the Communal People's Committees and CTY representatives, under the general directive of permitting any increases only when productivity had increased.[11] In 1957 it was provisionally decided that minimum incomes for workers should be prescribed by the federal authorities for each enterprise, at a rate of 80% of the enterprise's wage fund for the previous year. Subject to this, enterprises themselves (and here lay the principal novelty) would determine the division of the

11 This implied that wages should not be raised if special market conditions allowed enterprises to increase prices.

rest of their income (still heavily taxed) between extra wages and other purposes, and would work out their own wage rates. This new arrangement, confirmed by the Federal Assembly early in 1958, was a compromise.[12] It still seemed to the more liberal Yugoslav leaders to leave insufficient incentive to the enterprises, and not to favour sufficiently those who had earned their profits by increased productivity.

At the end of 1957 some progress had at least been made in checking economic anarchy. In December however a new phenomenon faced the Yugoslav leaders. There was a major strike at the coal mines in Trbovlje which might easily have spread to other mining districts, and could have been prevented by more resolute LCY or CTY action on the spot. In the major organisational shake-up which ensued, Tempo was transferred from the FEC to the leadership of the CTY, and he used his new position resolutely in favour of more power to the enterprises.

5

It was the major task of the VIIth Congress of the LCY, held at Ljubljana in April 1958, to formulate a new (the third) programme for the LCY and to express in theoretical terms the anti-dogmatic and anti-étatist principles in the practice of self-management. The motto was: 'Nothing that has been achieved should be so sacred to us that it cannot be surpassed and cannot yield place to something more progressive, freer and more human.'

The new programme confirmed the importance of the Communes: 'Increasingly assuming management of social affairs, and having the means to do so, the Commune is neither merely nor primarily a school of democracy; rather it is democracy itself; it is the basic cell of self-government of the citizen over common affairs.'

The programme also confirmed the general line of the VIth Party Congress (1952) about the leading role of the LCY in society, and posited as its main task the building of a self-managing society in Yugoslavia. Writing over ten years after the Ljubljana Congress, Dušan Bilandžić emphasised the inherent contradictions between this programme and the persistent strength of the centralist or 'étatist' elements in Yugoslavia:

in social-economic relations the state still had the dominant role...The

---

[12] In fact as far back as September 1953, Milentije Popović, a prominent Party theoretician, had pronounced the whole system of basic proportions, 'accumulation and funds', etc. to be only a type of compromise between the old and the new systems.

Party leadership was very slow in changing its old method of work. . . keeping in its hands particularly cadre policy and ideological-political work. Apart from the Party committees, an important, if hidden, power was retained by the organs of State Security. . .combining the highest Party functions with the highest functions of State Security.

Thus, he concluded, the ideas of the new Party programme did not coincide with the existing state of social relations, and relatively rapid and important changes could be expected in the latter.

The 1958 programme however had more immediate effects on Yugoslavia's external relations, particularly with the 'Socialist camp', than on her internal developments. At the beginning of 1957 the suppression of the Hungarian revolution by Soviet intervention had led to a minor crisis of Soviet–Yugoslav relations. A visible and important sign of this was the suspension in February 1957 of Soviet aid to Yugoslavia. Neither side however had any interest in a repetition of the Soviet–Yugoslav conflict of 1948. So far as Khrushchev was concerned, Tito had finally come down on the side of the 'Socialist camp' over Hungary. However unwelcome his criticism of the first Soviet intervention, he clearly favoured keeping his own house in order with a single-party régime. For Tito, Khrushchev was still the representative of the healthier anti-Stalinist trends in Soviet society, on which the development of the 'Socialist camp' depended, and he still had to fight for them against internal opposition. Thus Tito remained anxious to strengthen Khrushchev's internal position, to work for a second Soviet–Yugoslav accommodation, and to pay a considerable price in order to achieve this end.

A new phase in Soviet–Yugoslav relations began after Khrushchev had purged Molotov and others from the CPSU in June 1957. By the end of the month, Kardelj and Ranković had been in Moscow on an exploratory mission, and a renewal of Soviet aid was announced on 30 June. At the beginning of August Tito went to meet Khrushchev in Bucharest, Khrushchev obtained his endorsement for Soviet policy on the Middle East, and (even more important for Yugoslavia's relations with the West) on the recognition of East Germany. Tito seems not to have expected the result of this action, taken in mid-October; it was a diplomatic and economic rupture with the West German régime, as well as the growing belief in the West that Yugoslavia had gone over finally to the 'Socialist camp'.

Meanwhile Tito seems also to have agreed to the formal participation of Yugoslavia in the conference of Communist states, fixed to take place at Moscow in November. For him, the most important thing was the renewal of friendly contact with Khrushchev now in undisputed charge of Soviet policies. Presumably Tito thought that Khrushchev would again let him defend, as in summer 1956, comparatively 'equal relations' between the members of the 'Socialist camp', and appear as the protagonist of a highly differentiated 'road to socialism' in external as well as internal policies. In the statement published after the Bucharest meeting, Khrushchev did not insist on any reference to 'proletarian internationalism' (which implied an admission of the leading role of the Soviet Union),[13] and the validity of the Belgrade and Moscow declarations (1955 and 1956) was re-affirmed.

The advance Soviet programme for the November Conference must thus have been a shock for Tito. It was drafted with an eye on the Chinese, whose position in the 'Socialist camp' seemed at this time to be crucial, not least to the Yugoslavs. In summer 1955 full diplomatic relations were established between Yugoslavia and China, following Khrushchev's visit to Belgrade, and the Yugoslavs could reasonably hope that the Chinese would support their ideas about equality between socialist states. Mao's priority in foreign policy during his first years of power was Soviet economic aid; but he had no reason to trust Stalin, and had won his way to power even more independently than Tito. However Mao was more interested in a strong Soviet Union, which could help him militarily and economically, than in equality of relations between the Soviet Union and Eastern Europe. The Chinese leaders expressed doubts about the wisdom of Khrushchev's de-Stalinisation policy, and their doubts were strengthened by the events in Poland and Hungary in autumn 1956. They had subsequently played an important consultative part in the new settlement of Eastern Europe. The comparatively liberal phase of their internal policy (the 'Hundred Flowers' campaign of spring 1957) was soon over. They settled down to an extremely hard line at home and abroad, and pressed Khrushchev to take a tough line with the West[14] and to give them nuclear weapons. Khrushchev was not yet ready for a showdown with them, and the draft programme for the November conference was thus a hard-line document. Tito however could not accept a text which divided the world so definitely into two camps and so sharply

---

[13] When Tito received Gomułka in Belgrade six weeks later, he endorsed 'proletarian internationalism' as a guiding principle for relations between socialist states.

[14] They professed to, and probably did, take seriously Soviet propaganda about overtaking the West scientifically, after the launching of the first 'Sputnik' in September 1957. This was regarded as proof, in Chinese terms, that 'the East wind was prevailing over the West'.

attacked 'revisionism' (i.e. Titoist policies) with no compensating reference, such as was afterwards inserted, to 'dogmatism' (i.e. Stalinist policies). Tito refused to attend the Moscow meeting. Kardelj and Ranković went instead; they brought themselves to sign a general manifesto on Peace, proposed by Gomułka, but did not sign the declaration which, at Mao's insistence, severely condemned the 'Western imperialists'. Yugoslav abstention on this occasion was all the more conspicuous because of their rapprochement with Khrushchev in the previous August, and was a signal to other East European states that the Yugoslavs were 'revisionists' in foreign as well as in domestic policy.

It was precisely at this stage that the Yugoslavs had to proceed with the preparations for the Ljubljana Congress, which had long been deferred, and in particular with the drafting of the new LCY programme. They were anxious for internal reasons to clarify the LCY's stand on the issue of self-management. On foreign policy perhaps they saw some long-term advantage for their relations with 'progressive elements' within the 'Socialist camp' in opposing the Chinese-inspired dogmatic and dualist view of international relations, and repeating their own ideas of different ways to socialism, equal relations within the 'Socialist camp' and co-operation where possible with 'progressive elements' in the West. At any rate the programme contained passages bound to be very unwelcome at least to the Chinese; it condemned not only 'bourgeois revisionism' but also 'dogmatism' springing from 'bureaucratism and étatism'. This led to 'pseudo-revolutionary sectarianism and. . .loss of confidence in the strength of the working class',[15] to internal violence and terroristic rule, and to a tendency to brand 'as revisionism every true effort aimed at really developing the Marxist idea in contemporary social conditions'. Further the new Yugoslav programme decisively rejected the dualist view of the world. No attempt was made to differentiate between the two blocs and it was stated flatly that 'the division of the world into blocs impedes the realisation of the idea of co-existence and is at odds with full independence and sovereignty of peoples and states'.

All this was inevitably taken by the signatories of the Moscow Declaration of November 1957 as a declaration of ideological independence. The Yugoslavs professed themselves surprised. According to Tempo there had been serious discussion among the leaders on whether the Russians would react strongly to the draft programme, when it was

---

[15] Khrushchev levelled a similar charge against the Chinese only eighteen months later.

circulated in advance to fraternal parties.[16] In fact the first criticism to be received, from the Poles, was mild. The Chinese were the first to send in negative comments. They regarded the whole programme as anti-Marxist and revisionist, and would not attend the Congress. The CPSU followed shortly afterwards with a full criticism in *Kommunist*. The VIIth Congress was boycotted by all Party representatives from the 'bloc' and the third round of Soviet–Yugoslav ideological hostilities was clearly on.

In general the Yugoslavs were much better equipped than in 1948 for a political and economic boycott from the East, if this developed. They had however miscalculated on one point. In their anxiety to reconcile themselves with Khrushchev they had deliberately weakened some of their links with the West. Yugoslavia was no longer in diplomatic relations with West Germany. After Tito's triumphal reception in Moscow in June 1956 there had been increasing criticism in Washington of the policy of aid to Yugoslavia. In autumn 1957 Belgrade was informed through diplomatic channels that the U.S. aid programme was under review and, early in 1958, Tempo gave a public reply, declaring that Yugoslavia needed no more non-repayable grants from any source. Shortly afterwards Tito emphasised that no more military aid from the West would be accepted (in the same speech he deplored the 'bad Western influences' to which Yugoslav youth was exposed). Djilas had just been re-imprisoned, and there were further trials in February 1958 of former Social-Democrats. It seemed clear enough that, wherever Tito's treasure was, his heart was in Moscow.

[16] Tempo himself thought that the Russians would not react. 'Of course the whole of our practice is formulated in this programme, but they know about that anyhow.'

10

1958–61: Self-management and non-alignment

Yugoslavia's second open quarrel with the Soviet Union was serious but not long-lived. Throughout 1957 and 1958 Sino-Soviet relations were crucial in determining Soviet policies, and the Chinese emerged as the centralist hard-liners of the 'Socialist camp' in foreign as well as in internal policy.[1] However well before the end of 1958 the Chinese had begun to go much too fast and far for the Russians. The summer months witnessed the extremist 'Great Leap Forward' and the establishment of Communes in China, accompanied by wild propaganda about a short cut to Communism. Khrushchev resented this, and stood firm against Chinese pressure for more active Russian support in the Offshore Islands crisis of September 1959, and for the nuclear arming of China. By the end of 1958 the way to the Sino-Soviet split of 1963 was well marked out, and the Yugoslavs were probably aware of this.[2] Sino-Soviet differences of opinion worked in favour of the Yugoslavs, in so far as Mao was forcing Khrushchev into a comparatively moderate and pragmatic position on major questions of foreign policy.

Meanwhile the cooling-off of Soviet–Yugoslav relations after the publication of the Ljubljana programme helped to improve Yugoslav relations with the Western powers, especially with the U.S.A. Western statesmen were at least beginning to entertain the possibility that under Tito's leadership Yugoslav foreign policy would be alternately magnetised and repelled by Moscow. The crucial question for Yugoslav–Western relations was that of credits, and the case for granting them had positive and negative aspects. To grant credit facilities in place of those withdrawn for the second time by the Soviet Union might tie the Yugoslav economy more closely to the Western system, and in the

[1] As early as September 1957, the writer, then British Chargé d'affaires in Peking, was told by the very able Yugoslav Ambassador, Vladimir Popović, about Yugoslav distrust of the Chinese 'campaign mentality'.
[2] The Russians in Peking, for example, while behaving 'correctly', showed a clear lack of sympathy for Chinese extravagances, and did not conceal their views from their Western diplomatic colleagues.

long run political and even strategic connections might develop from the economic links. Conversely – and this was a more generally accepted argument – a clear refusal to help would drive Tito back into Khrushchev's embrace. In May 1958 the Yugoslav Government had confirmed that Western economic help without political conditions would indeed be acceptable. In August it made a formal request for credits from the U.S.A. and Britain amounting to nearly $200 million, and in the course of the following year large credits were granted, particularly by the Americans for the construction of an artificial-fertiliser plant originally to have been financed by the U.S.S.R.

In 1958 however it was still too early to talk of any definite westward trend of the Yugoslav economy. Tito was uncertain whether he would be able to reconcile himself fully with the Eastern or Western powers. It was at this period that he began to develop more systematically than before the policy of 'non-alignment' in order to strengthen Yugoslavia's international position. From 1949 onwards the Yugoslavs had been constrained by circumstances to work towards some such policy. They were anathema to the Soviet bloc, and did not wish to ally themselves too closely with the West. Their best hope of diplomatic support lay in developing connections with the Asian and later African countries which were also trying to assert their independence, and their best means of doing so was through the United Nations – specifically by increasing the powers of the General Assembly vis-à-vis the Security Council, which was normally dominated or rendered impotent by the Great Powers. Thus they supported the 'Uniting for Peace' resolution, which enabled the General Assembly in 1950 to authorise the despatch of American troops to defend South Korea; but they also backed Indian efforts to end the Korean war from 1951 onwards.

A Yugoslav Embassy in India was opened in April 1950, but it took some time before close relations were established between the two countries. Yugoslavia's closest Asian links were for some time with independent Burma, to which they provided military aid, and Yugoslav emissaries, including Djilas, also actively helped in developing the Asian Socialist International (1953–4). In summer 1953 they began to cultivate the recently established Egyptian Government under General Neguib and Colonel Nasser. Again it was the supply of arms which led to closer diplomatic links; these were facilitated by Yugoslav theories about independent ways to socialism and the importance of 'progressive forces' outside the Communist bloc. These could be interpreted as including the governments of any Asian or African country which strove to establish its national independence vis-à-vis the Great Powers. Thus the first Asian Head of State to visit Yugoslavia was the Emperor Haile Selassie of Ethiopia in summer 1954, and Tito returned his visit at the end of the year.

From this point on, Tito's own propensity for foreign travel[3] and talent for diplomacy contributed much to the form of Yugoslavia's policy of non-alignment. From Ethiopia he went on to visit India early in 1955, and returned via the Suez Canal where he met Nasser. On his return he stated – and this was a formal landmark of Yugoslav foreign policy – that the uncommitted countries were Yugoslavia's 'true allies and. . .greatest friends'. There were some economic as well as political calculations behind this statement, and certain Yugoslav enterprises hoped to find a steadily growing market in Asia and Africa.[4]

In 1956 Tito held his first meeting at Brioni with President Nasser of Egypt, for whom it was a major diplomatic occasion, and President Nehru of India, to whom it meant much less. The three Heads of State stated or restated their adherence to the principles agreed by the Asian and African Governments at the Bandung Conference in 1955, particularly the condemnation of colonialism, the importance of peaceful co-existence, further international co-operation, and the strengthening of the U.N. The three Presidents further emphasised their desire to see the 'power blocs' replaced by a system of 'collective security on a world scale, the enlargement of the area of freedom, and the ending of domination by one power over another'.

The concrete results of the Brioni conference were negligible. Tito did not aim to sell the Yugoslav model of socialism to uncommitted or non-aligned countries. Nor did he envisage the constitution of any 'third force' in any material sense, much less of a 'third bloc'. His main emphasis was from the start upon moral and political factors, and the need for national independence from all outside influences. This doctrine was of course welcome to the emergent nations of Asia and Africa, and the Yugoslav stand in 1948 had given Tito the clear right to preach it. At first however it was against Western interests. It was a significant chance that the Brioni communiqué was issued on the same day as the announcement that the U.S. had withdrawn its offer of assistance to Egypt in the construction of the Aswan Dam – an

[3] This was well-known in Yugoslavia by 1953, and was illustrated by the question-and-answer joke 'Is there a man in the moon?' 'No: otherwise Tito would have paid him a visit.'

[4] Yugoslav trade with the developing countries amounted to only 2% of its total foreign trade in 1954; the figure grew to about 15% at the end of the 1960s and has not increased substantially.

announcement which led directly to Soviet backing for Nasser, and the Suez crisis. The first practical concern of Asian and African countries was with hastening the end of the European empires in Asia and Africa and, when independence had been attained, with ensuring that it was not undermined by political conditions attached to economic aid ('neo-colonialism'). They knew Western imperialism at first hand, and did not recognise the existence of the Soviet variety. The Yugo-slavs knew plenty about what they called Soviet 'hegemonism', but for them the concept hardly arose in the Asian or African context. This state of affairs of course suited Soviet interests very well. There was indeed some argument in the West during the late 1950s and early 1960s whether the Yugoslavs in their pursuit of non-alignment were deliberately furthering Soviet influence in Asia or Africa. It seems much more probable that the Yugoslavs were furthering their own interests independently of the Soviet Union, though outside Europe their policy, in so far as it was anti-imperialist, was likely to coincide for a time with that of Moscow.[5]

2

Whatever excitement it aroused outside Yugoslavia, the new LCY line of spring 1958 seemed to set a clear course towards an extension of self-management in the Yugoslav economy. At least on a superficial analysis, the diminution in administrative regulation since 1952 had led to a marked increase in prosperity, and the trend continued until the end of the decade. The index of industrial production stood in 1959 at 238, with 1952 as the base year (100%). The number of workers employed stood at 2,730,000 (1956: 2,216,000). In the three years to 1959 agricultural production was beginning to grow, and the production of consumer goods (particularly cars, motorcycles and frigidaires) was increasing quite rapidly.

Nevertheless after as well as before the VIIth Congress of the LCY there were sharp divisions within the Yugoslav leadership between what might be called 'conservative' communists and others who were or seemed seriously keen to foster the movement towards further self-management in all sectors of society. By 1960–1 there was something like a confrontation between 'liberal' and 'conservative' communists.

[5] Mićunović's Moscow diary (25 July 1956) records that the Tito–Nasser–Nehru meeting at Brioni was displeasing to the Russians, as proof that the Yugoslavs were doing 'more for the establishment of co-existence and peace than any country in the "Socialist camp" '.

The principal issue was between those who thought that Yugoslavia's main continuing need was for rapid capital accumulation, to be achieved by effective planning from the centre, and those who thought that such a policy undermined all incentive at enterprise level, and could only lead to stagnation and chaos. The debate between them was largely on more concrete problems – investment, taxation and wages policy. It was conducted to a considerable extent by professional economists, but political and national factors were also closely involved.

At the political level arguments were conducted in largely ideological terms which led to semantic difficulties. Everyone on either side was for virtue and self-management, and against sin and bureaucracy. The 'conservatives' saw its worst manifestations under the existing system in the *de facto* alliances which were likely to take place between the chairman of the local Commune, the managing director and chairman of the Workers' Council of the main local enterprise, and probably some local bank managers, who all had an interest in maximising local profits and increasing local investment projects, with little regard to the economic needs of the country as a whole. This made a mockery, they said, of true self-management, and landed the Yugoslav economy in continual crises.

On more general grounds and less publicly they deplored what they saw as the degeneration of the post-war model of planned industrialisation into exclusive reliance on the stimulus of the market and too much concentration on profit-making. Everywhere, they argued, the influence of the LCY was being weakened, and the LCY itself was becoming corrupted. The only effective solution for this general crisis was more direction and detailed prescription from above, and a firmer line to be enforced (persuasively, no doubt, rather than through administrative orders) by the LCY.

The 'liberals' were also against bureaucracy, but equated it more naturally with centralism. As long as the state or the organs of local government continued to take so much of enterprises' profits in taxation, there was no real self-management and no incentive to greater productivity. In fact it was the firms with the greatest productivity that under the existing taxation system were being most heavily penalised. Naturally in this situation the men on the spot would look after themselves, and there would be an increase in undesirable 'localism'. The Yugoslav economy was becoming more and more distorted and less and less able to adapt itself to world market conditions. The right way out was to give more real power to the enterprises by letting them dispose much more freely of their profits and altering the federal and local tax structure accordingly. Then they would have a real interest in running their operations economically, in maximising exports, and in increasing general prosperity. In such conditions the temptations to petty tyranny and corruption would be greatly diminished.

Some of those who accepted these arguments were anxious to push them further towards a kind of total self-management. Devolution to enterprise level was not enough. Rational reforms were sometimes blocked by bureaucrats within enterprises, who wished to preserve their existing office empires. There must therefore be more internal democracy, and self-management must be extended downwards to separate departments of enterprises.

These were the main elements in the great debate which ultimately led to the Economic Reform of 1965.

Over the next three years it was the CTY under Tempo's leadership which campaigned most steadily for a fundamental change in the existing wage system, and for the introduction of one which would assure adequate payment for results achieved both by the individual worker and by the firm as a whole. In his memoirs, written some years later, Tempo emphasised the commonsense economic motives behind the CTY's prolonged battle for a more liberal economic system, particularly the need to base increased wages on increased productivity, and to work out new plans for productivity in the enterprises themselves. There are also interesting political implications in his account. The reader is told that Tito, while generally encouraging, warned Tempo that he was tackling the most crucial problem for the development of socialism in Yugoslavia; also that resistance at the top to any fundamental change was indeed powerful, usually taking passive forms – decisions were indefinitely postponed pending the conclusions of special commissions charged with working out new policies. It was not until 1961 that substantial changes were made, and then Tempo did not consider them wide enough in scope. Moreover according to Tempo's account, bureaucracy at the top had been supported by many representatives of factory management at enterprise level. Workers at branch level were much readier for change, and recognised their true friends in the CTY, rather than in the managing boards or even the Workers' Councils of their enterprises.

It is the political and personal aspects of this account which are the most interesting. Tito is represented as a father-figure above the day-to-day battles, who will advise the children from time to time, but will not intervene in their squabbles at an early stage (all this rings very true). A good deal of blame for conservative opposition is put on Ranković (this may well owe something to wisdom after the events of 1966). The most striking point however is that the spearhead of the attack on the existing Yugoslav economic system, which was highly vulnerable to argument on purely economic grounds, was the CTY, an interest group which had so far not been active in the field of politics, led by a powerful and disgruntled politician. Tempo was no trained expert in economics, but a political leader who enjoyed untying Gordian knots, and speaking bluntly and provocatively both to Yugoslav 'bureaucrats' and to the foreign negotiating partners of Yugoslavia. His memoirs are studded with the phrases 'I reacted sharply to this', 'I did not leave him unanswered', or 'He had no answer to this' – formulae that in his case did not represent simply the diplomat's *esprit d'escalier*. He was evidently determined to show that his new job in charge of the CTY could be as important as his former general economic responsibilities in the FEC. He developed at the CTY a distinctive standpoint over a wide range of economic policy questions, risking the charge that he was creating a rival to the CC, LCY. In the CTY he established a new political base from which to operate as a sort of tribune of the people (he was strongly in favour of devolution to enterprise branch level). The essential point here is that the debates on the economic system, while substantial, also covered personal feuding between the Yugoslav political leaders. This is hardly a surprising conclusion, but it should be established at this stage of the story.

In 1960–1 it looked as if the CTY and the comparatively liberal economists had wone a crucial political victory. The principles of determining wages by productivity, and of not penalising productivity by taxation, seemed to have been accepted when, at the beginning of 1961, the Federal Assembly adopted laws that gave enterprises greater independence vis-à-vis the Federal and Communal authorities. The state regulations about minimum wages were abolished. Progressive taxes on enterprise income were replaced by a flat rate tax, to stimulate production. Only 15% of an enterprise's income was to be paid in taxes of various kinds; the remaining 85% was at its free disposition, to be divided as was thought best between wages and investment funds. At the same time the dinar was devalued and the prices of some raw materials and factory products decontrolled. A start was made with measures to transform banks from government agencies into profit-making enterprises. All this constituted a considerable step forward for the 'liberals', and the CTY announced the reforms as the most important since the introduction of self-management in 1950.[6]

The liberalisation of the economy was intended to bring Yugoslav prices into line with those prevailing in Western Europe, and to facilitate Yugoslav acceptance of GATT (the General Agreement on Trade and Tariffs). These aims were also served by further large credits granted in 1961 by the International Monetary Fund (IMF) and the U.S. and other Western governments.[7] It soon proved however that this was a 'mini-reform' only and that the changes in the economic system did not go very deep. Economic self-management had certainly been extended, but elements of the old system remained. There was provision for a sort of surtax on enterprises' income above a certain level. The Yugoslav state too retained many important powers, including that of fixing prices for 70% of the products on the market, the distribution of the still important GIF, and the control of foreign trade and of foreign exchange resources. Moreover the 'mini-reform' was still opposed, at least passively, by those who wished to preserve untouched the economic influence of the state and the local organs of administration, and by others who professed, genuinely or not, to be afraid of the political consequences of setting the enterprises free. Bilandžić, a strong protagonist of economic reform, later wrote as follows:

Certain high political functionaries of the state and the Party did not dare or have the power to come out into the open against the transfer of rights to working organisations or the liberalisation of the market, and so sent into battle various experts, above all political economists, who warned public opinion that Yugoslavia, by decentralising its economy, was reverting to the period of liberal capitalism, while in all the rest of the world a process of centralisation and concentration of capital was taking place as a precondition and foundation for the development of the material forces of production and of the contemporary technological revolution.

Unfortunately the 'conservatives' soon had plenty to complain of in the performance of the Yugoslav economy and attributed its deterioration to the 'mini-reform' measures. The economic boom, which had coincided with the first of the second series of Yugoslav Five Year

[6] The new income law was described typically as 'a synthetic economic category of new self-managing social relations, a political-economic category in the process of the liberation of labour'.

[7] Political and economic relations with individual Western governments were not always in line. Western Germany remained diplomatically irreconcilable for some time after the Yugoslav recognition of Eastern Germany in 1957, but this did not put an end to commercial exchanges.

Plans, came to a halt in 1961. The plan had indeed been realised a year ahead of time, and a second more ambitious one was nominally put into effect. But this had been a period of too extensive investment, of ever-growing wages, and of growing imports on short-term credits. In 1960 Yugoslav exports were insufficient to afford any relief to the balance of payments. Foreign debts had to be repaid, and it was impossible to import the raw materials necessary to keep the Yugoslav processing industries fully active. At the same time wages were rising. Even by the beginning of 1961 – before the 'mini-reform' legislation was passed – there had been signs of severe inflation ahead. During 1961 industrial production increased by just over 4% only and agricultural production decreased by 3.3%, while personal incomes in the social sector (i.e. excluding most of the agricultural sector) increased by 20%. This was the first serious crisis of the Yugoslav economy since 1952.

3

It coincided with something like a crisis in Yugoslavia's foreign relations, during which Tito, perhaps for the first time and for only a short period, seemed to have lost his sense of equilibrium between East and West. The international scene was changing rapidly. In 1959 Khrushchev had embarked, it seemed, on a new course of super-power détente. In September he visited the U.S.A., and afterwards, at the tenth anniversary celebrations of the Chinese People's Republic, openly criticised Chinese 'adventurism'. The Sino-Soviet dispute began to simmer, and as a side effect Soviet–Yugoslav relations improved. Large scale Soviet credits were again made available, after Tempo's visit to the Soviet Union early in 1960. Even Khrushchev's angry curtailment of his summit meeting with Eisenhower in April 1960[8] did not reconcile the Chinese to the main lines of his policy. They continued to criticise what they regarded as the Soviet overall policy of détente, to preach unconditional support for 'national liberation movements', regardless of the risk of confrontation, and more privately to dwell on the inevitability of war. In June 1960 the Soviet leaders were organising at Bucharest the preparations for a further World Conference of CPs and in effect mobilising as many parties as possible against the Chinese. Here was an opportunity for the Yugoslavs to acquire merit in Khrushchev's eyes, and they gave open support to the Soviet doctrinal position on the issue of war and peace. Kardelj in August 1960 published a

8 After the shooting down of a U2 reconnaissance 'plane over the Soviet Union.

series of articles (subsequently collected in the form of a pamphlet), *Socialism and War.* In this he repeated the essential Yugoslav theses that socialism could be brought to birth within various countries by forms of political and economic struggle which need not culminate in armed revolution. At the same time on the international plane 'under present conditions the bellicose forces in the capitalist world have less and less power to kindle a new world war...the Socialist world both in principle and in practice is giving up and must give up the law of conquest as a means of imposing socialism'.

In other words the Yugoslavs accepted the Chinese premises that the relation of forces between the 'Socialist camp' and the forces of capitalism had changed once and for all to the advantage of the former. The Chinese argued from this that now was the time to put maximum pressure on the West, even at some risk of war. The Yugoslavs, like Khrushchev, argued the reverse. If the relationship of forces had changed, there was no need for war to defeat capitalism and imperialist forces. An adventurist policy in such circumstances was sheer folly.

Yugoslav support was not openly welcomed by the Russians, though they did not join in Chinese attacks on Kardelj's thesis.[9] The CPSU was still unwilling to break openly with the Chinese, and at the Conference of World CPs in Moscow (November 1960) a compromise statement was issued, in which Yugoslav revisionism was condemned. Moreover throughout 1961 Khrushchev guarded himself further against accusations from the Chinese and from opponents within his own Party by maintaining or creating a new state of considerable tension with the West. This was the year in which he renewed the near-ultimatum about Berlin, originally posed to the Western occupying powers in 1958. His principal object was attained when in August the flow of refugees from East to West Berlin was checked by the building of the inter-sector wall; the West did not react to this by more than diplomatic protests, and the immediate crisis passed. However the series of nuclear tests in the atmosphere, begun by the Soviet Government in 1960, in contravention of the moratorium agreed at Geneva in 1958, was another source of East–West tension and could be taken as indicating that Soviet armed strength was being built up with a view to a major confrontation in Europe.

On both these issues, and conspicuously on the latter, Tito took the Soviet side against the West. For him the most important thing was

---

[9] It was mentioned by two official Soviet commentators with the careful remark that they would not read it because they knew that it would merely express the Yugoslav revisionist standpoint.

probably to prevent a Sino-Soviet reconciliation and a renewal of open hostility between the Soviet Union and Yugoslavia, and therefore to support Khrushchev where possible. This remained one of the main strands of Yugoslav foreign policy, and in 1961 it was expressed most effectively through the machinery of non-alignment. Here is an apparent paradox. The Ljubljana Programme of 1958 re-affirmed Tito's decision not to rejoin the 'Socialist camp', severely criticised the 'statist bureaucracy' and dogmatism of the CPSU, and committed Yugoslavia to the pursuit of 'active co-existence' not only with the CPs of the world, but also with 'nationalist movements with progressive views' in Asia, Africa and Latin America. This was a new and formal commitment to the cause of uncommitted or non-aligned countries. For some years it worked by no means in favour of Soviet policies. At the XXIst Congress of the CPSU in February 1959 Yugoslav 'revisionists' were accused of seeking to instil in 'the young republics of the East a mistrust of Soviet policy and the policy of other socialist countries'. In October 1960 the Yugoslavs, though mistrustful of Dag Hammerskjöld's activist policy as Secretary-General of the U.N., refused support for Khrushchev's proposal to replace him by 'troika' machinery, in which the non-aligned countries would have weight equal to that of the Eastern or Western blocs.[10] Thus the first Summit Conference of non-aligned states, which opened in Belgrade in September 1961, did not seem likely unduly to favour the Eastern against the Western bloc. Its conclusions however seemed at the time to represent an eastward lurch by the non-aligned. The Heads of the non-aligned states present issued a declaration full of general principles. They were against blocs (including any bloc of non-aligned states, or economic blocs of developed states), and condemned threats or intervention against the right of nations to self-determination. They were in favour of the application of the principles of peaceful co-existence in international relations, the early grant of independence to colonial territories, and the immediate conclusion of a treaty on 'general and complete disarmament'. They took a more specific stance against the establishment or maintenance of military bases on the territory of other countries, the policy of apartheid, 'imperialist' policies in the Middle East, and any recourse to force in the solution of the German and Berlin problems. They pronounced themselves in favour of the Algerian independence move-

10 Subsequently, after the death of Hammerskjöld in September 1961, the Yugoslavs helped to promote the compromise under which U Thant succeeded him; they continued to uphold the Secretary-General's right to undertake diplomatic initiatives, maintained their contingent in the U.N. peace-keeping force in Sinai, and contributed towards the cost of the U.N. Congo operation.

ment,[11] the 'struggle of the people of Palestine for the realisation of all their rights', the evacuation of the American base in Cuba, the admission of China to the U.N., an immediate ban on all nuclear tests, and the setting-up of a U.N. capital development fund to help underdeveloped nations.

On all these points they were *de facto* supporting Soviet positions. This was only to be expected on China, the Middle East and colonial issues. What caused most resentment in the West was the non-aligned stance on the Berlin issue with which Asian and African powers had no direct concern, and above all the more general points, on which they seemed to ignore the Western case and to show undue faith in Soviet intentions. No Western government could agree, for example, to the simultaneous dissolution of NATO and the Warsaw Pact at the height of the 1961 crisis over Berlin, or indeed so long as the closest political links, which could be quickly re-transformed into a military alliance, continued to bind the countries of Eastern Europe. The same arguments applied to the disestablishment of military bases in West and East Germany, and a parallel case could be made against the non-aligned recommendations on disarmament. These indeed specified that there should be an effective system of inspection and control, but the crux was what constituted an effective system. Without far tighter provisions for control of disarmament measures on the spot than the Russians were ever likely to admit, the Western powers would, as was well known, never sign a general disarmament treaty. As for a complete ban on nuclear tests, the Western powers were most unlikely to accept it after the Russians had just completed a large series of tests in the atmosphere in contravention of an agreed moratorium.

All this looked like a large measure of support by the non-aligned for the positions of the 'Socialist camp', and support which hardly served immediate Yugoslav interests. Tito had plenty of experience of Soviet bad faith and considerable need of economic links with the Western world, including economic aid. It remains strange to the Western observer that at this stage of Yugoslavia's internal development Tito should have leaned so far to the East in his 'non-alignment'.

Various reasons can be advanced for his behaviour. The Belgrade Conference was the climax of a long drawn-out series of preparations.

[11] The Yugoslavs, though constant in their support for the Algerian national liberation movement (FLN), had up to this time been cautious about the form it took, in the hope that the moderate FLN leaders could find some accommodation with the French, especially after the return of de Gaulle to power. At the time of the Belgrade Conference, the Yugoslavs extended *de jure* recognition to the FLN, and the French withdrew their Ambassador from Belgrade.

Tito's prestige was involved in making a success of it. He would gratify his Asian and African guests by all-out support on colonial and Middle Eastern issues. They were willing enough to air their views on other problems which concerned them less directly. These views were superficially reasonable and the main argument against them was the possibility of Soviet bad faith if they were ever generally accepted. Anxious as Tito was for a second complete reconciliation with Khrushchev, he was the last person to dwell on this danger. As regards the Western powers, he had experience of their patience, and may have calculated that they would be unwilling to hasten his reconciliation with Khrushchev by reacting too sharply against his stance at the non-aligned Conference. Possibly too Tito felt that economic necessity as well as political inclination were working to swing Yugoslavia eastwards again. Political relations with France and the Federal Republic were at a low point, and Yugoslav–German economic links might be endangered. The Treaty of Rome, providing for the establishment of the European Economic Community had recently been signed. A Western economic super-power was perhaps going to emerge which might pose unacceptable conditions for Yugoslav commercial and financial relations with Western Europe.

In October 1961 moreover there were signs of a definite change in Western attitudes and President Kennedy ordered a review of U.S. policy towards Yugoslavia.[12] Tito used the doubts openly expressed about Yugoslav foreign policy for his own purposes. In a speech made at Skopje on 13 November 1961 he attacked 'certain quarters in the West' for trying to put pressure on Yugoslavia and to exploit its economic difficulties. There is little doubt that one of his main objects was to demonstrate to the Soviet leadership his independence of the West. On the internal economic front too he took measures which would incidentally have the same effect. At the end of November there was a plenary meeting of the CC, LCY, which put an end to the 'mini-reform' of 1961 and introduced a policy of 'stabilisation', i.e. the re-introduction of many of the abandoned economic controls. At the same time Tito expressed his anxiety about the way in which free and evil communications with 'rotten liberalism' had corrupted good communist manners and morals. Some attempt was made to restore stricter party control over the arts and the general life-style of individualistic Yugoslavs.[13]

[12] This eventually resulted in no significant changes.
[13] Dobrica Ćosić – a sort of Communist poet-laureate – in addressing the Sixth Congress of the Yugoslav Writers' Association, told his audience (16 September

Meanwhile, particularly after the XXIInd Congress of the CPSU in October 1961 and the opening of a second phase of de-Stalinisation (marked by the removal of Stalin's body from the mausoleum on the Red Square), there had been an intensification of official Yugoslav contacts with Moscow. In April 1962 Gromyko visited Belgrade, in return for a visit to Moscow by Koča Popović the summer before. Brezhnev arrived in Belgrade in September, and at the end of the year, Tito went to Moscow 'on vacation'.

It is tempting to see in the re-orientation of Yugoslav foreign policy towards the Soviet Union and in the re-de-liberalisation of Yugoslav economic policy at the end of 1961 two facets of a single master policy.[14] It seems more likely that at the end of 1961 there was a special conjunction of events in which, exceptionally, there were few contradictions between two of the long term objectives of Yugoslav foreign policy and what could be regarded as the immediate needs of Yugoslav society. Reconciliation with Khrushchev, and the satisfaction of Tito's desire to appear as a leader of the non-aligned nations could be attained simultaneously, particularly at a time of great international tension, when it may have seemed that Yugoslavia was being forced to take sides between East and West. There was also a case, arguable on purely economic grounds, for reverting to a policy of tight economic controls in Yugoslavia, and a case arguable by conservative communists, including Tito himself, for an attempt to reintroduce tighter social controls. The internal policy measures adopted, including the re-imprisonment of Djilas early in 1962, were certainly of a kind that would be acceptable to Khrushchev, and would facilitate a Soviet–Yugoslav reconciliation. But to assume that they were adopted primarily for this reason would be to make too tidy a pattern out of the chaotic variety of events.

The Yugoslav leaders have in all probability never had a masterplan, as was sometimes suspected in the West, for securing Western aid by temporary measures of liberalisation in Yugoslavia, and then enforcing much stricter discipline and aligning their country more closely or completely with the Soviet Union. But Tito was a Moscow-trained Communist. Economic liberalisation was forced upon him in the early 1950s, not deliberately adopted in order to attract Western aid. He and other Yugoslav leaders probably envisaged from the start the

1961) that they should purge themselves of bourgeois influences and pay more attention to the practice of the Soviet Union and other Communist countries.

[14] As late as 1964 at least one studious and well-informed Western commentator (Viktor Meier of the *Neue Zürcher Zeitung*) was writing of a fundamental and final re-orientation of Yugoslav foreign policy.

danger that it might lead to unwelcome social side-effects. They tended therefore to seize any chance of returning to some central controls in order to curb economic individualism and 'permissiveness', either in the arts or in the wider social sphere. To this extent they have resembled their Russian and even Chinese new puritan counterparts. Where they have differed from these is in their readiness to recognise that prolonged debate before important decisions is a vital feature even of 'democratic centralism'; that campaigning on broad social themes can easily become counter-productive; that some liberalisation would remain necessary, if the Yugoslav economy was to function efficiently; and that a certain social price would have to be paid for this.

11

Economic Reform: the beginnings, 1961–3

The years 1962–6 were those of Economic Reform. This was of course not effected in an international vacuum, but for a time international problems did not weigh too heavily on the Yugoslav leaders. By 1962 at least the main international tensions of the previous eighteen months were somewhat relaxed. The East–West confrontation in Germany had reached an uneasy stalemate and U.N. intervention had produced a kind of settlement in the Congo, which could hardly now be regarded as involving any danger of a wider war. In Western eyes, Tito's foreign policy still seemed pro-Soviet, especially on the German question and disarmament. The second reconciliation between Yugoslavia and the Soviet Union was formally completed when Brezhnev, as Head of State, visited Yugoslavia in September 1962 and received a very warm welcome. It was however more important that the foreign policy of the non-aligned states began at this time to be concerned less with problems at issue between the 'blocs', and more with the long-term economic problems of development aid within the U.N. context.[1] This in itself tended to reduce the temperature of Yugoslav–Western relations. Correspondingly less publicity was given to Yugoslav fears of their exports being squeezed out of a highly exclusive closed market in the EEC countries, though Tito continued to recommend as long-term

[1] Agreement was reached in summer 1962 at the U.N. Economic and Social Council to hold the first U.N. Conference on Trade and Development (UNCTAD – it took place from March to June 1964). The importance of economic development for the independence of small nations, and the need for development aid to them through the U.N., had been constant themes of the Yugoslavs at the U.N. since 1949. They were strong protagonists of the idea of a Special U.N. Fund for Economic Development (SUNFED). Discussions of this idea led indirectly to the establishment of the U.N. Special Fund for capital development (1957) and eventually of the U.N. Industrial Development Organization (UNIDO) in 1966. As it became apparent that development aid through these organisations would be quite inadequate, the emphasis in Yugoslav thinking (as elsewhere) shifted to the need for easier trade conditions for developing countries, and the series of UNCTAD Conferences was inaugurated.

economic strategy the concentration of Yugoslav exports on the developing markets of Asia and Africa.

The Caribbean crisis of autumn 1962, over the installation of Soviet missile bases in Cuba, blew up and was solved too quickly to affect the general trend of Yugoslav foreign policy, and its aftermath was a temporary stabilisation of super-power relations. Khrushchev was now ready for limited co-operation with the West and no longer tried conspicuously to outsmart President Kennedy or to keep the 'colonial' powers on the run in the United Nations. The new trend towards détente led to the conclusion of the Test Ban Treaty of summer 1963 between the Soviet Union, the U.S.A. and Britain. This in turn deepened the already open rift between the Soviet Union and China, which was very much in Yugoslav interests. In August 1963 Khrushchev visited Yugoslavia again; he had some kind things to say about Workers' Councils, and it was announced that Yugoslavia would be given observer status at COMECON meetings. The fall of Khrushchev from power in October 1964 was a personal blow for Tito and certainly was followed by a long period (not yet ended) of stagnation in Soviet internal developments. But it did not lead to any immediate changes in Soviet policy towards China or the Western powers. The resulting situation made it easier for Tito to regain his balance between East and West, and to pursue a foreign policy based on Yugoslavia's immediate economic interests.

2

The years 1962–6 were those of a great economic debate in Yugoslavia, with which were bound up very serious political issues. In February 1962 Tito returned from a long tour of Africa and found an economic situation in Yugoslavia which demanded his immediate personal intervention. The warnings which he had given, particularly at Skopje in November 1961, seemed to have been neglected. The controls then re-introduced were not working. 'Political' credits were still being granted for unnecessary new factories. There was too much competition between enterprises for export markets. Too many enterprises were profiting unduly from their monopoly positions, and prices continued to rise. A special meeting of the LCY Executive Committee was held early in April to discuss the state of the country, and a stern letter was circulated to all levels of the LCY as a result. Tito himself at a public meeting in Split on 6 May expressed his grave dissatisfaction; his speech was widely interpreted as heralding a reversion to a system of much tighter control, not only of Yugoslavia's economy, but also of its social and intellectual life.

On the economic front, Tito repeated the criticisms which he had voiced at Skopje, and reinforced them. There were by now excessively large wage differentials, and excessive waste of funds by a new managing class which travelled far too much abroad (some of his audience might have smiled at this), bought too many cars for themselves, and even sold Yugoslav industrial secrets to foreigners. New and tighter controls must be introduced, including new laws against economic criminals. The little 'private groups' linking directors of enterprises with the chairmen of Communal Committees must be broken up. Firm measures must be taken, even if people called them repressive. Democracy was a good thing, but 'it must be developed in a more co-ordinated way'.

A number of 'firm measures' had already been taken, including stricter import controls (preceded, as Tito himself said, by an unprecedented rush to import cars), wider price controls, and the formation of special commissions to determine the level of wages (this involved the effective revoking of the 'mini-reform' measures allowing much greater financial freedom to enterprises). After the 4th Plenum of the CC, LCY, in July 1962, Tito laid down further general lines of economic strategy. Imports of ready-made goods must be cut down in favour of buying licences to manufacture on the spot. There must be much more investment in tourism, and long-term plans must be made for greatly increased exports to the under-developed countries. Work on the new Five Year Plan was to be abandoned, and attention concentrated on a realistic plan for 1963.

However on many crucial problems there was no concrete guidance. About the freedom of enterprises to manage their own finances, for example, Tito was completely indecisive. The system of credits, he said, must be changed. The Republic and Communal banks (not the Federal authorities or the enterprises themselves) should have more funds at their disposal. Otherwise there would be continued 'localism and all possible anomalies'. But

...by giving funds to the Republics and Communes the correct development of our economy won't be entirely assured, although there will be some improvement. Thus I think that we shall have to aim at setting aside certain funds for the enterprises themselves. Some comrades perhaps won't agree with this idea, and I therefore won't insist that it should be adopted here and now. But I think that this is the only correct way, if we want to facilitate the correct development of self-management.

The whole passage is curiously uncertain, and suggests that Tito by the end of summer 1962 was backing away from the re-centralising position which he had favoured in the spring.

The results of Tito's guidance in any case seemed to be meagre. There was a Party campaign against private craftsmen which was soon put into reverse. There was some propaganda against directors as a class, which Tito himself had to discourage. The CC reached conclusions on some minor deflationary measures, on the importance of increasing the productivity of the small socialist sector of agriculture as an example to the large private sector, and on the compatibility of economic decentralisation with inter-enterprise integration, to achieve economies of scale. It soon became increasingly apparent that little had been achieved by the holding measures introduced from the end of 1961. Industrial production increased in 1962 by only 7% – much less than the rate of inflation that had obtained since the 'mini-reform' of 1961.

3

In this difficult economic situation, the LCY had failed to give a clear lead, and a major debate was now initiated by economic experts, rather than LCY or CTY committees, about the general lines of policy. It began in December 1962, when the Yugoslav Association of Economists met to discuss the economic clauses of a new Constitution, then in its final draft. It was continued a month later in Zagreb with the participation of representatives from the Federal Institute of Economic Planning. The argument continued in various forms between those who favoured central planning as still the best means of economic development, and the advocates of more reliance on market indicators. The control of prices and wages, foreign exchange and foreign trade of course continued to be important issues. In particular the 'liberals' could argue with reason that the whole price structure in Yugoslavia was hopelessly distorted by the persistence of measures taken in the period of maximum and rapid industrialisation, which involved uneconomically low prices for raw materials and all sorts of special rebates, subsidies and credits for enterprises which could never pay their way. However the crucial problem for the political as well as the economic development of Yugoslavia was now the control of investment, which at this stage involved a growing conflict of interest between the more and less developed regions of Yugoslavia. As this conflict intensified, Republican national feelings began to revive and within ten years endangered the whole structure and existence of Tito's Yugo-slavia.

Early in 1962 Tito had still felt able to say:[2] 'We have solved the national question.' Indeed it had been swept under the carpet for the first decade and more of his régime. Some attempt had been made from the mid fifties to foster a 'Yugoslav consciousness', as opposed to a sense of Serb or Croat nationality. There was a deliberate attempt to minimise the differences between the Serb and Croat languages (or dialects of the Serbo-Croat language),[3] and to put an end to the cultural isolation of the national minorities in Yugoslavia. The programme adopted at the VIIth LCY Conference in April 1958 envisaged the solution of the national question in the development of a 'socialist Yugoslav consciousness, in the conditions of a socialist community of peoples'. Socialist patriotic consciousness added to nationalist or ethnic loyalty would, it was hoped, ultimately lead to a specifically Yugoslav culture. Such hopes however were likely to awaken memories of the Serb exploitation of the Yugoslav idea in the inter-war period, and to be greeted very warily by Croats and Slovenes. By 1961 the 'Yugoslav idea' had been submerged in economic arguments which had an increasingly 'nationalist' complexion.

National dissensions were stimulated particularly by one of the main documents discussed at Zagreb early in 1963, a Croat presentation[4] of the 'liberal' line that, after the first and centrally planned stage of industrial development had been completed, in the later stages there should be progressively more freedom for market forces and progressively less intervention by central planners or political organisations. Such a policy corresponded most obviously with the interests of the more developed Republics, at a time when the gap between the more and the less developed seemed to be widening, in Yugoslavia as in the rest of the world.

The differences existing in 1962 are illustrated by the table on page 142.[5]

The first column of this table indicates the obvious difference in prosperity between the Republics as seen by average observers and felt

---

[2] In conversation with delegates from the High School of Political Sciences.

[3] On this (the Novi Sad Agreement of December 1954) see also Chapter 13, p. 172.

[4] Known as the 'White Book', it was jointly initiated by Bakarić and, among others, Savka Dabčević-Kučar, later to become Prime Minister of Croatia.

[5] Quoted, as are the figures in the following two paragraphs from Rudolf Bičanić's *Economic Policy in Socialist Yugoslavia*, Cambridge 1973. It should be noted that 1962 was the year after the fulfilment of the second Five Year Plan, which included a special programme of aid to the underdeveloped areas.

	National income per head 1962 000 din. (old)	Capital in industry per employed 1962 000 din. (old)
Yugoslavia	194	3,390
Slovenia	378	3,307
Croatia	232	3,307
Vojvodina	203	3,374
Serbia proper	187	3,420
Serbia (republic of)	175	3,570
Montenegro	142	8,848
Bosnia and Hercegovina	137	4,097
Macedonia	134	3,519
Kosmet	71	4,201

by the inhabitants of the poorer Republics. This difference moreover seemed to be growing. In the five years 1953–7 the 'social product' per head of population had grown in the more developed regions of northern Yugoslavia from 110% of the country average to 116%; in the less developed regions of the south it fell from 70% to 67%. This fall was of course consistent with some rise in the standard of living in the south; but it was the difference between south and north which was felt and counted most.

The second column of the table represents the view of comparatively sophisticated observers and of the taxpayers in the more developed Republics. Slovenian enterprises for example might still be more efficient and profitable than those in Montenegro or Macedonia; but the investment per head in these latter Republics had been considerable and had been made essentially from wealth created in Slovenia or Croatia and redistributed by the central authorities in Belgrade. Some further figures illustrated the same point. Industrial production in Yugoslavia as a whole rather more than quadrupled (421%) between 1952 and 1964. Similar growth in Slovenia and Croatia amounted to 367% and 414%, in Serbia to 505%, in Bosnia to 521%, in Macedonia to 636% and in Montenegro to 1125%. The proportion between the gross industrial production of the individual Republics to that of Yugoslavia as a whole varied little between 1952 and 1964. The most noticeable changes were in the Slovenian share which declined from 24.9% in 1952 to 19.7% in 1964, and in the Serbian share which rose from 29.5% to 33.7%.

There were powerful and purely economic arguments in favour of more concentrated development of Yugoslav industry as a whole. However in the less developed Republics it was felt more and more

strongly that the effect of leaving economic rationalisation to the enterprises and the immediate stimuli of the market, rather than to the
central planners, would be to concentrate productive industry even
more than before in the northern Republics of Yugoslavia. In the long-
term economic interests of Yugoslavia, development should be fostered
in what had hitherto been the poorer regions; their resources in raw
materials, particularly rare metals, were great and had been badly
under-exploited in the past. The creation of an infrastructure for such
development, particularly in the field of communications, would benefit
not only the poorer regions themselves. It would also open an increasing market in these regions to the firms already well established in
northern Yugoslavia.

There were strong arguments in social equity too for massive industrial investment in the southern regions. They were rich in labour-
power and the best way of using this was by bringing work for it to the
spot, rather than by encouraging further migration with all the social
problems involved. In any case they deserved to be compensated for
the unhappy accident of their historical past. Even within socialist
Yugoslavia, they had been exporting their raw materials cheap to the
more developed regions, and buying manufactured goods from them
too dearly. 'Equalising conditions of work' was one of the main
slogans of debate. It was a phrase which could mean almost anything,
but to the protagonists of the less developed Republics it meant essentially that there should be more investment from central funds in e.g.
Bosnian enterprises, to make up for natural or historical advantages
enjoyed by e.g. Slovenian ones.

The principal instrument of the 'centralist' policy favoured by the
less-developed Republics was the GIF, constituted in 1954. Even after
the VIIth Congress of the LCY, which expressed doubts about the
system of virtually unconditional grants-in-aid from the GIF, much of
the enterprises' income had continued to go to the state, and over
four-fifths of all investments made in Yugoslavia were made from the
GIF through the Yugoslav National Bank, or its subsidiary Investment
Banks. The central authorities controlled investment in two stages.
First they allocated funds for the main sectors of the national economy
through the Federal Social Plan and corresponding social plans at
lower levels. Then within these sectors they invited bidding for funds
at competitive rates of interest. The bidders' projects were also evalu-
ated by expert committees, but the whole procedure was liable to a
good deal of political manipulation.

As such, it was thought by the governments of the less developed

Republics to give them a better chance of attracting investment funds. The Five Year Plan adopted at the end of 1957 guaranteed the less developed regions preferential treatment in the matter of investments, even if Bosnia-Hercegovina was temporarily removed from the list of such regions. The over-rapid growth of investment expenditure in 1960 (gross investment being nearly 30% greater than in 1959) involved great difficulties for the Yugoslav economy as a whole, but the leaders of the less developed Republics tended to favour any programme which provided for industrial projects in their own regions.

The 1961 reforms constituted a limited victory for the economic 'liberals' who were associated, whether they liked it or not, with an essentially 'northern' (Croatian and Slovenian) outlook in the Yugoslav context. The reforms moreover included provisions for changing the system of guaranteeing investments for under-developed regions from the GIF. This was to be replaced by a centrally-financed Special Fund for the Development of Under-Developed Areas, which would at least be likely to limit the amount of funds devoted from the centre to these areas[6] (in fact it was not constituted until 1965, since agreement could not be reached on exactly how it was to be financed). There was also a new classification of regions eligible for financial support on account of under-development. This included large districts of Croatia, Bosnia and Serbia, as well as the Kosmet, Macedonia and Montenegro, and thus could be regarded as a concession to the Croats.

1962 witnessed another victory for the 'liberal' outlook, in the cancellation of the unrealistic Five Year Plan for 1961–5, which had been regarded as unduly favouring Serb interests.[7] However any 'liberal' trends of this period were short-lived. The emergency measures taken at the end of 1961 and in 1962 were certainly a victory for the 'conservative' centralists, largely representative of Serbia and the less developed Republics. This victory was also short-lived, and was soon put in question by the widening of the great debate on the need for economic reform.

The 'liberal' or reformers' case in this debate has already been broadly stated in a purely economic context, without reference to the 'nationalities problem'. The industrial growth achieved since 1952 had

[6] The new criterion for receiving aid was a comparison with the *per capita* income of the 'average' Yugoslav Republic; there was still no limit to aid to be granted to any one Republic.

[7] The projects envisaged included the joint Yugoslav-Romanian hydro-electric project at the Iron Gates, on the Danube, the Danube–Tisza Kanal in the Vojvodina, and the railway from Belgrade to Bar on the Adriatic – this last was historically connected with plans dating from 1878 for 'Greater Serb' expansion to the coast. All have now been completed.

been far too extensive and unselective. The spread of investment funds from the centre on a Republican basis was no less wasteful than the excessive investments by the Communes, which were a standard theme in the speeches of Tito and other Yugoslav leaders. The former was in fact largely a hangover from the pre-1949 era of totally controlled economy. It had been introduced for reasons of national defence, which now seemed less necessary, as well as on humanitarian, social and long-term economic grounds. But was it justifiable, even on all these grounds put together, to locate for example, a major steel mill at Nikšić in Montenegro, where communications were notoriously deficient?[8] This may have been an extreme case. In 1962 however the system still involved the injection of Federal funds on a large scale, often to keep thousands of workers in employment at factories which were unlikely to become efficient within many years. Moreover these Federal funds were administered, more obviously than the credits which reached the new industries at Communal level, by the central authorities at Belgrade, and an apparatus that was largely Serb; inevitably this was becoming a major grievance to the Croats and Slovenes. A more rational method of spreading resources would raise the general standard of living (this became an important slogan), would increase the funds available from the industrialised parts of Yugoslavia for direct investment in the under-developed areas, and would thus ultimately provide more help for the less developed Republics. Prosperous enterprises should integrate with similar ones in the less developed regions, or set up their own branches there. Such arrangements should be made without interference by the Federal, Republican or Communal authorities.[9]

Thus the economic debate tended to merge with historic national differences, and the issue of economic reform ranged, so to speak, ex-Austrians against ex-Ottomans within Yugoslavia.

4

Another important political issue underlay the economic debate between reformers and centralists. This was the fact that economic liberalisation tended to undermine Communist discipline, not only in the

[8] This, to quote Dennison Rusinow, 'began production in 1953, waited eight years for a rail connection with the nearby Adriatic, more than ten years for a paved highway to anywhere, and until 1975 for a standard-gauge railway line to the rest of the country'.

[9] Tito was on the whole in favour of this arrangement, but qualified his support for it in May 1962 by saying that political controls must be organised 'to ensure against. . .injustice in relation to the use of material resources. . .'

economic field. Tito had spoken severely in summer 1962 against the new caste of managers which seemed to be emerging from the system of economic self-management and transforming it into a bourgeois anarchy. At the same time he rated the leaders of the LCY for not having spoken up about the situation, and voiced an ominous concern that 'the directives given at the VIth Congress 1952 had somehow been unsatisfactorily and wrongly interpreted'.[10]

Such pronouncements seemed to foreshadow some return to central controls by a re-activated LCY. And Tito's desire to apply a 'firm-hand' policy was increased by trends outside the economic field. Intellectuals, historians and other writers were beginning to take advantage of the passivity of the LCY. By the end of 1961 it was becoming clear that the idea of a 'Yugoslav' culture, transcending nationalist traditions, was making little headway, and was often regarded as a mask for Serb ambitions. Even the most official of the Yugoslav newspapers, *Borba*, printed in December an exchange between Dobrica Ćosić, a Serb writer who had been close to Tito himself, and a spokesman for the Slovenes, in which the latter accused Ćosić of trying to re-impose the cultural domination of Serbia on Yugoslavia as a whole. In the 1961 draft of the new Constitution, adopted in 1963, the idea of Yugoslav (as opposed to Serb, Croat, etc.) nationality was completely omitted, though it found its way back into the final version.

By summer 1962 Tito expressed his alarm at developments: 'We've allowed anything and everything to be printed in the press...One is simply disgusted when one sees how chauvinism has begun to be spread among our younger generation. I don't believe that this has come out of the clouds, but from our own home, from the older generation...'[11] In his final speech at the 4th Plenum of the CC, LCY, he repeated that writers had enjoyed too much licence:

We've shrugged our shoulders and thought that it won't hurt anyone if we let everyone talk and write as he wants. But we've gone too far. Certainly we won't brainwash writers, and prescribe what they shall write, but also we shan't let anyone write nonsense and caricature or write against our social life. We shan't permit the spreading of divisive slogans, of national intolerance and chauvinism, which sometimes happens at present in our schools and other areas of our social life. Communists must smash this sort of thing and make it impossible. Till now they've not always been up to the job, since they've looked too liberally at such things...

[10] Speeches at 4th Plenum of CC, LCY, July 1962, and of 26 May 1962.
[11] Speech at Split, 6 May 1962.

Tito was referring particularly to the dangers involved for Yugoslavia in the re-appearance of inter-racial polemics, and the need for a tighter central control in order to check them. But if the LCY was encouraged to use censorship for one purpose, it might well (to judge by past form) go too far and use its powers for more general direction of the press and the repression of any cultural tendencies which were not 'socially positive', in the Party jargon. As Yugoslav contacts with the West had increased, there were already far too many 'socially negative phenomena' clearly visible to the older generation of communists. By 1963 indeed Tito had begun to talk in terms reminiscent of Khrushchev about remote intellectuals and decadent artists.[12] He told the VIIth Congress of Yugoslav youth (23 January) that they should have no use for thinkers who find everything about them too banal and every-day, who get enthusiastic about decadent art and literature from abroad, and think Marxism outdated. 'There is no question here of administrative intervention, but public opinion cannot afford to be passive in the face of such problems.'

It was clear from the same speech that Tito was not talking simply about a handful of intellectuals. He objected to the amount of public money being spent on 'certain so-called modernistic works, which have no connection with artistic creativeness, much less with the actuality of our time'.

Significantly too these passages were closely linked with attacks on the revival of bourgeois habits (Communists at least should call each other 'comrade' not 'Mister') and with insistence on the need for the 'integration of ideas and politics' in a Yugoslav socialist culture which should embrace and supplement national cultures.

Economics, culture and politics could theoretically have been separated. There was no logical reason in 1962-3 why Yugoslavs who favoured on purely economic grounds a large measure of economic reform and increased initiative at enterprise level should necessarily be Croat nationalists, or should necessarily oppose more centralised control of cultural affairs and more political activity by the LCY. Indeed a good Communist could have arrived again at the essential conclusion reached at the VIth Congress – economic decentralisation is good, but makes it the more necessary that there should be the maximum of centrally directed activity by the LCY. *De facto* however this logic was not applied. What emerged from the great debate on economics,

---

[12] Indeed in this case he may have been influenced by Khrushchev, whom he met shortly after the latter had uttered his notorious criticisms of modern art at the Moscow 'Manège' exhibition.

with its strong national undertones, was very broadly speaking a confrontation between on the one hand leaders interested in economic efficiency, considerable independence for the Croat and Slovene nations, and a considerable degree of political as well as economic liberalism; and on the other hand those who were concerned with the preservation of the machinery of centrally directed investment, the pre-eminence of Belgrade and of the largely Serb administrative apparatus, and the maintenance of conservative communist standards. This confrontation naturally centred around certain dominant political leaders on either side. The conservative centralists certainly had good reason to suppose that Tito was on their side. But whatever his instincts, he had given only a very muted lead at the 4th Plenum, and had left himself the option of backing the economic reformers without having to eat too many words. And at a time when Khrushchev, in the name of de-Stalinisation and a struggle against the political old guard in the Soviet Union, was using the talents of Tvardovsky and Solzhenitsyn (*Ivan Denisovich* was published in *Novi Mir* in 1962), Tito could perhaps afford to accept some strange allies if he decided in favour of reform.

12

Economic Reform: the crisis, 1964–6

The economic debate of 1962–3 was the most important political reality in Yugoslavia at the time. It was however paralleled by a simultaneous debate, in more strictly political terms, taking place within the committees charged with the preparation of the new Constitution, to be presented to the Federal Assembly in 1963.[1] The 4th Plenum of the CC, LCY, adopted in summer 1962 a resolution about self-management by economic units within enterprises which satisfied the CTY and appeared to have Tito's backing. This was meant to be a turning-point in the history of Yugoslav democracy, but all sorts of practical problems remained before it could be put into effect. The right sort of units would have to be formed within enterprises, and the relations between them regulated. There was moreover opposition to such arrangements not only from enterprise managers, whose private empires could be diminished, but also from 'a certain number of Communists in very responsible positions within the organs of state administration'.

Meanwhile it was necessary to embody in the new Constitution something about the theory of self-management within enterprises. Tempo, a member of the Constitutional committee, was commissioned to have the appropriate clause drafted by his own organisation, the CTY. The draft cut down the powers of the local Communal authorities and of the managers within individual enterprises; it declared the collectives of workers in economic units to be 'the immediate representatives of the process of reproduction' (and thus to have the right of disposing of their own 'surplus product'). This would establish the rights of individuals both as producers and as consumers of material goods. They were however also 'consumers' of social services, and here too some means must be found of letting them exercise their rights. The CTY solution was to provide for agreements to be reached within

---

[1] The following paragraphs are based largely on the memoirs of Tempo, admittedly a very prejudiced source.

Communes between e.g. the health and education services, and the workers who were to 'consume' their 'product'. A certain minimum standard must be enjoyed, and if necessary central funds had to be used to ensure it; but services above that level were to be agreed by bargaining on the basis of the 'consumers' needs and of the funds which they themselves could provide.

The CTY leaders were only moderately satisfied with the final results of their drafting exercise. Their formulations had been over-refined, Tempo thought, by the legal experts. It is however important in the history of Economic Reform, and of subsequent political crises in Yugoslavia, that the 1963 Constitution embodied articles which encouraged and could serve as a text for further agitation for more detailed self-management. It was also important that the CTY, led by a formidable political debater in the person of Tempo, had engaged itself thus far in the same direction.

The new Constitution as a whole was a complicated exercise in political theory, which thoroughly re-organised the Federal People's Assembly, known henceforward as the Federal Assembly. Its basic constituent part was now the Federal Chamber – 120 deputies from territorial constituencies. Within this was still contained a Chamber of Nationalities, consisting of 10 delegates from each Republic and 5 from each Autonomous Province, due to meet separately only in occasional and specified circumstances.[2] Much of the Federal Assembly's work under the 1963 Constitution was to be done through or in conjunction with one or other of four special Chambers, the Economic Chamber (replacing the Council of Producers of 1953), and separate Chambers for Education and Culture, Welfare and Health, and Organisational Policy. Each comprised 120 members;[3] each could act separately within its own sphere, or could be consulted on subjects which fell partially outside this sphere; and there was a complicated procedure for resolving conflicts between the Chambers. The task of determining whether Republican legislation could or did come into conflict with the Constitution was shifted from the Government or LCY to a newly-established Constitutional Court.

Thus the syndical principle underlying the original Council of Producers was considerably extended, and at Federal level (to go no

[2] For the Republics this was less important than the restatement of their rights to self-determination and secession; and on a narrower basis than the provision that the FEC would be composed with due consideration of the need for Republics to be represented there.

[3] They were nominated by and from a 'work organisation or work community in the relevant sphere of activity' and then elected by Communal assemblies.

further down the line politically) Yugoslav citizens were represented as inhabitants of a territorial constituency, as nationals of Croatia, Serbia, etc., and as workers in their particular field.

Whether or not as the result of the new form of organisation, the new Assembly, which met under Kardelj's Presidency for the first time in June 1963, showed itself a far more lively body than its predecessors. Yugoslav parliamentary life became an important and exciting reality. Ministers were openly criticised and Government bills rejected. There was particularly strong criticism of the Social Plan for 1964, on account of its obviously interim quality, and a strong demand for clear-cut decisions about economic reforms. Thus when in 1964 Economic Reform was debated in the Assembly, the subject took on new dimensions, and became a matter of wide interest, with arguments put to the public in the principal periodicals, and on radio and television.

2

Meanwhile the practical case for Economic Reform was strengthened by (in communist phraseology) 'life itself'. At the end of 1963 indeed the Social Plan for 1964 had contained satisfying figures for the economic results achieved that year.[4] However there was a rise – soon to become much steeper – in the cost of living, and a growing trade gap, caused mainly by imports to satisfy the growing demand for consumer goods. By mid-1964 it was established that investment was 50% higher than over the same period in the previous year, thus aggravating inflation. The measures taken half-heartedly by the advocates of central control in 1962–3 had never begun to produce the necessary major structural changes in the Yugoslav economy. Thus the case for applying the principles of Economic Reform wholeheartedly was much strengthened.

A crucial step was taken at the beginning of 1964. Without any great fanfare the GIF was abolished on 1 January together with the similar Republican and Communal funds. The contributions levied on enterprises for them were abolished, as was the Federal tax on surplus profits. Enterprises continued to pay taxes on capital and personal income distributed. But the proceeds were now to be handled by the banks. These could still allocate funds for political as well as for economic reasons, but the abolition of the GIF was none the less an important symbol.

[4] Including a 12% growth in social product, with increases of 15% for industrial production, 7% for agriculture, 16% for exports, 17% for realised investments, 13% for personal consumption in the socialist sector, and 9% for productivity.

Tito proceeded to order the preparation of papers embodying the reformers' theses for the VIIIth Congress of the LCY at the end of the year. In doing so however he indicated more than once that there was still plenty of opposition to them within the LCY, and left himself some room for compromise. Speaking to the 6th Plenum of the CC, LCY, Tito seemed still to preserve a position above the fray. There should be no 'campaign', he said, about raising the standard of living (the reformers claimed that this could only be done by cutting down further on central control of investment). To settle the problems involved it would not be enough simply to raise wages. The wage problem must be used as an occasion for examining thoroughly the whole economic development of Yugoslavia, starting with the most essential problems – 'accumulation, investments, the internal organisation of enterprises, the full use of unexploited reserves, etc'.

A month later, introducing the Vth Congress of the CTY, Tito came down more firmly on the side of greater self-management. He was furious, he said, to learn that in 1963 only 30% of the huge amount of dinars invested in industry had been provided by the enterprises themselves. There must be fewer new projects and fuller use of existing industrial capacity. Only by a decentralised investment policy could these aims be effectively attained, and the standard of living raised (this was important backing for the reformers, who had argued that only such a policy could ensure the right sort of mobility for capital). However there was a sop to the centralists when Tito declared that the excessive differentiation of wages must be ironed out.

In April 1964 the Federal Assembly passed a resolution on 'basic guidelines for the further development of the economic system', which confirmed a generally liberal course, and a similar resolution was passed (in November) on the medium-term Plan (1964–70). The crucial occasion however was the VIIIth Congress of the LCY. This was opened in Belgrade on 7 December, when Tito made a keynote speech of substance. The first half of it was devoted to foreign affairs and the state of the 'workers' movement' throughout the world – themes which only Tito could handle with the authority necessary for the occasion. In the second half of his statement he came out clearly in favour of the reformist theses worked out previously by SAWPY, and 'particularly by the Trade Union organisations which, as direct representatives of the producer, are most affected by these problems'.

Tito's main themes were familiar. What was new and important in his fuller exposition of them was the specific linking of the themes of self-management and more rational investment with the problems of nationalities and uneven development within Yugoslavia, and with the question of inadequate Party discipline. In treating these problems, Tito used the bogey of bureaucracy with great adroitness. Communal authorities who looked too narrowly to their local interests, and the managers of enterprises who did not look further than their own Republican framework in developing links with other enterprises, were essentially bureaucratic in their outlook, insufficiently concerned with the true interests of the workers, and likely to feed the fires of national chauvinism. What was wanted was integration or co-operation between enterprises on a nation-wide scale. Such a policy would maximise national income from industry and the benefits would be felt soon by the under-developed Republics. Moreover, it was more likely to be put into force by workers organised in independent work-units within enterprises and thus better able to manage their own affairs, than by the existing type of enterprise organisation, dominated by managers and directors.

Republican nationalism was itself, according to Tito's thesis, an essentially bourgeois and bureaucratic or managerial phenomenon, alien to the workers in the various Republics: 'in our present social conditions, nationalism is mainly a form of expression of bureaucracy and of hegemonistic tendencies'.

This last was a shrewd point designed to appeal to the under-developed Republics, particularly Macedonia, and to the Kosovo region. By and large these opposed the idea of having to depend for investments on the economic calculations of the prosperous enterprises of northern Yugoslavia. But Macedonians as well as Croats had had experience between the wars of Serbian hegemony, and could be brought to associate a centralised investment system with Serbian national domination.

Tito repeated that the national problem in Yugoslavia had been solved once and for all in principle, but also dealt in more detail than hitherto with cultural forms of nationalism (a tacit admission that these were gaining in importance), particularly the problem of 'historiography'; Serb and Croat children were, it seems, receiving historical instruction which did not make for reconciliation of Republican interests. The solution of any temporary difficulties was to let the sound socialist consciousness of Yugoslav workers, whether in Serbia, Croatia, Bosnia or Slovenia, assert itself. Unlike bourgeois bureaucrats, they would never wish to play up national differences. The LCY should remain 'politically aware', but should make no further attempt to create an artificial 'Yugoslav' consciousness. The peoples of Yugoslavia should be encouraged freely 'to link with each other and enrich each other by mutual cultural influences. . .The development of a unified Yugoslav culture should be conceived only as a free flourishing of the national cultures of all our peoples and nationalities united by common interests and a common social system. . .'

The message was that not even the blindest and narrowest forms of nationalism could be successfully abolished simply by prescribing Yugoslav unity.

Tito had now come down firmly in favour of Economic Reform, and this should have been the end of any organised opposition to it. Such opposition had indeed been voiced not only by functionaries in Belgrade who had vested interests in administering a centralised investment system, but also by respectable economists and by representatives of the underdeveloped Republics. These however found it difficult too, as centralists, to avoid the label of bureaucracy, and to escape blame for the mess in which the Yugoslav economy found itself. On the other side, the proponents of Reform had good economic arguments at their disposal, and much powerful intellectual support from the developed Republics. They were not without backing in the less developed Republics – Kiro Gligorov, for example, one of the most competent pro-reform officials, was a Macedonian. They had also the impeccably radical support of the CTY, and attractive slogans about raising the standard of living and stamping out bureaucracy. This seemed an invincibly strong combination of political and economic forces.

The LCY was told by Tito to take decisive measures to 'remove all that might hinder the rapid improvement in the standard of living of our working citizens' and was warned that further weaknesses and mistakes in its daily work would no longer be tolerated. There were indeed several references in Tito's main speech to political opposition:

Certain individuals in the LCY have even become carriers of these [nationalist and chauvinist] tendencies. . .On the other side we come up against the conception that there has been exaggerated emphasis on the rights and role to be played by the socialist Republics and autonomous regions, and that this will lead to the disintegration. . .of our community.

Blame was thus distributed on either side of the prescribed Party line, and the face of the centralists was to some extent saved. But they were left in no doubt that for the future centralism was to be regarded as heresy No. 1. This was a severe warning for those communists who had opposed the decisions of the VIth Congress in 1952, had succeeded in turning the clock back to some extent during 1953, and had fought since then against radical changes of policy.

3

Tito's keynote speech on Reform had been preceded in summer 1964 by some practical measures to prepare the ground for it, and these had indicated that the process was going to be painful. In July 1964 increases were announced of nearly 30% in the prices of hitherto subsidised commodities which largely determined the cost of living – flour, bread, milk, coal and electricity. The average consumer was also hit by a new law, giving some effect to the CTY views on the need for 'social self-management'. Communal authorities were required to finance social services out of their own funds, subject to Federal support if they could not afford to provide for minimum needs. In the debate of the VIIIth Congress in December, the Slovene Boris Krajgher, one of the most important spokesmen for Reform, prophesied that the thorough and necessary transformation of Yugoslavia's economy would bring with it much sweat and tears. The abandonment of the central investment system and of price subsidies would in the short run cause much hardship. Exports would have to be increased greatly at the expense of many existing fragmented and uneconomic industries. Unemployment would inevitably rise.

These prospects might be unpleasant, but in 1964–5 'negative phenomena' in the economy persisted on a scale making Reform even more obviously necessary. Excessive demand for consumer goods and investment funds continued. The rate of inflation and the deficit in the Yugoslav balance of payments continued to rise. So did Federal subsidies, rebates and special tax reliefs, in spite of the abolition of central taxes in 1964. Further preparatory steps had to be taken in spring 1965 before the main Reform package had been fully worked out. A new Law on Banks and Credit Transactions was passed in March 1965, to provide a more effective substitute for the distribution of funds from the Federal centre. Banks were made responsible, not only to the State, but also to the institutions and enterprises which deposited funds with them; and attempts were made to induce enterprises to deposit with the new banks the funds of which they now disposed after the abolition of Federal taxes.[5] Meanwhile the FEC had to put into force centralist deflationary measures, including restrictions on consumer credits, investment credits and the creation of new jobs, and simultaneously to give some protection to the consumer by a total price freeze.

[5] As far back as 1963 there had been a specialist debate on whether enterprises should be encouraged to invest in banks and receive interest on the funds deposited. This was now allowed, but was criticised later as an important step away from 'social ownership', to 'group' or even private ownership.

As these measures began to bite, opposition to Reform began to build up, even in Croatia and Slovenia.[6] Its protagonists therefore rushed the main package of measures known as Economic Reform through the legislative machine. It was approved by the CC, LCY on 17 June and presented to a joint session of the Federal and Economic Chambers of the Federal Assembly on 24 July. The laws were passed, signed by Tito, and promulgated all on the same day.

The case for rationalising the Yugoslav economy had been argued at length and generally accepted in theory. But the further concrete measures embodying rationalisation came as a considerable shock. There was an overall price rise of 24% over 1964 levels. The general public was hit most severely by the increases in agricultural prices (32%) and transport (26%). Industry was most affected by radical changes in the 'price-ratios'. Industrial prices as a whole rose by only 14% (in the processing industry generally by 8% only) while the prices for basic and semi-processed raw materials were raised by an average of 45%. This put enormous pressure on industry, as intended, to economise and rationalise its structure and operations.

To facilitate the growth of foreign trade and further to adapt the Yugoslav to the world market the dinar was devalued by two stages – from 750 to 1250 (12.50 from the end of 1965) to the U.S. dollar. Quantitative restrictions on imports were removed and the average duty on imports reduced by more than half (from 23% to 11%). This, as well as many of the internal economic reforms, could be regarded as part of the price for support from the IMF, which had sent a mission to Yugoslavia in the winter 1964–5, and granted additional drawing rights of $80 million. The restructuring of foreign trade also made Yugoslavia more credit-worthy abroad, and new loans, eventually totalling about $140 million, were being negotiated with the U.S., Britain, France and Italy, as well as with the Eastern bloc; but these represented long-term gains, not felt by the individual consumer or by the small enterprise in distress.

The other side of the coin for industry and public alike was the revision of the tax structure, which reduced the State's share in the net income of enterprises from 49% to 29%. Corporate income tax on enterprises was abolished, and capital tax reduced from 6% to 4%. Turnover tax, applied to every stage of industrial operations, was replaced by a sales tax on final consumption, at a maximum general

---

[6] The structure of industry and communications in these Republics was by no means totally rational. In 1964 for example an airline had been set up in Slovenia to compete with the Yugoslav Air Line.

level of 20%.[7] For the individual, taxes on personal incomes and social insurance were reduced (the former from 17.5% to 10.5%). These reductions however were quite insufficient to balance the increased cost of living, particularly since in August 1965 housing property was revalued and rents were raised in sharp stages towards the level at which they would cover depreciation and maintenance.[8]

The short-term economic results of Reform were painful for most enterprises as well as for most individuals. Many even of the more prosperous enterprises were affected severely by the increase in prices of raw materials and in transport costs; they had to pay for these increased costs sooner than they could benefit from a larger market at home or abroad. At the same time the less prosperous industries experienced a crisis. The simplest way of cutting costs was to dismiss part of their work force. This was too often done by simply sacking the women before the men, or by cutting on research funds, or by getting rid of technical experts rather than ordinary workers, which hardly served to increase efficiency. A survey conducted in October 1965, and published in *Borba*, indicated that 455 enterprises, employing 225,000 workers had already dismissed some 12,500 (nearly 6%), and planned to dismiss 20,000 more.

Growing unemployment led to greater calls on the social services. The income of social insurance funds from personal contributions had been substantially reduced and State, Republican or Communal income, for this purpose among others, was drastically cut. There had been no time for income from other sources to swell the social funds as the longer-term effects of Reform increased general prosperity. But in the face of growing need, and in spite of much economic criticism, not least from the Economic Chamber of the Federal Assembly, social security payments were not diminished.

The same kind of situation prevailed throughout the economy as a whole. It was almost fatally easy to make exceptions as the crisis hit various sectors. It would be impossible, it was said, to abandon certain investment prospects without causing unacceptable local damage, and increasing unemployment. The 'prices ratio' might be more logical

[7] Of this 12% went to the State and a maximum of 6% to Communes. The maximum figure was made up by a temporary 2% levy to relieve distress caused by floods in Croatia and an earthquake in Skopje.

[8] The CTY had originally wanted to introduce private ownership of houses, in order to increase the incentive to maintain them properly. This idea however was not accepted, and self-managing Housing Associations were eventually formed to collect rents and carry out major repairs and new buildings. The experiment, which was not successful, provided obvious opportunities for corruption.

than before, but it affected unfairly at least certain of the processing industries.

The general result was that large-scale attempts, often successful, were made to evade the economic effects of Reform on social and political grounds. There was constant special pleading to the political authorities and to responsible Party members, for mitigation of the effect of stern economic laws. By mid-winter 1965–6 economists and politicians were deeply pessimistic about what was happening. Both the 'centralist' and the 'liberal' solutions for Yugoslavia's economic problems seemed to have failed.

4

At the beginning of 1966 Tito and the LCY Executive Committee were faced with grave political as well as economic problems. The failure of the Reform policy would strengthen the hand of 'centralisers' against 'liberals', Serbs against Croats and Slovenes, and in the field of Party policy 'conservatives' – those who had never fully accepted the reforms of 1952 – against 'progressives'. There was a succession of meetings of the LCY Executive Committee in the winter 1965–6. Intelligent Yugoslav observers probably knew much of the debates that were going on.[9] It was well enough known that the argument was about the principal aspects of the Reform policy, but the main national element of the battle was fully revealed to the public only when Kardelj in March announced, after the 3rd Plenum of the CC, LCY, that a special Party Commission was being formed to investigate 'inter-nationality' relations in the field of the economy.

The personal clashes concealed behind the debate on the 'national question' were even more sedulously concealed. However it might have been deduced from the campaign for strict Party discipline, waged in March and subsequently, that there were grave differences at the top, as well as at lower levels, of the LCY. The 3rd Plenum of the CC, LCY, held late in February, had to be adjourned after two days of debate until 11 March, by which time further consultations had taken place in the Republics. The CC finally adopted a resolution commit-

---

[9] A Belgrade Cabaret show of this time, 'Alice in Progressive Wonderland', neatly linked a futile campaign to exploit and create reserves with the tendency of conservative communists to publish unreadable patriotic memoirs. The first scene showed a progressive publishing house eagerly accepting a three volume auto-biography (the title of the third changed by a neat vocal inflexion from 'Why I fought' to 'Why *did* I fight?') on the ground that a large printing of unsaleable books would satisfactorily increase the firm's material reserves.

ting the LCY as a whole to active and total support of the decisions of the VIIIth Congress, in particular those on Economic Reform.

It was remarkable enough that only two months after the VIIIth Congress its conclusions had to be re-affirmed and loyal execution of them demanded. Moreover there were fairly open suggestions in the reported proceedings of the CC that even a new agreement on this subject might not hold, since words and formulae meant different things to different people. Perhaps the most significant feature of the Plenum, and the clearest sign of trouble ahead was the re-introduction by Tito himself of the concept of the 'class enemy' fostering dissension even within the LCY:

I have already talked about the conflict of opinion in the communist ranks, which is entangled with petty-bourgeois and who knows what other conflicts of opinion...We shall easily overcome the problem since it has been decided once and for all that our peoples are marching together in the creation of a socialist society...The question is how it has come to pass that the development of socialism in our country is being rendered impossible. This has been the aim of the class enemy. His work takes various forms, and in the course of the last two years the conditions for it have ripened very much...Nowadays our cadre policy is carried on in cafés, and all sorts of schemes are hatched for pushing people into this or that responsible post. Not only that. Certain communists, or more correctly, certain members of the LCY, are falling under the influence of fractional petty-bourgeois ideology from the West, and of internal reactionaries from before the war.

Tito's emphasis on the machinations of the 'class enemy' was idiosyncratic and bound up with his vision of the general world situation at this time and his continued 'near-alignment' to many aspects of Soviet foreign policy. He also went further on the differences within the LCY than any of his subordinates.[10] The two points were no doubt deliberately linked. Tito wanted to ease the restoration of Party discipline in the highest circles by making it a matter of 'class confidence', so to speak, rather than of differences between nationalities. Indeed he went out of his way to play down the 'nationalities' issue, saying that as the result of discussion at the Plenum it did not appear vital to him. Tito thus implied that the essential issue was now the unity of the Party; if it were not proved in the implementation of Economic Reform, this could only be because of the machinations of the 'class

---

[10] Veljko Vlahović, one of the secretaries of the Central Committee, gave a more orthodox exposition, saying that the 'class struggle' was finding expression even within the Party in 'preventing the working class from realising its rights, in bureaucratic self-will'.

enemy' within the Party. It was unthinkable that such activity should be allowed to continue unchecked.

The implication was that, if necessary, heads might have to roll. The most important of these proved to be that of Ranković, Vice-President of Yugoslavia, responsible for organisation of the LCY, and for the secret police organisation. According to Tempo, Tito had a blunt talk with him just before the 3rd Plenum, and in the course of it he was given the task of publicly reproving the Serb nationalists, in order to align him with the official position. Towards the end of March, Ranković left Yugoslavia to represent the LCY for two weeks at a Soviet Congress. At about the same time, Bakarić, the Croatian Party Secretary, began to make a series of public appearances in Belgrade and Sarajevo. Here he emphasised the need for the LCY to reform its organisation and mentality if Economic Reform was to be implemented and the conditions thus created to calm down nationalist agitation, which he clearly rated as a major danger. Bakarić was the main power in the LCY of Croatia, but also a man whose wisdom and proven moderation (particularly on agricultural questions) had won him much respect outside his own power base; and within Serbia he could rely, so far as concerned Economic Reform, on two prominent Serb politicians, Milentije Popović and Mijalko Todorović. Bakarić had now gone in one important respect further than Tito who, for all his criticisms of the LCY's work, had not yet demanded the re-organisation of the Party. This demand amounted to an almost direct attack on Ranković, who was responsible for organisational policy. When Tito decided at the end of April that the next meeting of the CC Plenum (the 4th) would be devoted to 'cadre policy' (another of Ranković's responsibilities) rather than the national question, it was evident that he had moved behind Bakarić.

The immediate reason for the moves against Ranković was no doubt the continued lack of discipline within the LCY on the issues of Economic Reform. If Ranković continued to encourage opposition to it, he must now be regarded as deliberately splitting the Party. He was probably suspected of the most sinister reasons for doing so. He was already Vice-President – a new office created for him under the 1963 Constitution. Might he not be trying to edge Tito upstairs and to establish his own position as Tito's successor? And might he not be preparing to re-impose Serb domination of Yugoslavia through his secret police apparatus? Ranković's position was already powerful. Tito's counter-attack therefore had to be carefully planned, and to concentrate on an issue which had some popular appeal. Economic

Reform aroused too much opposition to provide this. Party organisation was a comparatively esoteric subject, as was the doctrine of 'Democratic Centralism'. The most vulnerable point was Ranković's stewardship of UDBA, the secret police.

In April the search for incriminating evidence was begun. It is of course the winning side which has left us the official history of the battle of wits which then ensued, and in a war between rival intelligence services Lenin's question 'kto kovo?' (who has done down whom, in this case) is particularly difficult to answer. Probably UDBA itself was loyal enough to Ranković at the crucial levels. The Chairman of the former Ministry (now Federal Commission) of Internal Affairs, Svetislav Stefanović, was also a Ranković man, who had worked with him in UDBA from the start, and was to fall along with him. A key man on the opposite side was probably Milan Mišković, a Croat who had only become Federal Secretary for Internal Affairs in 1965, and did not belong to the hard Serbian core of the UDBA leadership. His strength lay in the fact that he had access to UDBA's main rival, the Army's counter-intelligence service, in which Mišković's brother Ivan was a high officer. Whatever the exact line-up of intelligence services, UDBA's opponents had collected enough material by mid-June to enable Tito to launch his attack. The crowning mercy was the discovery on 9 June that Tito's own residence was fitted with UDBA microphones, and a technical commission was promptly formed to investigate the extent of surveillance by UDBA of high Party officials. On 16 June the LCY Executive Committee was summoned to hear the evidence, and appointed a special Commission under Crvenkovski to make a more formal and thorough investigation.[11] Ranković already recognised defeat, and offered his resignation while voting for the appointment of the Commission. Its report was soon ready. On 22 June the Executive Committee met again, decided that the case was made against UDBA (and Ranković and Stefanović in particular), and convoked a meeting of the CC, LCY, for 1 July at Brioni.

Again the attack or counter-attack had to be carefully prepared. If a generally convincing case was to be made against UDBA and if its political activities were to be properly checked, it was important not to concentrate too much on its wire-tapping, on which it would be difficult to provide full evidence.[12] For the same reason, the defendants at

---

[11] It contained one member from each Republic (a typical and important detail), and Crvenkovski was a Macedonian; it would have been politically inept to appoint a Croat or Slovene as chairman.

[12] Particularly since UDBA had been given enough warning to destroy their own records, and Stefanović flatly denied the charge that UDBA had put Tito under

the Brioni Plenum, Ranković and Stefanović, tried to narrow the issue to the technical one.[13]

The vital charges against UDBA at Brioni were thus the more general ones which, together with many supplementary and unsavoury details, were published afterwards in the Yugoslav newspapers. Created as the Party's own weapon against the 'class enemy' within Yugoslavia, UDBA had succumbed to the temptation of economic corruption, including international smuggling and misappropriation of funds. Through its control of personnel departments in Ministries, institutions and enterprises, it had operated a thorough-going system of 'jobs for the boys'. It had done so too often in the interests of a narrow Serb nationalism, the worst side of which was revealed in the brutal repression of the Albanian majority in the Kosmet – soon to become a flashpoint of ethnic unrest. At the highest policy level the UDBA system had been used to thwart Reform and to build up Ranković as a possible successor to Tito. In this context there was no public reference to any special connection between Ranković and the Soviet leadership, but Tito could well have been uneasy on this point too.[14] Ranković had been a scourge of Cominformists after 1948, but the Soviet leaders could guess that Economic Reform was likely to lead to closer Yugoslav links with the West, and would thus tend to back the Yugoslav anti-Reform party.

This is speculative. What is certain was Tito's concern about the irresponsibility of the LCY in having 'virtually left our Security Services to go their own way for more than twenty years'. He blamed himself publicly for not having grasped the nettle at the Executive Committee meeting of March 1962:

at which various problems were examined which touched on relations within our leadership and within our Party. At that time we determined in general terms the points on which certain anomalies and deviations existed, but we did not determine their sources. It seems to me that we were wrong in not going right ahead at the time, and in stopping half-way, because of certain tendencies to compromise and to prevent things from affecting the unity of our Party and the unity of our leadership which was in truth already undermined.

For far too long at the sessions of the Party's Executive Committee 'we

surveillance. Indeed if, as seems likely, someone had done so, it was not necessarily UDBA agents who had committed this contemporary form of lèse-majesté.
[13] Even here the evidence of the Crvenkovski report was likely to tell against them heavily in the eyes of some of the veteran leaders. Tempo records in his Memoirs that he was not amused to find that his telephone had been monitored since 1950.
[14] Ranković was certainly on good terms with the Soviet Ambassador in Belgrade at the time of his fall.

never once raised the question of this service [UDBA]. But can any organisation or any organs be left for so long without control by the Party, without control by the leadership of the Party? Naturally this is our own fault.' And now it was wrong to talk only of the responsibility of individuals for 'certain deformations' in the Party's work; 'I cannot at the moment say for certain, but my opinion is that it isn't only individuals who are in question, and not only particular personalities that are generally responsible, but that what we are dealing with is a fractional group struggle, a struggle for power.' And later 'I must say that people have begun to whisper that an atmosphere of mutual distrust has been created, from the top downwards. Doesn't this look to you a little like what once happened in Stalin's time?'

The Brioni plenum accepted Ranković's resignation from his Party offices and recommended to the Federal Assembly his resignation as Vice-President.[15] Koča Popović (Foreign Secretary until 1965, and a Serb) was elected to replace him. Mijalko Todorović and Milentije Popović (both moderate Serbs) replaced Ranković respectively as Secretary of the CC and as a member of the Executive Committee. Stefanović was removed both from his offices and from the Party. The Plenum further approved a motion by Veljko Vlahović to appoint a large special commission under the chairmanship of Todorović to make proposals for a radical change in the LCY's organisation. In a personal report Vlahović laid down what were in a Communist context liberal guidelines for the Commission's work.

Tito himself insisted more than once in subsequent comment that Western interpreters who talked of a movement of liberalisation in Yugoslavia were totally wrong. UDBA would continue to be active against the class enemy and his foreign sources of inspiration – Tito professed to find that these were particularly busy in summer 1966 and anxious to take advantage of any weakness in Yugoslavia. The LCY was following its own consistent course without deviation to right or left. Now that the influence of Ranković and the Party bureaucrats was scotched, it would be able to provide the political and social framework for the maximum of self-management at enterprise level. In fact it would be able, properly re-organised, to accomplish successfully the task which it had set itself in 1952. It would also be able to explain and to ease the temporary problems which were bound to arise for a great many Yugoslav workers as the result of the continued and now

[15] Before the end of 1966 he was removed from the Federal Assembly and expelled from the LCY. Criminal proceedings against him and others were dropped, possibly because of the large numbers of people who would have been involved.

unimpeded operation of Economic Reform. The 'nationalities problem', Tito said, would fall into place, now that UDBA had been reformed and its powers checked.

The CC had shown themselves, according to Tito, at the height of their powers at the Brioni plenum. It was indeed an achievement to have isolated and defeated Ranković and his supporters without more damage to the Yugoslav political structure. July 1966 represented an even more decisive turning point for Yugoslavia than November 1952 or January 1954. The political as well as the economic consequences of Reform were far-reaching.

13

The results of Reform

Tito's cautions about the continued need for a new-style UDBA and for more effective action by the LCY were signs that he feared the political side-effects of Reform.[1] From the economic point of view, Reform was openly aimed at the adaptation of Yugoslavia's industrial and commercial structure to closer links with the West. Enterprises soon began to pursue their own commercial policies, and trade with the West increased rapidly, particularly the import of consumer goods. In 1966, in spite of an increase of some 30% in exports to hard currency areas, Yugoslavia had a net trade deficit of about $300 million.[2] In 1967, exports to hard currency areas were up by 8.1%, but this resulted entirely from maize exports after a good harvest. Imports were up by 19.4%, and this looked like a more permanent trend. Income in hard currency from Western tourists, and remittances from Yugoslavs abroad, might lessen the balance of payments deficit, but further steps in this direction had become essential. Fresh loan agreements had to be negotiated with Western governments and outstanding loan repayments rescheduled. It was also necessary, as Tito had warned in 1962, to find less expensive ways of importing Western technique and products. The large-scale purchase of licences to manufacture had already begun, particularly for car, lorry and tractor production. In 1967 a serious effort was made to launch joint production schemes with Western countries in particular,[3] under which foreign firms would help in the construction and capitalisation of new Yugoslav enterprises, receiving payment in the form of processed material or finished goods, or in the proceeds of exports to 'third' markets. Such schemes took

[1] In the same way, as the Soviet leaders try to open up the Soviet Union to Western technology, they insist that the ideological war must continue unabated.
[2] Restrictions placed on Yugoslav agricultural exports by EEC countries were a matter for much concern and continuous negotiation.
[3] It opened with an international conference in Belgrade, led jointly by Leo Mates, then Director of the Institute of International Politics and Economics in Belgrade and the late Professor Wolfgang Friedmann of Columbia University.

some time to materialise, but they served to link Yugoslavia more closely with the West.

This in itself was probably distasteful for the older generation of Communist leaders. Greater difficulties however arose from the application of the slogans of Reform to the daily life of the Yugoslav people. The consistent emphasis on 'self-management' and 'profitability' had important and lasting side-effects. These aims had of course been pursued before Economic Reform in 1965 and the fall of Ranković in 1966. None the less the summer of 1966 was an important turning point, in that they could afterwards be more freely pursued without fear of any backlash from the Party leadership. The political climate now favoured a number of new social currents stimulated by Reform.

The results of increasing automobile production was a case in point. An agreement had been concluded with Fiat in 1963 under which the Yugoslavs produced under licence their own Fiat model (the 'Zastava', popularly known as the 'Fietsche'). In 1964 the new cars began to come on to the Yugoslav market in large quantities; by 1966 the number of owner-drivers had extended well down the Yugoslav social or salary scale. A car-owning society naturally wanted to travel. New roads were needed, and to provide them Communal authorities had to raise increased taxes and spend more money – which encouraged economic 'localism' at the Communal level. More petrol-stations and more home-produced or home-refined petrol was required. This involved developing Yugoslav oil resources, located mainly in Croatia.[4] The new roads and new traffic in turn created a demand for more restaurants, cafés and drinking houses along the roads – a demand amply met by private enterprise. And the new travelling class began to think in terms of finding, or quite as probably constructing, their own holiday cottages or week-end houses (the word 'vikenditsa' is current Serbo-Croat). There was an increase in unplanned and unauthorised, or 'wild' building, particularly at the sea-side.[5] All these trends were reinforced by the need to attract more tourists, and for some years after Reform the whole concept of a private sector within a generally socialist economy was becoming more respectable in terms of economic theory, as well as of practice.

The application of the 'self-management' principle also produced

---

[4] The Croats naturally gained an increased sense of their own economic importance within the Yugoslav community, and this later had its repercussions in intensifying the nationalities problem.

[5] In spring 1967 I was told by a taxi-driver in Korčula that his new house, now almost finished, had been the subject of objections on environmental grounds which had gone to the highest Federal Court and been dismissed.

interesting results in the institutional field. Great strides had been made since 1945 in the eradication of illiteracy, but the general rate for Yugoslavia in 1966 was about 20%. Indeed in Bosnia only about 65% of the children of school age attended school.[6] Now the provision of educational services was essentially a regional or local task. In 1966 three-quarters of the money spent on education was provided by the Communes. The Federal Government still subsidised the less developed Republics, but the pay-rate of teachers was locally determined by self-financing educational communities, supported as necessary by a special Communal tax on personal incomes. Generally this meant that teachers wanted to get away from the poorer regions where they were most needed. Locally there were difficult disputes about the rate of the special tax and the basis on which teachers' pay should be calculated. A system of 'payment by results' was canvassed, but came up against obvious difficulties. The problems of the educational system were highlighted by a strike by teachers in the Užice district in autumn 1966, protesting against the salary rate offered to them. This strike was (also significantly) the occasion of a public polemic between Tempo, the spokesman of the CTY, and two of the most respected papers of Belgrade, *Politika* and *Ekonomska Politika*, which accused him of trying to strengthen the CTY's political position by encouraging the 'collectives' (general assemblies) of enterprises or institutions to overrule their own more expert management boards.

Self-management among the information media also gave rise to problems for the LCY which were new not so much in kind as in extent. It was for example galling for the LCY that at Christmas 1966 the Catholic authorities sponsored the issue of a record of carols which proved to be a best-seller. More generally greater revenue now accrued to newspapers from advertisements, and more concessions were made to the taste of the normal reader; there was a marked increase in the number of cartoons, light-hearted features, and gimmicks in the form of competitions, to attract a new and wider public.[7] There was increasing coverage by the main Yugoslav newspapers of scientific, cultural and social developments in the outside world, including good descriptive journalism about the political scene in London, Paris, Washington and Peking. More important, the open debate on the main issues of

---

[6] A further problem was that of 're-illiteracy'. It was calculated in 1966 that 100,000 adults who had learned to read and write just after the war were annually forgetting these skills.

[7] I used to see in 1969–70 a paper specially produced for the Yugoslav Army, which at that time included a regular column of psychological advice, dealing mainly with sex problems, and a series entitled *Loves of the Great Commanders*.

Reform introduced or confirmed the habit of comparatively free discussion on other issues. Three of these remained taboo for any but the boldest spirits – the foundations of official ideology, the main tenets of official foreign policy, and the personal role of Tito and other main Communist leaders. Editors however were ready to sail as near the wind as they could.

The habit of comparatively free discussion had also caught on in the Federal and Republican Assemblies. By 1966 indeed the Federal Assembly was the scene of lively debate and much individual activity by deputies. Its system of operation was highly complicated at this stage. Apart from the main five Chambers there were no less than 89 Commissions, standing or *ad hoc* Committees, which were ancillary bodies of the Chambers, and groups, which included for example *ad hoc* commissions on the organisation of Trade, Banking and Credit, and the financing of the Educational system. Draft bills were dealt with by an elaborate procedure which included consultation with the appropriate Republican authorities, and gave ample scope for debate and criticism by individual deputies.[8] The procedure, designed to give expression to improved forms of self-management, also favoured the growth of Republican influence at the centre of government in Yugoslavia, and this was one of the principal ways in which the development of self-management could change the direction of democratic government.

2

There remained limits to free discussion, and these were conspicuously illustrated for Western observers by certain well-publicised cases from 1965 onwards. In its January and February numbers, the Belgrade literary monthly *Delo* published a travelogue by Mihajlo Mihajlov, a young lecturer of Russian émigré origin in the Faculty of Philosophy of Zagreb University at Zadar. He recorded various conversations with Moscow literary figures, and conveyed the general impression that socialist freedom had been on the march in the Soviet Union under Khrushchev, but his article also contained references to concentration

[8] Drafts were initially produced by the State Secretariat concerned; after consultation with the Republican authorities, they would be sent via the appropriate Committees to a plenary meeting of the FEC. This then sent them on to the President of the Assembly, who would pass them on to the President of the appropriate Chamber. Detailed discussion would start in the appropriate Committee, and Committee members exceptionally could demand plenary discussion in the Chamber. Bills would normally then be checked by a Standing Commission, in the first place to ensure that they did not contravene the Constitution. Finally they would be voted on by the appropriate Chamber.

camps, which he said were instituted in Lenin's time, and extracts from unpublished ballads of camp life.[9] Probably there was a protest from the Soviet Government, and Tito was anxious to prove to Khrushchev's successors after the VIIIth Party Congress that he would meet them on such matters. The February number of *Delo* was banned on 11 February, and Tito talked to delegates from the Public Prosecutor's office. On 4 March, after Tito had talked with the Soviet Ambassador, Mihajlov was arrested on suspicion of hostile propaganda. He was dismissed from his academic post on 27 March and tried publicly at Zadar on 29 April. The charge of hostile propaganda was dropped, but he was accused of distributing banned material and bringing a foreign State into derision, and was given a sentence (afterwards suspended) of 9 months' imprisonment. This was only the opening stage of Mihajlov's long conflict with authority,[10] and in July 1966 he was again imprisoned for expressing the intention of founding a new journal as a basis for a new political party. The impression given to the outside world was that Soviet pressure had reinforced Tito's own feelings and that in acting on it, he was ready to distort the truth (he accused Mihajlov of defending concentration camps).

The trial of Mihajlov might have been regarded as an isolated warning that Yugoslav writers should be particularly careful about Soviet–Yugoslav relations at a time when 'life itself' was driving Yugoslavia into closer relations with the West. A more generally significant case was the suppression in May 1965 of the literary and political review, *Perspektive*, published in Ljubljana by a group of young Communists of the post-Partisan generation, who proceeded from analysis of the effects of broadened 'self-management' to attacks on LCY bureaucracy, and finally to demands for the formation of a second party – the heresy known as 'Djilasism'. More important still for the development of political debate in Yugoslavia and for the reputation of Yugoslavia abroad were the polemics that ripened in 1966, a few months before the fall of Ranković, between ideological spokesmen of the LCY and a group of neo-Marxist philosophers associated with the Zagreb magazine *Praxis*. From 1963 these had held summer schools in Korčula, which were attended by Western philosophers; they had founded *Praxis* in September 1964, and were also closely associated with the Belgrade *Delo* and *Gledišta*, a publication of the Serbian

[9] It should be remembered that in the Soviet Union *One Day in the Life of Ivan Denisovich* had been published in 1962, while in 1952–3 the Yugoslav press had published much more thorough revelations about Soviet camps.
[10] He was released from his last term of imprisonment under the amnesty of November 1977.

Youth League. *Praxis* from the first took the offensive against con-servative Marxism, and attacked in particular Milentije Popović, a prominent official in the Serbian LCY, who was also a strong supporter of Reform. The essence of *Praxis'* attacks on the ideological establish-ment in Yugoslavia and elsewhere was that their thinking was still dominated by Stalinist positivists, for whom Marxism involved primarily the collection of hard facts about the social structure in order to make the most accurate projection of the future. They thus rejected critical and value judgements and left on one side the humanist element of Marxism. If this was to be restored to its proper position, and if the social realities of the present time were to be humanised, some system-atic philosophical guidance was necessary; such guidance could only be provided by a revived Marxism, which would have to start by accepting and explaining the problems set by the apparent survival and economic success of capitalism.

The principal target of *Praxis* was 'conservative communism' as practised in the Soviet Union, and its criticisms were far more offensive than anything said by the unfortunate Mihajlov. However the editor of *Praxis*, Rudi Supek, also reserved some barbed shafts for the Yugo-slav conservative communists: 'A man who has just exchanged his peasant shoes for a limousine cannot be expected to grasp the human-istic problem of socialism.' An alleged Zen Buddhist saying was applied to Yugoslavia's Marxists:

'If you have something to say, you will be given 30 strokes; if you have nothing to say, you will be given 30 strokes just the same.' The strokes are intended to ensure that those questioned should always give the same stereotype answer 'moo', or some other equally sonorous reply.

The official ideologists hit back hard. The most insistent counter-charge was that the *Praxis* circle, and particularly Rudi Supek, were exalting the intellectual and the individual at the expense of the LCY as a whole. They were accused of 'subjectivism' and hence of bureau-cratic attitudes. The reasoning was circular and obscure.[11] It was how-ever understandable that reforming Communists, deeply engaged at the time in the implementation of Reform and the struggle with Ranković, should have resented theoretical criticism from people who had no responsibility for the practical running of affairs. The most dangerous accusation raised by Milentije Popović against the *Praxis*

---

[11] Roughly as follows: All 'bureaucrats' must be 'subjective' — if they weren't, they would be representing a fault in the social system of which they form a part. Therefore (by a well-known fallacy) all 'subjectivists' are bureaucrats.

circle was that they were 'Djilasists', who aimed at forming a second party.

Polemics were not continued at this level of intensity. In spite of full-scale debate on the *Praxis* doctrine in the Croat Assembly and Party organisation (May and June 1966), the periodical survived until 1975. The 1966 episode in fact illustrated that freedom of discussion could go a long way, even so far as to question the theoretical basis of both conservative and liberal communism as practised in Yugoslavia. Despite severe counter-criticisms by Tito, Kardelj and Vlahović, it was the comparatively liberal wing of the LCY, including Bakarić, who carried the day in 1966 and decided that, if they were to live up to their principles about free argument, *Praxis* must be allowed to survive.[12]

It should be added that at the beginning of 1967 Djilas was released from prison, probably because it would appear invidious to subject him to conditions notably worse than those imposed on the recently-fallen Ranković, and perhaps in part to create a good impression in Western Labour and Social Democrat Parties. Certainly his release portended no liberalisation of official political thought. He lived, and at the time of writing lives, in central Belgrade, on a pension and the foreign currency earnings of his heretical writings. His fortunes have varied in his new position, and he has never been either re-admitted to favour or entirely forgotten by his former comrades. One of the most fascinating men of his generation, he remains a magnet to Western visitors, and an unwilling monument to the comparative moderation of his accusers.

3

Meanwhile it proved that the forces of nationalism had by no means been dispersed by the events of summer 1966. This point was illustrated unexpectedly at the elections held in April 1967 to replace half the members of the Federal, Republican and Communal assemblies, who had to retire under the provisions of the 1963 Constitution. These elections approximated much more nearly than before to contests of the liberal democratic pattern. SAWPY continued to organise them, but Party members behaved more scrupulously than before in permitting some choice of candidates.[13] The results were not encouraging to

---

[12] Bakarić may have reckoned that its positions did not seem to differ very much from those of some prominent young Croat Communist politicians, particularly Mika Tripalo.

[13] For the 60 vacant seats in the Federal Chamber the Communal assemblies nominated 82 candidates (41 of them in Serbia for 25 seats); this contrasted with only 62 candidates for 60 seats in the corresponding elections of 1965.

what could now be called the Yugoslav reformist establishment. It was on the whole ex-Partisan candidates from the LCY 'old guard' who contested and often won seats from the official reformist candidates. The most notable victim was the Federal Secretary of Foreign Trade, Nikola Džuverović; and the most notorious of the contested elections was won at Lazarevac by a certain Radivoje ('Bradonja' or 'beardie') Jovanović. According to very credible charges subsequently made against him[14] he owed his victory to the joint support of former Chetniks and the local Veterans' Organisation, in which Ranković had had a powerful influence, and to the indiscriminate promises of economic improvements which he made to his constituents. An ominous triumph in fact for anti-Reform conservatism, economic localism and Serb nationalism.

The new Assembly indeed met in April 1967 under the shadow of an explicitly nationalist crisis over the language issue. This had been settled for the first time in 1850 by an agreement concluded at Vienna between the most prominent Serb and Croat men of letters, along lines recommended by the great Serb autodidact, Vuk Karadžić. His solution had been to declare that Serb and Croat were one language with two different scripts. The Novi Sad agreement of 1954 repeated and somewhat refined the original Vienna agreement. There should be not only two scripts, Latin in Croatia and Cyrillic in Serbia, but also two main variant spellings. As a kind of symbol of the new agreement Tito's pronouncements, as printed in Cyrillic for Serbia, were made to preserve the essentially Croat spelling variants.[15]

Language as well as history is a subject highly charged with national feeling in Yugoslavia. It was thus regarded officially as a very unwelcome danger sign when on 17 March 1967 Zagreb's main literary weekly published a sort of linguistic declaration of independence signed by a number of prominent literary groups, including the important Matica Hrvatska,[16] and by thirteen intellectuals, the great majority of them Communists, and including Croatia's best-known writer, Miroslav Krleža, a member of the Croat Central Committee and personal friend of Tito. The signatories denounced the Novi Sad agreement and called for the constitutional recognition of Croat as a separate language, to be used strictly in parallel with Serb for all Federal purposes and in Croatia exclusively. Forty-five Serbian writers, again including many

---

[14] He was unseated and expelled from the LCY in autumn 1967.
[15] The Croat 'Riječ', for example, rather than the Serb 'reč' for a 'speech'.
[16] 'Croat Queen Bee', founded during the Croat renaissance of the 1840s. See Chapter 15, p. 197, n.2.

Party members, immediately made counter-demands, particularly for the use of Cyrillic only on Belgrade television and for education in the Serb language for the 700,000 Serbs living in Croatia. The leaders of the LCY reacted very strongly against both nationalist proposals. Sacrifices had to be made on either side, more conspicuously in Croatia where Krleža, a Yugoslav national figure, had to resign from the Republican CC.

This reaction was immediately followed by important official concessions designed to meet nationalist feeling. Before the elections of April 1967 the outgoing Assembly passed certain amendments to the 1963 constitution, designed to increase the powers of the Republics vis-à-vis the Federation. The most important was No. I, which resulted from a complaint to the Chamber of Nationalities in January 1967 by the Governments of Bosnia-Hercegovina and the Kosmet over the allocation of development aid from the Federal Fund. The amendment provided for an important increase in the competence of the Chamber of Nationalities, which had hitherto played an insignificant part in the proceedings of the Assembly.[17] The Chamber of Nationalities was now effectively separated from the Federal Chamber, and was required to consider virtually all economic and other potentially contentious subjects on terms of equality with the Federal Chamber and 'from the viewpoint of the equality of the Republics, nations and nationalities and the safeguarding of the constitutional rights of the Republics'. Another amendment (No. IV) made the Republics jointly responsible with the Federation for public order – an important safeguard against the re-emergence of another Ranković and his misuse of a Federal position for nationalist ends. More immediately important for the satisfaction of Republican nationalism were the changes of organisation or personnel introduced in May 1967 in the new Federal Assembly. The FEC was effectively downgraded, with a new and not very prestigious President (Mika Spiljak) and State Secretaries. These were significant formal steps towards the confederalisation of Yugoslavia.

They were paralleled by changes within the LCY, which since the 4th Plenum of the CC in summer 1966 had been considerably restructured. The Todorović Commission, then appointed to propose 'radical changes' in its organisation, worked under a general directive that harked back to the principles of the Vth Congress in 1952. The LCY 'should not concern themselves with those issues which fall within the jurisdiction of elected responsible bodies, but. . .rather. . .should channel the work of members towards the essential problems of

[17] This was the first occasion on which it had met.

self-government in practice and the role of the working man in society'.

Early in October 1966 the 5th Plenum approved the Todorović Commission's recommendations without calling a special Party Congress. Their essential point was to prevent another Ranković securing an uncontrolled power position within the LCY. The CC was to remain as before, but the Secretariat was abolished. The Executive Committee was now to have a purely administrative function, and to consist of eleven members only, six of them the secretaries of the Republican Executive Committee. Members of the Executive Committee were not allowed to hold other executive posts, and in particular they could not serve simultaneously on the new policy-making body, the Presidency of the CC, consisting of thirty-five members, with Tito as President of the LCY rather than, as before, Secretary-General. Republican Party machinery was reorganised on the same lines. The new pattern was not finally determined until the IXth Congress of the LCY in April 1969, at which the more general theses of the Todorović Commission on adapting the LCY to conditions of 'self-management' were also discussed.[18]

Some considerable changes in local organisation were indeed made in June 1967, when single LCY organisations were formed for each enterprise and Commune, the latter to include all locally resident LCY members (many of these would thus be members of two LCY organisations). This proved to be an insufficient condition for the effective exercise of uniform influence by the LCY. It helped rather to build up the independence of the local organisations vis-à-vis the CC and Presidency of the LCY. Even more important for the 'confederalisation' of Yugoslavia was the increase in power, after the Constitutional Amendments of spring 1967, of the Republican branches of the LCY. These were now empowered to appoint and dismiss higher and middle-rank functionaries – a task hitherto for the central Organisational Secretariat. Ambitious young men now began to look for political careers in their Republican capitals rather than in the Federal Centre, Belgrade.

4

Amid all the change of political machinery, the main economic problems confronting Yugoslavia remained very much the same. The reformers recognised from the first that the whole process of adaptation

---

[18] Meanwhile the CC (July 1968) had recommended that it should itself be replaced altogether by a Presidency.

would be painful, and the fact that their expectations were realistic enabled them to hold their chosen course more steadily than their opponents, or even their friends, could have hoped. But the negative consequences of Reform lasted for nearly three years. The slow-down in production[19] was tolerable in contrast with the excessive investment and production of unnecessary goods which had characterised the previous period, but the consequent increase in unemployment was a serious matter, particularly as in the years 1964–7 the generation born in the demographic 'bulge' years 1946–7 was coming on to the labour market. Total employment fell by 1%, from 3.61 million to 3.56 during this initial period of reform, and in the predominant 'social sector' (covering 97% of all employment) there was a fall of 3%, hardly compensated by a rise of 42% in the minuscule private sector (largely services and catering). Moreover among those who were coming on to the market, and could not find jobs, there was an increasing number of graduates of universities or higher vocational schools. This could be a potent cause of discontent among the more articulate of the younger generation.

The great bulk of the unemployed however were still the young peasants who continued, as before, to leave the farms and seek higher-paid, more interesting and more prestigious work in the towns. The Yugoslav authorities had avoided any major crisis of agriculture since 1954, but could not claim any great success. Their aim had been to keep up numbers on the small private farms. The limit on holdings would prevent the formation of a 'kulak' class, but output would be improved by the spread of modern techniques from the co-operatives. In fact the socialist sector of agriculture had not failed, by and large, but was hardly an exemplary success. The older generation of private peasants prospered reasonably, but the younger generation did not want to stay on the farms. By 1967 about 2.3 million Yugoslavs had migrated to the towns, and well under one half of the total population worked on the land, as opposed to over two-thirds in 1948. The trend appeared to be irreversible. The supply of new jobs in the towns dried up after 1965, as industry was rationalised, but there was little to attract young peasants back to the country. Instead they migrated mainly to Western Europe, as previous generations of Balkan peasants had emigrated to America, but in far larger numbers.[20]

---

[19] Over the four years 1964–7 the average rate of increase was 2.9%, as compared with 9.7% for 1961–4 and 12.7% for 1957–60.

[20] The trend was general, and there was a considerable exodus from Turkey in particular. There were other minor streams of emigrants from Yugoslavia, notably one of Macedonian peasants to Australia, where they were highly valued

The Yugoslav 'guest workers' in Central Europe, and particularly in Western Germany, became an important factor in the political and economic calculation of the Yugoslav and recipient Governments. So far as the Yugoslavs were concerned, it was better that such people should find work abroad than that they should stagnate in the villages at public expense, and their remittances in hard currency were a useful item for the Yugoslav foreign exchange budget. On the other hand the large-scale export of manpower was a poor advertisement for the Yugoslav socialist model. The administrative, economic and social problems involved in the operation tied Yugoslavia even more closely into the West European economy. In West Germany, the new immigrants could make dangerous political contacts with the remnants of the Ustaše, who had been outside Yugoslavia since the end of the war. A minor brain drain could be involved, in that many of the more skilled workers wished to follow the example of the unskilled. This applied particularly to Croatia, where the 'wasting of the national substance' became a nationalist slogan.[21]

Another major result of Reform began to become apparent in 1967, and affected the 'nationalities question' more deeply. Reform had been successful at first in leaving control of investment much more to the enterprises themselves. In 1967 enterprises controlled the distribution of about 58% of the national income (as opposed to 45% in 1961 and 49% in 1964). However the financial power originally enjoyed by the Federal Government was being taken over increasingly by the re-modelled banking system, and particularly by the three former Federal banks operating from Belgrade, which had in 1964 inherited the Federal General Investment Fund. The Law on Banks of March 1965 had envisaged a new system under which the enterprises investing their capital in the banks would control the Bank Assemblies and thus secure genuine financial self-management. In fact the crucial investment decisions were made essentially by the banks' credit committees, composed of expert bank employees under the chairmanship of an expert director. As the need for large capital sums for investment increased, the number of banks was decreased by mergers (in 1967 it was reduced to 102 from the pre-Reform 217). Within the larger units, the powers

---

for their tough manual work. The Australian Test cricketer, Len Pascoe, is of Macedonian origin.

21 The Yugoslav authorities at the time gave exit visas only to the unskilled. It was said that some skilled workers, in order to emigrate, would work for a short time at jobs for which they had no qualifications, in order to earn an 'unskilled' certificate. Once in Germany they would resume their normal occupation and produce a second 'skilled' certificate.

of the shareholder enterprises were less, and those of the management greater. And the management of the major banks was inevitably bound by previous patterns of investment. They could not close down all the 'political factories' which economically did not deserve to survive. They were committed further to a number of long-term major projects, mainly in the field of communications, which would only mature slowly and would bring no immediate benefits to the economy.[22]

All in all therefore the enterprises' freedom to invest was still considerably hampered. By and large they had less funds to dispose of than they had hoped, and they were unlikely to indulge in socially useful but financially doubtful projects of integration across Republican borders. Thus investment tended to be frozen within Republican boundaries and did not serve to lessen the economic disparities between more and less developed Republics. It began to appear that the 'bureaucratic' Federal apparatus had been replaced by a small 'technocratic' group of bankers, still centred in Belgrade. This aroused strong nationalist sentiment particularly in Croatia and Slovenia. It also had more indirect but important results for the less developed Republics.

Croatian suspicions of the new system boiled over in connection with the 'retention quotas' for foreign currency re-introduced by the banks in 1967. In order to encourage incentives for visible and invisible exports, exporting or tourist enterprises were allowed to keep on average 7% of their own foreign currency earnings to be used as they saw fit; the remainder was to be deposited in special banks for resale to firms who needed it for imports (including those firms which had originally owned it). Five of the seventeen special banks were located in Belgrade, and the new system produced strong protest and counter-argument among the Croats, who claimed to produce, through exports and receipt of foreign currency from tourists and workers abroad, up to 40% of Yugoslavia's total foreign currency earnings.

5

Thus by early summer 1968 the 'nationalities question' had acquired new dimensions. At this stage another problem came to the troubled surface of Yugoslav society, and produced an immediate political crisis,

---

[22] In one respect too the state managed to claw back some of the funds and powers which it had surrendered in 1964. Repayments in respect of pre-1964 credits from state funds were paid into the new banks, but under a law of 1965 the Federal Government had effective control of how such repayments were used; it could and did specify investments or subsidies to be financed from the 'extra-budgetary accounts'.

which demanded the active intervention of Tito himself. 1968 was the year of 'student power' all over the world. In the U.S.A. students organised protests against the drafts for the war in Vietnam. In Paris and Warsaw too there was a strong movement by the younger generation against the doctrines and policies of their established elders in the government. The students of Yugoslavia were no doubt affected by this general malaise of the younger generation. They felt quite as generally alienated as their Western counterparts from the generation of their fathers. A good number reacted cynically to the heroic pieties of the ex-Partisans. These were, it seemed, of no relevance to their new and increasing post-Reform problems. The policy of self-management as applied to education often entailed cutting down on material facilities for students. In 1966 there had been strikes by students about their accommodation in Zagreb and Skopje, sufficiently serious to rate some not very sympathetic guidance by President Tito. By 1968, as the full economic effects of Reform were felt, employment prospects for students had become increasingly doubtful. Many of the jobs which, they felt, they should have had, were held down by technically ill-qualified veterans. Dissatisfaction on these counts with the 'establishment' merged among the higher-minded with a genuine and outraged idealism. What had happened to the ideals of communism in an age of 'dinar-socialism'? Even the establishment of the LCY thought primarily about profitability, and sacrificed the idea of 'social ownership' to it. Enterprises no longer paid sufficient taxes to compensate for the advantages which they enjoyed in respect of use of sites and plant. They envisaged differential rates of pay which outraged socialist convictions. No wonder the energies of the less political majority were so largely devoted to the acquisition of better cars and television sets, a new 'vikenditsa' or the possibility of a trip abroad and the import of further valuable consumer goods. There must be something very wrong with an ideology and a political system of which this was the normal result. It was at this point that the more politically-minded among the students were affected either directly by the doctrines of *Praxis* and *Gledišta* or by the climate of ideas in which these periodicals had begun to flourish.[23] There was indeed some danger of common opposition to the 'Reform establishment' of the LCY by the students and the

[23] During the winter 1967–8 there had been another round of open newspaper debate about the success of Reform, in which the eminent economists, Branko Horvat and Aleksander Bajt, had strongly criticised the ignorance and inefficiency of the reformers (though not questioning their principles) and had been bitterly accused in return of rocking the boat and spreading alarm and despondency.

CTY, which was also much concerned with growing unemployment and differential earnings.

The criticism of the philosophers began to be openly echoed by Yugoslav students, primarily but not only in Belgrade, during April and May 1968. On 8 May a symposium was held at the Belgrade Law Faculty, at which one faculty member urged the students to demand a free and progressive university and added that there was only one step between the demand for university reform and that for the reform of society as a whole. Early in June, then, the Belgrade students published an 'action programme' which summarised the demands of the 'new left', and was indeed endorsed by the CTY journal, *Rad*.[24] This was followed shortly after by a flare-up between the Belgrade students and the forces of law and order. The occasion was trivial – a street fight between students and Youth Brigade workers over admission to an evening variety show. However the reaction of the city riot police was unnecessarily forcible, and the next day 4,000 students took to the streets, with posters making economic and political demands. Again there were confrontations with the police, and in the second of these 169 people, mainly students, were injured badly enough to require treatment.

The students had already shown evidence of organisation, and proceeded from street demonstrations to a sit-in strike in the University buildings. The authorities could not treat the events of early June as an example of Serb chauvinist excess, since the students of Zagreb, Ljubljana and Sarajevo showed their solidarity. Tito himself decided that some steps must be taken towards meeting at least the students' particular economic grievances. By treating them within a broad national framework, he hoped to calm down the students without making particular concessions to them. The sit-in was ended. On 14 June Tito himself publicised 'Guidelines for further measures of economic and social reform'. These were approved, together with proposals for Party re-organisation, at a Plenum of the CC, LCY, on 16 July. Neither the 'Guidelines' nor Tito's speech contained anything striking. Immediate action should be taken to revive the economy, to remove obstructionists from the Party, to discipline people who violated socialist norms of behaviour, and to help low-income workers. Such

[24] The main points outside the educational field were an incomes policy which should eliminate social inequality; an expansionist investment policy to solve the unemployment problem; democratisation of the LCY and the news media; and the reversal of the trend to convert 'social ownership' into 'group ownership' (this implied that enterprises had too much financial freedom and should pay heavier taxes).

general action would, it was said, fulfil the student demands, which Tito described as justified. The students however saw few concrete results from all the pronouncements made; many of them suspected that all they had gained was a postponement of positive action against them.

For Tito and the leaders of the LCY the whole incident was at first alarming, as illustrating the emergence of what could be a new and powerful force in Federal and Republican politics. There were however some compensations. The LCY organisation at Belgrade University had been able to secure the dissolution of the special student Action Group by 'persuasive' rather than 'administrative' means, and subsequently, after Tito's general promises, to defuse the tense situation created by the more specific student demands. It was also important for the régime that the student demonstrators had failed to attract further workers' support with such slogans as 'Bureaucrats, hands off the workers', 'Down with the Princes of Socialism', 'More schools, fewer automobiles', etc. The student strikes did not spread to industry, and soon the LCY organisations were busy in the factories mobilising opinion against the students. The régime had therefore not come off too badly from the student affair; but within six weeks this was entirely overshadowed by a major crisis of foreign policy.

14

The Czech crisis and the IXth Party Congress

Yugoslav foreign policy since 1965 had been a strange resultant of economic needs, political calculation, and ideological loyalty. Economic Reform had made for closer trade links with the West and the EEC countries in particular. So far as non-official dealings were concerned, business-like and friendly relations with the West, including the neighbour countries of Italy, Austria and Greece, formed an essential element of the Yugoslav way of life.

Non-alignment continued however to be the official foundation of Yugoslav foreign policy. The momentum of the decolonisation movement at the U.N. and elsewhere ensured that officially Yugoslavia, along with India, Egypt and other Asian and African countries, remained to some extent non-aligned against the ex- or nearly ex-imperial powers. The continuance and spread of the war in Vietnam from early 1965 onwards aroused genuine feeling in Yugoslavia, as elsewhere, against the U.S. administration and usually provided a safe point of agreement between Yugoslav statesmen and their foreign hosts or guests. They may also sincerely have thought, as they sometimes said, that American intervention in Vietnam and intervention in the Dominican Republic heralded a new phase of American and general 'imperialist' counter-attack against what they regarded as the forces of progress and liberation. Trade relations with Italy caused difficulties in 1967, and these threatened to spill over to the territory of the former Zone B of the Trieste territory – there were odd non-official suggestions from Italy that the 1954 settlement was never meant to be final. The 'Colonels' coup' in Athens (April 1967), and the Greek–Turkish troubles in Cyprus which preceded and followed it, were also interpreted as proof that the 'imperialists' were again on the march in Europe and the Mediterranean. The same moral was drawn officially from the decisive Israeli victory over Egypt in the six-day war of June

1967.[1] And in January 1968 the Yugoslavs supported the efforts of the Italian Communist Party to explore at a series of Mediterranean Conferences the possibility of joint action to counter 'imperialist action' in the area.[2]

There was thus a certain amount of fear, legitimate or not, about 'neo-imperialism' to keep the growing number of non-aligned countries together. Occasions for common political initiatives by the non-aligned were however rare, and their fate was not encouraging; for example the attempt in 1965 to bring pressure to bear on President Johnson over Vietnam (the 'initiative of the 17 countries') was a total failure. Moreover, as the number of non-aligned countries grew, the differences of interest between them also grew. Indonesia for example tried against Yugoslav wishes to organise in 1964 a special anti-colonial conference to replace the Cairo meeting of non-aligned Heads of State. The formation of the Organisation of African Unity (OAU) in 1963 diverted the diplomatic energies of many African countries away from the non-aligned framework.[3] And it proved increasingly hard for the Yugoslavs to be sure of backing the right party in any particular country. In spring 1965, for example, just after a visit by Tito to Algeria, Ben Bella, the Algerian Prime Minister, who had expressed the most cordial feelings for his guest, was overthrown and imprisoned. In these circumstances political activity by the non-aligned declined in importance and the next major meeting of non-aligned Heads of State was postponed until 1970 (the Lusaka Conference).

The Asian and African countries were however beginning to organise themselves as an economic pressure group within the U.N. framework for collective negotiation with the more prosperous countries. The most important development of the mid-1960s was to channel non-aligned activity towards general economic ends. With Yugoslav diplomatic backing, Asian and African governments in particular had pressed successfully for the first U.N. Conference on Trade and Development (UNCTAD). They also organised the 'Group of 75' (afterwards 77), to put forward a co-ordinated point of view for the less developed nations, and the COMECON countries (whose economic relations with them were insignificant) were glad to support

---

[1] This was far from universally deplored. The story ran in Belgrade that Dayan was a Sarajevo Jew, and that students, strongly encouraged to demonstrate against 'Israeli aggression', did so with black eye-patches.

[2] This initiative was quickly dropped when both the Soviet and French Communist Parties took offence at it.

[3] African states south of the Sahara, for example, were especially reluctant in 1967 to support the UAR cause in the Middle East.

them, in order to embarrass the West. General principles and policies for increased trade between more and less developed countries were laid down at UNCTAD I in Geneva (1964). Little concrete progress was made at UNCTAD II (New Delhi, 1968) in putting these policies into practise.[4] However Yugoslav statesmen supported them fully, and seemed happy to find in 'neo-imperialism' or 'economic imperialism' a new embodiment of the ancient ideological enemy.

In so doing they could incidentally demonstrate to Moscow that in spite of Reform they remained good communists. They had been anxious to re-assure the post-Khrushchev Soviet leadership, as soon as they could see that it would not be aggressively conservative, and the new Soviet leaders on their side seemed unwilling to exacerbate relations by any polemics against the new Yugoslav course. Yugoslavia had a strong interest in improving economic relations with COMECON, in order to lessen their dependence on EEC, and particularly in finding products which they could usefully import in return for their large exports eastwards. Tito's own instincts also played their part. Immediately after the outbreak of the six-day war in 1967, he flew to Moscow, proclaimed that Israel had been the aggressor, and broke diplomatic relations with Tel Aviv. This served to align him closely with official Soviet policy,[5] but it caused some concern in Yugoslavia that Tito should have taken such important decisions in Moscow, and without full consultations at home.[6] In August he displayed greater realism by floating a plan for a settlement which in some respects foreshadowed the generally agreed U.N. Resolution of November 1967 (No. 242) that marked the end of this phase of the Middle Eastern crisis.

From autumn 1967 onwards the course of rapprochement with Moscow was beset with difficulties. The Bulgarian Communist Government had been irritated by Yugoslav decisions in 1967 to establish a

---

[4] The increased independence enjoyed by Yugoslav enterprises after Reform in 1965 tended to work against increased trade or credits with Asian and African countries. Representatives of India, the UAR and Yugoslavia agreed in October 1966 on an expansion of economic co-operation; mutual tariff reductions were agreed in April 1968, and there have been some joint investment ventures, as by *Iskra* in the Asian Electronics Company of Bombay. The essential problem remains however of finding goods or materials which Yugoslavia needs to and can economically import from the less developed countries, and Tito himself has had to defend (as at Priština in March 1967) the granting of large credits to Asian and African countries.

[5] And to dissociate him from the Romanian leadership, otherwise the most congenial to Yugoslavia among the Warsaw Pact countries.

[6] Marko Nikezić, the Yugoslav Foreign Secretary at the time, is thought to have put the view directly to Tito on his return from Moscow, and to have paid for such boldness five years later.

separate Macedonian Academy of Science, and to allow the Macedonian Church, autonomous in effect since 1958, to become 'auto-
cephalous' (i.e. to appoint its own Patriarch). Early in 1968 the
Bulgarians were preparing celebrations for the ninetieth anniversary of
the Treaty of San Stefano,[7] under which a greater Bulgaria had been
temporarily established. They used this occasion to call in question the
Macedonian settlement of 1945 and again to stake their own claims to
'Bulgarian Macedonia'. The Yugoslavs concluded, probably correctly,
that they would not have done so without backing or instigation from
Moscow.

Then there was the question of a new world conference of Communist Parties, for which a preparatory conference was held at
Budapest in February–March 1968. The Yugoslavs could not attend,
if only because the new conference was to accept the conclusions agreed
by the last held in the series (Moscow 1960), which included strong
condemnation of Yugoslav 'revisionism'.

Meanwhile a new factor in Yugoslav calculations had emerged, in
the shape of the unexpected and thus doubly welcome 'Prague spring'.
The Czechs, like the Yugoslavs, had discovered that their highly
centralised economy would not work, and that to liberalise it effectively
they needed a new and more persuasive type of Communist Party. The
Yugoslavs were enthusiastic about the developments in Prague; they
noted that these did not include demands to abolish the political
monopoly of the Communist Party, or to leave the Warsaw Pact, and
thought for some time that the Russians would therefore accept them,
however reluctantly. In this case Tito seemed to be fully in line with
his own public opinion. Perhaps he began again to see visions of
'liberal Communist' governments in Central and Eastern Europe,
looking to Yugoslavia for example and guidance. At any rate, according to his own later account, he warned the Russian leaders when he
visited Moscow in April 1968 that any attempt to use force against the
Dubček government would be a catastrophe. During the following
summer, the new Czech régime had strong public support from the
Romanians as well as the Yugoslavs. Tito and Ceauşescu visited Prague
amid great enthusiasm at the last possible moment, in mid-August
1968. They calculated even then that the Soviet leaders had evolved
sufficiently from the Stalinist outlook not to risk the political conse-

---

[7] This was the first Russian-imposed solution of the 'Eastern crisis' of 1875, which
started with a Bosnian revolt against the Turks, developed into a Russo-Turkish
war, threatened a major European one, and was finally settled at the Congress of
Berlin (1878) which much cut down Bulgarian territorial gains.

quences of invasion, and that the shows of military force on the Czech borders were designed mainly to prevent the Dubček régime from repeating the mistakes of Imre Nagy in Hungary.

Thus the invasion of Czech territory on 21 August 1968 was a total surprise to the Yugoslav leaders (nearly all of them were away on holiday) and faced them with an entirely new and potentially very dangerous situation.

2

Among the Yugoslav people as a whole the invasion of Czechoslovakia caused what seemed to many Western Europeans exaggerated alarm. The idea that the Soviet leaders intended to invade Yugoslavia as well seemed 'Yugocentric' and incredible. None the less there was a feeling of national emergency in Yugoslavia,[8] and the general perception of the situation was almost as important in this case as the situation itself.

Yugoslav thinking was that the Soviet Government had disciplined Czechoslovakia without any dangerous reaction from the Western powers, and that Romania might be next on the list. President Ceauşescu had earned black marks in Moscow by his flirtation with China, his maintenance of diplomatic relations with Israel, and now by his association with Tito in enthusiastic support for the Dubček régime. If he were replaced by a leader subservient to Moscow, Yugoslavia's general position would be weakened and her military vulnerability much increased.

The prospect of a military-political emergency was thus not difficult to envisage. There were political gains also to be derived from behaving as if an emergency existed. Tito's economic and political lifelines to the West needed strengthening, and one of the best ways of making this possible was to show Yugoslavia as a bulwark against a Soviet threat. On the domestic front too an appeal to national unity had its advantages, in diverting attention from student and nationality troubles and in restoring a sense of purpose to the LCY.

There was thus no attempt to gloss over the situation in Czechoslovakia. On the evening of 21 August, the Party presidium and Executive Committee formally condemned Soviet aggression and after a further emergency meeting with Ceauşescu Tito declared on 23 August that 'we shall know how to defend and protect Yugoslav independence with all means against whatever side the threat comes

---

[8] The author met Yugoslav officials in Edinburgh on the evening of 21 August 1968, and the feeling certainly extended to them.

from'. He compared the action taken against Dubček and his 'progressive revolution' with that undertaken by Stalin against Yugoslavia in 1948, thus increasing the general sense of emergency to a new height.

The most important Yugoslav reaction to the invasion of Czechoslovakia was the public announcement and practical evolution of a new defence policy, designed to impress potential aggressors and potential allies with the Yugoslav will and ability to defend themselves in case of need. After the initial round of public meetings and resolutions pledging the Yugoslav people as a whole to defence, a new 'Law of All-National Defence' was rushed through the Federal Assembly. For long it had been impolitic to suggest that, in case of aggression, the regular Yugoslav Army would be unable effectively to resist overwhelming numbers and equipment in the northern plains or the comparatively level country of eastern Serbia.[9] It was now made clear that any invader would have to face not only the regular Army, but also a sort of popular militia integrated with it on a local basis and comprising all Yugoslavs from the ages of 18 to 65, all units being trained in advance to fulfil particular combat tasks, and armed as far as possible with comparatively cheap defensive weapons (especially anti-tank guns) produced in Yugoslavia. Under these conditions – and an immediate start was made to organise training – it was hoped that Soviet invaders would find the Yugoslavs as tough a proposition as the Americans had found the North Vietnamese. Meanwhile there was plenty for the LCY to do at every level, including the Federal, in helping the Yugoslav Army to organise and train the local units in their tasks. It was significant, and a hopeful sign for Tito, that recruitment to the LCY greatly increased during the second half of 1968.

3

By late autumn 1968, the Russians had taken no further action and the sense of emergency in Yugoslavia was blunted.[10] The deeper problems of the LCY could not be solved only by associating it with occasional crisis measures. Measures of re-organisation in 1966–7 had done little to turn it into an effective unifying force in Yugoslavia. It had lost prestige in 1966–7, as the very full press revelations about

[9] In 1951 a correspondent (and future editor) of the *Manchester Guardian* was taken to task severely for saying this in a published article.
[10] The Yugoslavs still did their best to conclude a trade agreement with the EEC and to secure further credits from the World Bank. But they also let their wish be known to expand trade links with COMECON countries, and not to be associated with 'cold war reactions' in the West.

UDBA misdeeds spread over to the question of Party privileges. In one sense it was too inclusive an organisation. Serb bankers and Croat industrialists were equally members of the LCY. But it was their function as bankers and industrialists which determined their attitudes and activities much more than their common membership of the League. So far as the LCY was effective, it had become so since 1967 on a Republican basis, and particular Republican loyalties tended to outweigh allegiance to a centrally determined Party line.

The older generation of Communist leaders was well aware of these dangers, and tried to meet them at least in part by emphasis on self-management. If the position of the ordinary worker could be strengthened, the 'technocrats' and nationalists (the two categories tended to overlap) would be under better control. By an act of faith it was assumed that Workers' Assemblies throughout the country would be more socially minded than Workers' Councils and committees of management, that they would be less ready to pursue 'particularist' or Republican interests, and that it would be easier to find among the local Party cells or CTY branches people activated by higher social motives who would guide the working class in the right direction. This was the aim still pursued by Tempo, as head of CTY.

The crisis over Czechoslovakia had moreover emphasised the 'external' aspect of what had previously been an internal debate. If, as seemed likely, the Soviet Government had been ready to back Ranković in 1966, they were even more likely now to foster political opposition in Yugoslavia among disappointed Party conservatives, student idealists or (most dangerously) among disaffected Serb or Croat nationalists. It was therefore all the more urgent for the Yugoslav leaders to reach some stable settlement of their multiple problems on the home front. In doing so they wanted not only to discourage 'Cominformism' directly, but also to nip in the bud 'ultra-leftist' demonstrations such as those of the Belgrade students in summer 1968, which might strengthen the case for re-centralisation and a policy of the 'firm hand'; for the leaders who had enthusiastically supported Dubček's 'Prague spring' found it hard to repress in their own country freedom of discussion and effective self-management. As in 1952, they had to steer between Scylla, the 'pseudo-liberal conception of a bourgeois state' and Charybdis, 'the restoration of state-bureaucratic or technocratic hegemonism'.

The IXth Congress of the LCY met in March 1969 and confirmed the policy of the reformers who in 1965 and 1966 had decided that Charybdis was more dangerous than Scylla. Their victory was

helped by the felt need to adapt the LCY to 'conditions of self-
management', and the suspicion that any movement towards recen-
tralisation would be exploited by the conservative communists, possibly
aided by the Russians. It was also facilitated by what was evidently
a decision to meet nationalist movements within Yugoslavia half-way,
and thus if possible to take the sting out of them. The Congress met in
the shadow of new national problems almost as dangerous as that
between Serbs and Croats. In November 1968 the Serbian LCY held
their VIth Congress and discussed with considerable frankness the
problems of the Albanian population of the Kosmet (now an autonomous Province). A few days later the Albanians, nearly a million in
number by now, organised demonstrations against the Provincial
government, which had their counterparts among the Albanian
minority in Western Macedonia. After the fall of Ranković, much had
been done to dismantle the Serb-dominated UDBA which had played
a highly oppressive part in the Kosmet.[11] But the taste of liberty only
provoked the appetite for more; the Albanians were now looking for a
separate Republic within the Yugoslav federation, in which they would
form a majority. The demand had uncomfortable external implications. A Yugoslav Albanian Republic could be subject to pressure from
Albania (now aligned with China against the U.S.S.R.), or could be
used by the Russians as a means and excuse for infiltrating Albania
themselves. At the same time a Macedonian Republic diminished and
deprived of its Albanian population would be more liable to Soviet-
inspired propaganda and infiltration from Bulgaria.

The Albanian demonstrations could not be suppressed without the
use of force, but here and elsewhere an effort was made to pursue a
double policy. What were reckoned to be dangerous instances of
nationalism were strongly discouraged;[12] at the same time, and particularly in Croatia, the moderate pursuit of national interests was
allowed. The preparations for the IXth Congress indeed involved one
unprecedented concession to national feelings. In accordance with the
new LCY statute adopted in 1964, Republican Congresses were held

---

[11] Some force however was certainly necessary. A state of emergency had been
declared in the Province in 1955, and the last group of Albanian terrorists was
reported to have been captured in the same year. Trials of Albanian agents were
still taking place in 1961.

[12] In October 1967, for example, Večeslav Holjevac, a former Mayor of Zagreb,
was condemned for 'nationalist deviations' in his conduct of the affairs of a
Centre for Croatian Emigrants; and in May 1968 the well-known and demon-
stratively 'Yugoslav' writer, Dobrica Ćosić, was severely criticised for nationalism
when he spoke in the Serb CC against non-Serb nationalist manifestations, e.g. by
the Magyars of the Vojvodina.

between November 1968 and February 1969, before the main LCY Congress. It was the Communal and Republican meetings – where discussion was comparatively open – which nominated people for the Federal LCY organs, and the nominations were merely confirmed by the IXth Congress. The principle of 'rotation' was applied with legalistic strictness, and there was little choice of candidates for elective posts at the Republican level or for places at the main Party Congress. The comparatively liberal leaders in the LCY had taken warning from what happened during the election contests of 1967, and were determined not to give the 'conservatives' such a free hand again.

The result was the biggest turnover of delegates and responsible officers in the history of the LCY. It looked as if the post-1945 generation of Partisan backwoodsmen had after 25 years been finally evicted from politics. Of the delegates at Republican level over 90% had never attended a Party Congress before. Among the nearly 300 people elected to the Republican CCs nearly 70% were new, and in the new CCs as a whole 60% were under 40 and 15% under 30 years of age.[13] Qualitative change at the Republican level was greatest where, from the liberal point of view, it was most needed – in Serbia. The new President of the CC was Marko Nikezić, a man of broad horizons who had been a senior diplomat, and Secretary for Foreign Affairs since 1965; he was backed by another comparative newcomer, Latinka Perović, who in her mid-thirties became Secretary of the Executive Committee. Here were two newcomers untainted by any infection from the days of Ranković's dominance in Serbia. Their appointments were thus welcomed by responsible politicians elsewhere, particularly by Bakarić and Tripalo in Croatia, as likely to bring about some decrease in Serb–Croat national tension.

The most important changes effected by the IXth Congress were in the field of organisation. A new Party statute was passed, confirming the changes at basic organisation level as agreed provisionally by the CC in July 1967. The most important of these was the abolition of the CC itself and of the Executive Committee of the LCY. It was agreed (July 1968) to replace the CC by a Presidency. This was to be confederal in character, with six representatives[14] from each Republic (instead of delegates in proportion to population), three from each Autonomous Province (Vojvodina and Kosmet) and three from the

---

13 Figures are taken from the Dennison Rusinow, *The Yugoslav Experiment 1948–74*, to which the whole of this and the next chapter owes much.
14 The number was changed to six from five at the last moment. The Presidents of the Republican CCs were also *ex officio* members, as was Tito himself. Thus the total number was fifty-two.

army, which thus had a new and important role as a unifying element. Between Party Congresses (and there had been a gap of $4\frac{1}{2}$ years between the VIIIth and the IXth) the Presidency would be responsible to a newly-created body, an annual Conference of 280 members, of whom 200 were to be elected for each annual meeting, and the remaining seventy elected for the inter-Congress period by a Republican Congress.

As regards executive machinery, it had at first been planned that decisions of the main Party Congresses and Conferences should be put into force exclusively by the Republican and lower instances. This would have been a quite remarkable step in the direction of confederation. The decision to abolish all central executive machinery was reversed at the IXth Party Congress by Tito himself in his speech to the final session of the Congress. He announced that, after consultation with the leaders of all the Republics, a new Executive Bureau would be set up in order to replace the Executive Committee and to reinforce the centre of leadership in the League of Communists.[15] It would consist of fifteen people, two from each Republic (including 'some of the present presidents and secretaries of the CCs or other leading comrades' from all six Republics), one from each Autonomous Province, and Tito himself. There would, he said, be 'some younger comrades. . .to ensure continuity' (he himself was nearly 77 years old at the time).

The new Executive Bureau was to be formed from the members of the Presidency, but to rank above it. It could be considered as a disguised form of Politburo, an expression of Tito's yearning for a return to 'democratic centralism' and a firm hand at the helm. Yet the new Bureau was highly confederate in structure and was constituted, like the Presidency itself, in accordance with what subsequently became known as the 'ethnic key' – equal representation for all the nations of Yugoslavia. This could face Tito himself with a very difficult task in reconciling the various Republican interests at the top level. On the other hand the Republican presidents and Party secretaries might be much more easily dealt with in Belgrade than in their own Republican capitals, where they would be subject to, or even encourage, the most extreme forms of nationalist and local economic pressures. For the operation and authority of the Executive Bureau, much would clearly depend on how the various Republics chose their two representatives on it, and on the power relations between these two and the senior leaders who stayed in their Republican homes. The crucial cases were of course Croatia and Serbia. Bakarić and Tripalo were elected for

[15] In the advance text of his speech there was no hint of a new body.

Croatia, and Bakarić removed himself effectively from Zagreb, leaving the key places there to Savka Dabčević-Kučar (Croatian Prime Minister since 1967) and Pero Pirker (Mayor of Zagreb from 1963–7). On the other hand Marko Nikezić and Latinka Perović, the newly-elected President and Secretary of the Serbian CC did not join the Executive Bureau, preferring to be represented there by Mihajlo Todorović and Miroslav Pečujlić.[16] Among the other important Republican representatives at the centre, the President of the Macedonian CC, Krste Crvenkovski, had liberal ideas about how the LCY should develop, but found his wings effectively clipped by his transfer to Belgrade. The Slovenes' choice fell – obviously – on Kardelj, but when Stane Kavčić, the Prime Minister, refused to leave Ljubljana (and was thought thereby to have incurred Tito's disfavour) his place at Belgrade was taken by a youngish member of the Slovene Executive Committee, Stane Dolanc, the first of his generation to make a career – and a highly important one – at the new centre of party politics.

The highly confederate nature of Yugoslavia's Party machinery, 1969 model, was only doubtfully offset by the creation of new Executive Bureaux which might or might not succeed in taking swift and effective decisions in face of various Republican pressures. In April–May 1969 a further step was taken towards the political transformation of Yugoslavia into a state which the veterans of 1945 could hardly recognise. The IXth Party Congress was followed within two months by elections to the Federal, Republican and Communal assemblies – the first full elections to be held since 1963. Most of the chambers of these assemblies were filled by indirect rather than direct elections. This applied especially to what was now the most powerful Chamber of the Federal Assembly, the Chamber of Nationalities. None the less the 'liberals' now dominant in the LCY leadership, who had thought it important to restrict the choice of candidates for the Republican and Federal Party Congresses, found it even more necessary to give the 'conservatives' very little rope in the elections to the Assemblies.

As often, the leaders of SAWPY, charged with the conduct of the election, found it easier to say what they were against than what they were for. They were against any 'struggle for power' – that is to say, direct political argument between rival parties, or rival interest groups. They were against 'spontaneity', or the unprepared mass meeting, at

[16] Of these Todorović had much political experience and had been a strong advocate of Reform. Pecujlić occupied a chair at Belgrade University and only accepted the place on the Executive Bureau on condition that he could retain it.

which volatile crowds could be swayed by the arguments of unscrupulous demagogues. They were in favour (tacitly) of a fair variety of candidates who could be trusted to act within a certain political framework. To ensure that such, and only such, candidates came forward, SAWPY devised an extremely complicated system of nomination[17] – so complicated indeed that it was seldom possible for all the interest groups involved (enterprises, veterans' organisations, etc.) to agree on more than one candidate (two safe ones would have been SAWPY's ideal). The elections ended with a great majority of officially sponsored candidates duly taking their place in the assemblies. But a few non-approved ones had still secured nomination; and a few of these had been elected – notably the Serb Sretoje Urošević who, as in 1967, defeated the official candidate at Čačak by nearly 80,000 to nearly 30,000 votes. The whole process had taken place in an atmosphere of unprecedentedly public discussion, which had often made clear the nature of the interest groups involved in the bargains over nomination. The 1969 election was thus a considerable step, forward or backward according to viewpoint, in the political education of the Yugoslav people.

[17] Candidates were first registered at 'pre-nomination' meetings at village or enterprise level. Then (an innovation) came Communal or inter-Communal 'nomination' Conferences to semi-finalise nomination. Subsequent 'voters' meetings' could finally add candidates to the list. There was much discussion of the new form of democracy in the Yugoslav press. SAWPY and the LCY exercised control to the extent of publishing lists of Party members considered unsuitable for candidature by the local LCY branches.

15

The nationalities crisis: Croatia

On the international front the period following the IXth Congress was one of decreasing tension; this had its effects on Yugoslav foreign and domestic policy. The Soviet Government decided in 1969 that a period of *détente* with the West was in its interest. The decision was probably motivated first by the need for large-scale technological imports from the West. Possibly there were deeper calculations about forestalling the establishment of a West European Community united by social, political and military links against the U.S.S.R. At any rate the appointment of Willi Brandt as Chancellor of the Federal Republic of Germany determined Brezhnev to pursue an active *Westpolitik*, and to arrive by direct negotiations with the West Germans at the kind of solution for East–West German relations which he had long tried to attain by conference diplomacy in a European framework. The most essential steps in this process were completed in August 1970.

Less than a year later Communist China began to emerge from the international isolation in which she had been engulfed for some years after the Cultural Revolution. The Sino-Soviet dispute was by no means ended thereby, and the renewal of direct contacts between the U.S. and China could conceivably portend a new diplomatic front against the Soviet Union. For some time the Yugoslavs kept their options wide open. A Sino-Yugoslav Trade Agreement was signed in March 1969, and Ambassadors were exchanged between China and Yugoslavia by August 1970. A month later, at a meeting of Communist Party representatives in Budapest, the Yugoslavs insisted on the importance of full Chinese participation if an effective 'anti-imperialist' front was to be organised. The Yugoslav Foreign Secretary, Tepavac, visited China in 1971, and meanwhile relations between Yugoslavia and China's protégé, Albania, were noticeably improved. Economic and touristic links were strengthened, and educational exchanges were initiated between Albania and the Kosmet with its large Shiptar population. On the south-eastern frontier, the Bulgarians did not let the

Macedonian question sleep, and Tito accused them in 1970 of trying to provoke a crisis in Yugoslavia for their own purposes. In the same speech he hinted at a revival of Cominformist activities. 'Devils abroad try to destroy us from within. . .Such people are predominantly those who should be among our best friends. . .Abroad there are all those ravens who have their long necks and beaks aimed at Yugoslavia, wondering whether they might obtain some easy pickings. . .'

For Yugoslavia however the overwhelmingly important fact was that from 1970 a new stage of international relations had begun in Europe. The short-term effects of this for the Yugoslavs were considerable, if negative. In the new phase of East–West détente there was little likelihood either of a dangerous Soviet–Yugoslav crisis or of a close Soviet–Yugoslav rapprochement in a 'conservative communist' spirit. Equally there could be less objection from the Soviet side to a strengthening of Yugoslav–Western European relations. Thus the Yugoslav Government was likely to be able to pursue without hindrance a steady normalisation of state relations at least with the U.S.S.R., and at the same time an intensification of economic relations with the West, such as the Croatian and Slovenian leaders in particular desired.

Yugoslav statesmen could also hope that, if détente developed, they might for a time have a new role as mediators between East and West in Europe (these hopes were to some extent realised at the Helsinki European Conference in 1975). Equally if détente brought some thaw in the internal political conditions of the Warsaw Pact countries, the Yugoslav way to socialism might begin again to be influential in Eastern Europe, as on the Yugoslav reckoning it had been in 1956 and 1968. These however were dreams for the future. Meanwhile preparations for the meeting of non-aligned Heads of State in Lusaka, 1970, and the fostering of new relationships between developed Europe and underdeveloped Asia and Africa continued to be the official preoccupations of Yugoslav diplomacy. They also began to seem rather irrelevant to the immediate international context in Europe.

Here the most important event for Yugoslavia was the signature in Brussels (March 1970) of a long-desired and comprehensive commercial agreement with the EEC. This was designed to ensure that Yugoslavia's position with the countries which were now her major trading partners should be safeguarded by formal arrangements to ensure the maintenance of trade, and above all to lessen the danger of restrictive measures being applied to Yugoslav exports. Thus there were general provisions for non-discrimination in trade and most-favoured nation treatment on either side, and special concessions to Yugoslav exporters of baby-beef, who had for long had grievances, particularly in relation to Italy. The importance of the agreement can be judged by the fact that in 1969 the EEC provided Yugoslavia with 49% of its total imports and took 39% of its exports. Thus Yugoslavia seemed to have assured its position as a trading partner of Western Europe, and to have secured formal links with the EEC which protected it against any renewed danger of blockade from the East, and politically balanced its observer status at COMECON meetings, granted in 1963.

2

The new international context of the early 1970s once more allowed Yugoslavia to deal with its domestic problems without any likelihood of being jerked out of them by international crises, such as those of 1956 and 1968. This fact in itself tended to increase the importance of the 'nationalities question' in Yugoslavia. The aim of LCY and Federal Assembly alike had been to kill nationalism by kindness, giving full scope in the Assembly for preliminary discussions between Republican representatives before decisions were taken which affected their interests. At the same time the new LCY Executive Bureau should have been able to take quick and definite decisions at the highest level when urgent action was required.

However, excellent as the system may have been in theory, it proved inadequate to deal with the economic problems arising at this time in Yugoslavia. At the end of 1968, before the IXth LCY Congress, the Republican congresses of Bosnia and Montenegro had passed resolutions demanding 'compensation for the unfavourable effects of individual measures and relations in an integrated market' which were incorporated in a draft resolution discussed by the IXth Congress in March 1969. This gave rise to bitter debates about the familiar questions of investment strategy. It was not only the under-developed Republics which continued to complain. In summer 1969 the FEC had to deal with the distribution of funds under a loan from the World Bank for the construction of the first major motorways in Yugoslavia. Projects in Serbia and Croatia were given first priority, and the very strong economic case for a new highway between Ljubljana and Nova Gorica was neglected.

The Slovene case – and here was a new disturbing element for the LCY particularly – had far-reaching foreign policy implications. Stane Kavčić and his government in Ljubljana were primarily interested in northward links with Austria and Western Germany, and thought (especially after the Soviet invasion of Czechoslovakia) that closer economic and political relations with Western Europe should have priority over inter-Republican relations within Yugoslavia. For Tito such a standpoint clearly illustrated the long-term dangers involved in letting 'technocrats' determine major questions of policy. 'Politics' in the Chinese phrase 'must take the lead'. More immediately the effects of the Slovene crisis in summer 1969 on Yugoslav constitutional machinery were in themselves cause for sufficient concern. Official protests from the Slovene Government were backed by mass demonstrations in Ljubljana. The crisis nearly led to the fall of the Federal Government, and could not be solved by the Assembly; only intervention by the LCY at the highest level could defuse it, and this was an important precedent.

It was however the Croats who, after as before 1969, pressed their economic case most consistently against the Federal Government. One of their main grievances remained the dominant position of the Yugoslav Federal Banks, and the apparent readiness of the Banks to use this position in favour of Serbia, or at least against the interests of Croatia. Another constant grievance, connected with the first, was the control by Federal authorities of foreign currency earned by Croat exporters. A third and more general one was the amount of investment funds which the Croats had to provide through the remaining central machinery for the less developed Republics.[1]

These were old grievances. There were new factors which made them more dangerous. In the first place the background was one of growing inflation, a soaring balance of payments deficit, rising cost of living, and increasing unemployment. Industrial production certainly rose by 43% between 1968 and 1971, but even the official cost of living index nearly matched this rise. By 1971 the proportion of imports covered by exports was only 55.5% (84.7% in 1965), and the number of Yugoslav emigrant workers rose to 800,000 – over a fifth of those in employment within the country. Thus economic controls from the centre seemed more than ever necessary. At the same time it became clear that after 1969 the Federal machine was becoming increasingly ineffective, even when not blocked by Republican vetos. In winter 1970–1, for example, attempts to impose price control were frustrated

---

[1] A Croat economist, Šime Djodan, expressed these grievances in February 1971 in a form bordering on self-parody: 'In old Yugoslavia [1918–41] 46% of our income was used outside Croatia, in Austria-Hungary 55% and now it is 63%! Thus for the Croats the Socialist Federal Republic of Yugoslavia is a bigger exploiter and thus less acceptable than Austria-Hungary or old Yugoslavia!'

by enterprises declaring that their products were new types and so not subject to the regulations.

If any one benefited from the importance of the Federal machine, it was the Republican authorities. The hope of Yugoslav political theorists had been that the process of devolving effective power would continue down to the Communal and enterprise level. In fact it proved that Croat and other nationalisms, expressed at Republican level, were able in the new circumstances to outweigh nearly 25 years of general socialist education and the ability or will of the LCY to act as a unifying social conscience for Yugoslavia as a whole.

3

The Croats and Slovenes were not alone among the constituent nations of Yugoslavia in trying to improve their position. Macedonians and Bosnians in particular had special grievances of their own. It was however the Croatians who did most to bring the central machinery to a halt by constant use of their Republican veto against Federal attempts to impose price control and limit or co-ordinate investment and foreign trade. They were encouraged by the sheer size and economic strength of Croatia (the only one of the Republics which could conceivably form an independent state).

For some time after the fall of Ranković (an apparent victory for Croat influence), it appeared that the Croats might be content to build gradually on this success. Bakarić was a Yugoslav statesman as well as a Croat politician, and saw that Tito was quick to react against Serb as well as Croat nationalism. At the beginning of 1970 however Bakarić felt himself bound to adopt a more aggressively Croatian line. This even in the short term harmed the Croat cause. Other Republics too could use their veto to block Federal Government action. This in effect preserved the powers of the Central Banks and operated against Croatian interests.

By 1970 there was a strong nationalist movement in Croatia, fostered by the revival, from 1967 on, of the Croat cultural organisation the Matica Hrvatska (Croatian Queen Bee), which had strong nationalist overtones.[2] The Matica had begun to publish in 1968 a periodical *Kritika*, which discussed the disadvantageous position of

[2] The original Matica had been formed in the 1840s as a cultural society, on the model of the existing Matica Srpska in Novi Sad, to further the 'Illyrian movement' for greater Slav independence; this was at a time when direct political activity was forbidden by the Austrian authorities.

Croat minorities in other Republics (particularly Bosnia) and seemed
at one point to be calling in question the linguistic settlement of 1954
(confirmed in 1967) between Serbs and Croats. A particularly
prominent figure was the President of the Croatian Writers' Union,
Peter Šegedin,[3] who claimed that small nations, including Croatia,
existed for themselves only – not, it was implied, for partners in a
socialist federation. His arguments and the general line of the Matica
Hrvatska were strongly attacked late in 1969 by a Croat politician,
Miloš Žanko, in the national daily, *Borba*. Žanko treated them as an
illustration of growing and dangerous national currents in Croatia
linked with rightist and clerical tendencies in Croatian history, and
called on the Croatian Party leaders to restrain these more effectively.

It was to meet this challenge that Bakarić summoned the Croat
Party leaders to an important meeting in December 1969, and subsequently called the 10th Plenum of the Croat CC. He played down the
strength of the Croat nationalists, saying that they were too profoundly
divided to constitute any real danger. On the other hand he emphasised the dangers of the centralist policy advocated by some Croat
LCY members. Many of these held prominent positions and might
relapse into 'bureaucratic centralism and Cominformism'. The Croat
CC duly condemned Žanko for opposing the policy of the LCY, and
suggested that his articles had been inspired by 'coffee-house politicians
in Belgrade' and by some quarters in the Federal administration.

This was a new line, and one very dangerous for political stability
in Yugoslavia, since the Croat LCY was now linking centralists, Serbs,
bureaucrats and Cominformists in one hostile bloc. Presumably
Bakarić allowed them to do so on the reckoning that he himself was
unable to stop the strengthening of nationalist tendencies in the Croat
LCY, and that he could at least control them better than anyone else.
The risks involved in such a policy were considerable. The less moderate Croat nationalists were almost bound to gain in strength by out-
bidding the more moderate ones, and by bidding for complete Croat
independence they could unite the other Republican leaders against
Croatia.

In 1970 indeed the Yugoslav political setting was favourable to the
maximum freedom for the Republics consistent with the existence of a
Yugoslav state. In April the sovereignty of the Republics was formally

---

[3] It was Šegedin who appeared to be arguing the case against the linguistic agreement by a sharply critical review of a book of Viktor Novak, published in Belgrade,
on *Vuk [Karadžić] and the Croats*. Vuk had been the main force behind the
Vienna linguistic agreement of 1850.

recognised by the LCY Presidency, and Yugoslavia was formally defined as the outcome of an 'institutionalised agreement and co-operation among the Republics'. The Federal Government's competence in defence, foreign affairs and common foreign trade and monetary policies was reaffirmed, but the Federal Secretariats and the army were enjoined to implement more consistently the principle of the 'ethnic key', to ensure that important posts were effectively shared between the Republics, and Party Commissions were appointed to see that the principle was observed.[4] At the highest level too Tito went far towards 'confederalising' his own state office. He was already 78 years old and had to envisage the prospect that his retirement or death might give rise to an inter-Republican scramble for the Presidency. To avert this he proposed at the end of September 1970 that he should be replaced by a Collegiate Presidency, also to be constituted according to the 'ethnic key' by an equal number of 'outstanding personalities' from each Republic, and some representation from the two autonomous Provinces.

The Croat Republican leaders meanwhile overplayed their hand by proposing reforms of the central banking, foreign currency and foreign trade institutions, and the re-distribution of former Federal assets in a way which united at least four other Republics in opposition to them. The Bosnians and Macedonians in particular had a strong interest in the survival of some Federal machinery for the channelling of funds to the poorer Republics. They could still theoretically be frightened by the threat of Serb 'hegemonism', but the new Serb LCY leaders pursued a sober and inconspicuous course. In these circumstances the less developed Republics had much more to fear from Croat nationalism.

Tito himself was well aware of the danger that national pressures would fatally weaken 'socialist consciousness'. In August 1970 he complained bitterly of regional pressures and of lack of discipline among Communist leaders, and his critical references to the decisions of the VIth Congress (November 1952) suggested that he was thinking seriously about a return to a policy of the 'firm hand' within the LCY. Nevertheless the formal process of 'confederalising' Yugoslavia continued. At the first meeting of the newly-created Conference of the

---

[4] It was further stipulated that the Federal Government should undertake some measures of economic co-ordination ('instruments necessary to guarantee a single market and economic system and ethnic quality'), but these were uncertain in scope. In October 1970 moreover, at Serbian insistence, the remaining Federal functions in distributing investment funds from the 'extra-budgetary accounts' were wound up.

LCY, Tito's proposals about the Presidency were endorsed,[5] and, more important, a commission was formed to work out a new set of amendments to the 1963 Constitution. Its membership was determined by the 'ethnic key' and its main directive was implied in the conclusions of the Conference. 'There is urgent need for a further step in the direction of reconstructing the Federation as a function of the statehood and sovereignty of every Republic and the autonomy of the Provinces, as the basis of the equality of the nations and nationalities of Yugoslavia.'

It was stated hopefully that the new amendments should produce a mechanism for inter-Republican consensus at the high policy-making level. However paralysis continued at the centre and inflation worsened while the new amendments were being worked out, to the accompaniment of detailed, lively and often bitter polemics in the organs of the Yugoslav press, reacting after their national kind. The public pressure for some action was such that early in 1971 the new Commission was deliberately isolated in Brioni to work out the package of nineteen constitutional amendments. These were accepted by the Commission as a whole early in March and finally promulgated after discussion by the Federal Assembly on 30 June 1971.

The new amendments, nearly all to be included later in the 1974 Constitution, confirmed the principle (accepted in 1970 by the Presidency of the LCY) of all powers to the Republics and Provinces, except for those specifically delegated to the Federation. More important was the inclusion of provisions to ensure that inter-regional consensus was to be reached even in the areas specified for Federal control. This confirmed and legalised a power of Republican veto. Moreover a long and important list of subjects was included in the amendments on which the Federal Assembly could decide only 'on the basis of agreement with responsible Republicans and Provincial organs'. The only direct and exclusive sources of income for the Federal budget would be customs and stamp duties. The rest of the Federal income depended in some degree on the Republics and Provinces.[6] The amendments laid down that the 'ethnic key' would apply to the most important Federal organs and institutions, including the FEC, and the Constitutional Court. They also confirmed that the territorial militia, set up under the new defence law of 1969, should be under Republican control.

[5] Its composition was enlarged from two per Republic and one per Province, as proposed by Tito, to three per Republic and two per Province (23 in all including Tito himself). This change was designed to meet the ethnic problems of Bosnia-Hercegovina.

[6] These would decide on the proportion of the turnover tax, collected by themselves, which should be allotted to the Federal Government.

Thus the constitutional basis for a new-style near-confederate Yugo-slavia was laid in the spring and summer of 1971.[7] But this did not create a stable balance between nationalities. The Serbs were anxious about the consequences of dismantling Federal machinery, particularly for the large number of Serbs living outside Serbia (mainly in Croatia). On the other side a number of Croats, especially those connected with Matica Hrvatska and its new weekly *Hrvatski Tjednik* (Croat weekly), regarded the amendments as only a first step towards fulfilling Croatia's national aspirations. The 'Matica men' claimed to represent a Croatian mass-movement, which could only support the Croat LC leaders in so far as they stood for 'progressive and national' tendencies, and their influence increased rapidly in 1971.[8] Outside Yugoslavia too Croat nationalism had begun to flourish in dangerous forms. Two émigré workers had shot the Yugoslav Ambassador in Stockholm,[9] while the leading émigré organisation had celebrated in Munich the 30th anni-versary of the foundation of Pavelić's NDH, and had boasted of its links with the Soviet Union.

Not for the first time Tito left decisive intervention against political dangers till the last possible moment. On 15 April at a meeting in Priština he spoke very sharply about nationalism and the general passivity of the LCY: '. . .behaviour in the League of Communists is not good and I am not satisfied. I must say this hurts me terribly. You know that I have long been at the head of the Communist Party and the League of Communists of Yugoslavia. But I think that so far we have not had such a situation as we have to-day. . .'

It might be necessary, he said, to apply 'administrative measures'. He was going to summon a special meeting of the Party Presidency together with 'the most responsible figures in all the Yugoslav Republics and provinces', and they would carry on their discussions until they reached agreement. The meeting assembled in secret on Brioni at the end of April. The communiqué however was a damp squib. National-ism and divided leadership were condemned. The constitutional amendments should come into force as soon as possible (they were

---

[7] Three other amendments accepted at the time kept alive the CTY ideas on 'total self-management' of Yugoslav society. These proved to be of great importance later.

[8] The extreme nature of their demands was shown by Franjo Tudjman, a former Partisan general, who declared that the Croats could not be satisfied any longer with a Federal State, and that Serbo-Croat relations could be handled only within a 'Confederation or League of States'.

[9] It was particularly alarming for the Yugoslav Government that these were young men in their twenties, not relics of the Ustaša régime.

promulgated at the end of June); and all other points of disagreement could be resolved by negotiation.[10]

4

At the Brioni meeting, it was afterwards said, the Croat leadership was taken severely to task; it was hoped that this would be a sufficient warning to them and that the constitutional changes promulgated on 30 June would be a sufficient sweetener. The latter however were not enough for the Croat extremists. Croat representatives at Belgrade remained totally intransigent on the economic issues that mainly affected them and continued to press their own reforms. By this time the most important organs of government proved to be extra-constitutional ones – five specialised inter-Republican Committees and an inter-Republican co-ordination Committee. The Croat delegates were the prisoners of their own extreme nationalist constituents and felt isolated within the Federal machine. They increased their isolation by using nationalist pressure in Zagreb as a threat to those who wished to hold the Federation together. Indeed there were plenty of nationalist excesses in Croatia – the destruction of signs in the Cyrillic alphabet, the showing of Croat emblems without the Communist red star to mitigate their significance, brawls and riots in mixed Serb and Croat areas. As these manifestations of Croat nationalism grew, the Serb population of Croatia began again to remember the terrible massacres of 1941 and to prepare for self-defence.

The evidence for the attitude of the Croat communist leaders dates largely from after 1971 and is suspect for being wisdom after the event by those who survived the catastrophe. Undoubtedly however one group, who occupied the most authoritative positions, Savka Dabčević-Kučar as head of the Government, with Mika Tripalo and Pero Pirker at the head of the Party, tried to ride the tiger of national-ism, as Bakarić himself seems to have done in 1969. They professed not to be frightened by the rapid growth of the extremist influence of Matica Hrvatska and its weekly *Hrvatski Tjednik*; and, fatefully for themselves, they accepted without any resort to discipline a nationalist

---

[10] The Yugoslav public was reminded of one of these points by the issue of a state-ment by a special commission appointed to examine Croat charges that an un-named Federal agency had supported Croat émigré organisations in Germany. The Commission absolved the still unnamed agency of the charges against it, but agreed that there had been a conspiracy abroad to blacken the Croat leader-ship by associating it with émigré organisations abroad.

student coup at Zagreb University, carried out in April 1971.[11] The new student leaders declared that they could have no more to do with the Yugoslav Student Union. They turned their organisation into an instrument of extreme Croat nationalism and used it as another means of bringing pressure on the Croat Communist leaders, who found it hard to oppose them without obvious resort to the 'firm hand' – a term of abuse for 'liberal' Communists.

Tito himself continued to demand a firmer and unitary Communist line, and re-emphasised on 8 May[12] with threats of disciplinary action that the policy agreed at Brioni must be carried out. In Zagreb it looked as if the Croat CC had hoisted in this message, and Tripalo emphasised the need for statesmanlike behaviour now that the Republic of Croatia 'was a State'. He and other speakers condemned Croatian nationalism along with other heresies outside Croatia. For this however they were publicly criticised by the Matica circle, and *Hrvatski Tjednik* began to speak of the victory of 'conservative forces' in the Croat leadership. Tripalo reacted with a statement that was dangerous on two counts. 'Nation' and 'class', he said, were now identical in Croatia, which implied the corollary that the more the leaders fought for Croat interests, the more they committed themselves to the class-struggle (against bourgeois Serbians?). Tripalo also committed himself publicly to a radical revision of the Yugoslav foreign currency system, involving separate foreign currency régimes for each Republic. This was pure economic fantasy, which could have involved for example Serb claims for Croat foreign currency payments in respect of food delivered to tourist hotels in Dalmatia.

By this time the 'triumvirate' (Dabčević-Kučar, Tripalo and Pirker) could only satisfy the 'mass movement' at the cost of their political credit with other Republics and, with Tito himself. The Croat LC leaders who opposed them were increasingly fearful of their own political position and began to think of appealing to Tito. He himself was increasingly worried about the multiplication of Matica branches and demonstrations, and about Croat attempts to apply the 'ethnic key' in order to reduce the number of Serb employees in Croatia. He visited Zagreb early in July to address the Executive Committee in terms (as published in May 1972) of furious anger:

[11] A significant new appointment was that of Ivan Zvonimir Cicak as 'student pro-Rector' of Zagreb University. He called himself a 'Catholic Titoist' and his nationalism was of a mystic variety.

[12] In a very effective speech to the Congress of Self-Managers at Sarajevo (the choice of audience was significant).

Under the cover of 'national interest' all hell is collecting...even to counter-revolution...In some villages the Serbs out of nervousness are drilling and arming themselves...Do we want to have 1941 again?...

Tito referred also to the international context and an offer of 'fraternal assistance' by Brezhnev:[13]

Are you aware that others would immediately be present if there were disorder?...I'd sooner restore order with our own army than allow others to do it. We've lost prestige abroad and it will be hard to get it back. They are speculating that 'when Tito goes, the whole thing will collapse' and some are seriously waiting for that. The internal enemy has plenty of support from outside. The great powers will use any devil which will work for them, whether he's a Communist or not....All kinds of things are being said. Now it is being said among you that I invented my conversation with Brezhnev in order to frighten you and force you into unity.

He was specific too about the dangerous state of Zagreb University, and 'the transformation of the Matica into a political organisation, to such a degree that...it has become stronger than you, so you're in no condition to curb it'.

Tito sought firm action from the Croat leaders and must have received definite assurances. There was no apparent change at this point in the policy of the 'triumvirate', nor any noticeable deflation of the Matica and its supporters. It was all the more surprising that on Tito's next visit to Croatia early in September he declared himself publicly to be very well satisfied, to have seen no evidence of nationalist deviations and to have concluded that reports of 'nationalist excesses' were much exaggerated.

Tito may have been convinced at the time that the 'triumvirate' was really trying to control the extreme nationalists, and may have wished to indicate his support for them. If so, he miscalculated. His words indeed increased the difficulties of those members of the Croat Executive Committee, with Bakarić now at their head, who thought that the 'triumvirate' had become the prisoners of the nationalists, and that there must be a show-down with the latter, and probably with the 'triumvirate' too, if Croatia was to enjoy its proper position among the Yugoslav Republics. The 'triumvirate' had dallied too long with the nationalists to be welcome back among the moderates. It was becoming increasingly hard for them either to dissociate themselves from the 'mass movement' without losing their political influence altogether, or to control the movement effectively.

[13] Tito had evidently mentioned this already to the April conference at Brioni.

Tripalo however in particular was confident in this respect and a confrontation between him and Bakarić was inevitable. At the meeting of the Croat CC held on 5 November a last attempt was made by Savka Dabčević-Kučar to maintain a façade of unity. The 'mass movement', she said, was in line with the policy decided at the Committee's 10th plenum, at which 'a unity of nations and Party was forged and sturdily grew into a mass political movement'. The comrades who thought that this should be treated with reserve were themselves deviating into heresy. Those who rejected 'mass support' were doing so 'in the interest of some abstract revolutionary purity which. . .incidentally represents nothing less than sectarianism and fear of the mobilisation of the masses. . .as though we, as a League of Communists, are a closed sect who think that society and the working people exist for us and not we for them'.[14]

The entire text of this speech, including the passages in praise of the 'mass movement' was adopted by the Central Committee as the 'conclusions' of their session, and there was no countervailing resolution against the Matica's activities.

At this stage Bakarić decided to appeal to Tito, who had just returned from the last of a long series of state visits.[15] The immediate background of the appeal was ominous. Early in November the final text was publicised throughout Croatia of the Matica's proposals for revising the draft amendments to the Constitution of Croatia. These amounted to something dangerously close to a declaration of independence. Croatia was defined as 'the sovereign national state of the Croatian nation', with the 'right to self-determination, including the right to secession'. It would have full control of all revenues collected in its own territory, with 'voluntary contributions' only to the Federation, determined by inter-Republican agreement. There would be a separate Croat monetary policy and bank of issue. The Croatian territorial army should be autonomous, and Croatian recruits to the Yugoslav army would normally do service only in Croatia. In Matica and student meetings in support of these amendments, more far-reaching ideas were discussed – revision of Croatian frontiers, the formal federalisation of the army and separate Croat membership of the U.N. All this was an open challenge to the whole concept of Yugoslavia.

Tito could hesitate no longer. On 15 November he received a special

[14] In arguing thus, Bakarić later said, the triumvirate were breaking private agreements previously reached with the Executive Committee.

[15] He had also received Brezhnev in Belgrade at the end of September, and this visit probably had more relevance than the others to the internal situation in Yugoslavia.

emissary of Bakarić in Bosnia and agreed to discussions with the Croat Executive Committee. The next evening the President of the Croat Federation of Students attacked Bakarić and warned the triumvirate in front of a mass meeting of students: 'If they do not see through a dirty behind-the-scenes game being played to divide them from the Croatian people, they may lose the confidence of the nation.'

On 22 November, just before Tito left Belgrade for a meeting with President Ceauşescu in Romania, the Croat Student Federation decided to call a strike next day at the University over the issue of retaining foreign currency. It was successfully arranged, and the students attempted to organise similar strikes in other academic institutions and in factories near Zagreb. The timing strongly suggested that the students and presumably the Matica knew of the Executive Committee's appeal to Tito, and were trying to force the issue during his absence. The 'triumvirate' however got cold feet. On the Yugoslav National Day, 29 November, Savka Dabčević-Kučar appealed on television to the students to end their strike. She had already been summoned to Tito's hunting lodge at Karadjordjovo, north of Belgrade, along with the other Croat Party leaders. On 1 December, Tito told them that his patience was at an end. On 2 December in an exceptional nation-wide broadcast, he accused the Croat leaders of having pandered to nationalists and separatists and of displaying a 'rather liberal' attitude towards what was in effect a counter-revolution. Their complaints about the economic system, he said, might well be justified, but not their attempt to press these by extra-constitutional means as essentially national questions. He found the cause of the Croat crisis in the general ideological crisis of the LCY which 'went back a long way', in the lack of 'Marxist education' and in the tolerance of 'anti-Marxist . . .and in large part pro-Western' ideas in schools and Universities.

Tito's immediate conclusion was that the Croat CC must now put their own house in order, and the message to the 'triumvirate' was clear. After Tito's broadcast of 2 December, there was a properly orchestrated public demand, even in Croatia, for their removal. Within a few days they handed in their resignation to Tito, and this was announced when the Croat CC met on 12 December. The nationalist student leaders were arrested early on the same day, and there was a display of force by the army and police in Zagreb calculated to discourage any popular intervention by the nationalists. Tito and Bakarić must have been uneasy about the course of events, but in fact the great nationalist 'mass movement' had not succeeded in penetrating adequately the Yugoslav armed forces, and collapsed rather ignominiously, with no more than minor student demonstrations to protest on its behalf. By mid-January over 400 of the nationalist leaders and their subordinates had been arrested, and the Matica Hrvatska was banned. A dramatic crisis in the history of Tito's Yugoslavia had, it seemed, reached a curiously undramatic conclusion.[16]

[16] In an interesting study, *Croat Separatism: Nationalism, Dissidence and Terrorism*, published (London, 1979) while this chapter was at the printer, Stephen Clissold notes that in 1971 Matica Hrvatska had no less than 36 branches abroad, which provided links with the Croatian émigrés, especially in West Germany. He also gives details of armed incursions into Yugoslavia by émigré Croat groups, and of activity by Croat terrorists (and counter-activity by UDBA) particularly in Sweden and Germany from 1971–8. This has led the Yugoslav Government into considerable diplomatic difficulties with those of the Federal Republic of Germany and Australia.

16

A new equilibrium?

The Croatian crisis of 1971 resulted in a victory for some kind of Yugoslav unity over extreme nationalist currents of thought in Croatia and elsewhere. The machinery of Federal government was not blocked on every important issue by a Croat veto. At the same time some Croat grievances were met. For example, the quota for retention of foreign currency earned by exports from Croatia, so long an issue inflammatory of Croat national feeling, was tripled in 1972.

There was however potential danger in Tito's solution of the crisis. It could be interpreted as victory not only for the 'Yugoslav idea', but also for a 'firm hand' at the centre, though such a possibility was firmly denied by most senior LCY spokesmen. Among the Croat leaders who resigned in December 1971 were a number (particularly Savka Dabčević-Kučar and Mika Tripalo) who had been associated with Reform and with a comparatively liberal application of communist ideas. The dangers of Croat separatism were great enough to justify their removal; but the Croat crisis could also be used to discredit the fallen leaders' liberal policies by association with extreme nationalism. In other Republics too Communist leaders might be similarly discredited – Crvenkovski for example in Macedonia, for his reformist views about the role of the LCY in society, and Stane Kavčič in Slovenia, for his advocacy of a more decisive 'occidentation' of Yugoslav foreign policy.

In January 1972 the LCY held one of those annual conferences which were intended to bridge the gap between major Party Congresses. The two main themes were how to strengthen Party control and how to ensure the fuller realisation of self-management. It was easy, particularly for foreign observers, to assume that the latter theme was for appearances only, while the former represented the essential aim of Tito and the other Party leaders. There was certainly a strong movement at the head of the LCY to give it a more positive and powerful role. Even before the Conference Tito, in an ominous speech to the

Trade Unions, had expressed his dissatisfaction with the results of the VIth Congress (1952) which had limited the LCY to a 'persuasive' rather than the 'administrative' task. In winding up the LCY Conference he emphasised the need for the continued dictatorship of the proletariat and for democratic centralism. Bureaucracy remained the main enemy. But new targets for an ideological offensive by the LCY were identified, or re-identified, in the shape of the 'technocratic' managing class, including the representatives of the central banking system. These had been closely associated with the execution of Reform, and it looked as if the Reform policy might be due for basic reconsideration.

Meanwhile the central machinery of the LCY was tightened up. The size of its Executive Bureau was reduced from 15 to 9 (including Tito), and a new political star emerged in Stane Dolanc, Secretary of the Bureau, who continued to hold this post for more than the single year originally envisaged (it was made permanent in 1974). The members of the Bureau who were replaced, or dropped altogether, included the comparatively 'liberal' Todorović and Crvenkovski.[1] Thus at least some steps had been taken towards creating a small body under Tito's influence, which could act as a central organ for the 'dictatorship of the proletariat'. At the same time there were changes in the composition of the LCY Presidency. A new rule, that its members should not simultaneously be members of the State Presidency, proved to be a convenient device for getting rid of Crvenkovski, for example, without any formal disgrace.

Foreign policy also was tending in 1971 towards a reconciliation with the conservative communists of the Soviet Union. Brezhnev's visit to Belgrade in August 1971 symbolised the end of the period of acute suspicion resulting from the invasion of Czechoslovakia. His offers of help to Tito over the solution of the Croatian problem may have been tactless, but were to some extent counteracted by a joint re-affirmation of the Belgrade and Moscow declarations of 1955–6 which had marked the first post-Stalin reconciliation. Tito's own use of the 'firm hand' in December was warmly supported by the Soviet press, as a sign that the policy of 'democratic centralism' and firm Party leadership was being reintroduced. Tito returned Brezhnev's visit in June 1972 (his first visit to Moscow for five years), and negotiations were duly begun in September for a huge new Soviet credit ($1,300 million) for the construction of new industries in Yugoslavia. The implied re-orientation of the Yugoslav

---

[1] They also included Bakarić and Kardelj, who both remained ready to play an active part in politics.

economy was an important political event in the context of inter-Republican relations from 1972 on, and suggested that the pressure of the Croat and Slovene governments for closer links with the EEC countries was now to be officially countered. At a Party seminar in Ljubljana (September 1972), Kardelj emphasised that exclusive links with Western Europe at the existing stage of Yugoslav economic development could result in excessive dependence on capitalism. Indeed by this time economists with a less ideological outlook had begun to wonder whether over the long term Yugoslavia could compete successfully in the Western market, and should not re-insure by adapting her trade more to the conditions of Eastern Europe.

2

The economic rapprochement with the Soviet Union coincided in September 1972 with a conspicuous further attempt to tighten LCY discipline and to discourage liberal or 'technocratic' tendencies. In a letter addressed to all LCY members by the Executive Bureau, Tito called for 'heightened ideological and political unity of action', a greater sense of responsibility by local and Republican branches towards Yugoslavia as a whole and more attention to the principle of 'democratic centralism'. These words were the prelude to a purge of the Serbian Party in October–November 1972 for which there was much less apparent reason than for the action nearly a year before in Croatia. Marko Nikezić, the President of the Serbian Party, and the Secretary, Latinka Perović, had a good record in handling Party affairs. They had been appointed with two main ends in view – to calm down the agitation of Serb students and intellectuals, which had attained such dangerous proportions in summer 1968, and to ensure that the 'conservative' and Serb nationalist supporters of Ranković could not use the Serb Party as a base from which to oppose the policies of 'liberal' Communism. By the end of the 1960s Nikezić had succeeded in achieving these objectives quietly enough, and had managed thoroughly to rejuvenate the Serb CC. His declared aim was to extend the scope of self-management, but he also insisted on the need for a more developed economy as a basis on which to build. He understood socialism as being 'not the return to the equality of small units in an under-developed economy, but a programme for the unity of mankind on the basis of modern means of production'.

Members of the Party must give up thinking in terms of power positions and abandon any thought of applying a 'firm hand' policy.

They must help in the extension of self-management, but this need not be equated with general opposition to large economic units or to giving a reasonably free hand to experts.

Nikezić was enthusiastically supported by most of the Belgrade Party Committee and to a large extent by the news media. Within the Serbian LC however there were many at CC and lower levels who opposed his policies and found it easy to misrepresent them. In September 1972 a campaign from inside and outside Serbia was mounted against Nikezić, Latinka Perović and their followers. It could not be said with any show of reason that they had directly encouraged Republican nationalism. In fact during the Croat crisis they had kept deliberately quiet in order not to foster ill-feeling between Serb and Croat communists. The charges against them were rather that they had been too exclusively occupied with the dangers of Federal bureaucracy and the 'firm hand'. They had encouraged the wrong sort of self-management and too much freedom for 'technocrats'; they had adopted over-passive ideas about the proper role of the LCY, and refused freedom of discussion to opponents of their ideas. Their negligence, it was alleged, had enabled a 'technocratic' bureaucracy to strengthen unduly their power positions within the parliamentary and executive machine, within enterprises at the expense of Workers' Councils or assemblies, and particularly within Yugoslavia's main financial institutions. Tito accused Republican Party branches of frustrating the 'workers' amendments' to the 1963 Constitution put forward in summer 1971 at the height of the Croat crisis, and designed to subject principally the big banks and insurance companies to popular control. He also pointed out that most of these financial giants were located in Belgrade. The conclusions were that strong action would be necessary by the central authorities of the LCY, and that the first step to be taken must be the purge of the Serbian Party, which had deliberately connived at or even encouraged excessive 'technocracy'.[2]

The purge was not accomplished smoothly. Tito feared that the Party Presidency was too thoroughly permeated with 'liberalism' of the wrong kind, and did not try to secure its backing before meeting on 9 October with the Serbian leaders and a large number of lower officials from the Serbian Republic and Belgrade, whom he expected to support him against Nikezić. In the event – unique in the political annals of Communist Yugoslavia – the meeting was suspended after

[2] It is significant that during the run-up to the XIth Party Congress (March–June 1978) the weekly *Nin* serialised a one-sided account of this political crisis, under the title 'The Reckoning with Liberalism'.

four days' inconclusive discussion. It was reconvened on 16 October, when Tito made a fuller speech, voicing his resentment that for the first time he had been criticised unfavourably within the Serbian Party. The texts of this and of the Executive Bureau's letter of early September were published on 18 October. Tito had thus made the dismissal of Nikezić a matter of public confidence.

There was no question about what the outcome would be. On 21 October the Serb Central Committee met to receive the resignations of Nikezić and Latinka Perović, shortly followed by those of the Presidents of the Vojvodina and Belgrade Party branches. These resignations were succeeded by others of greater national importance. Tepavac stepped down from the post of Foreign Secretary, and (quite unexpectedly) Koča Popović, a former Foreign Secretary, who had chosen Nikezić to succeed him, resigned from the State Presidency. Stane Kavčić quitted his post as Prime Minister of Slovenia and the chief editors (among others) resigned from the staff of the respected Belgrade daily, *Politika*, and the weekly *Nin*.

The whole action was generally interpreted as resulting from a mixture of the need to keep an even political balance between Serbs and Croats, a personal desire by Tito to be rid of Nikezić, and a swing back towards a type of communism more likely to be acceptable to the Soviet Government. It was understandable that nationalist feeling should continue to simmer in Zagreb after December 1971, and that Tito, as a Croat by birth himself, should look for the next opportunity to show that he dealt even-handedly with heretical doctrines in Belgrade as in Zagreb. This however can only have been a contributory cause to the action against the new Party leadership in Serbia. Nikezić himself had probably been for some time a destined victim. He was widely thought to have opposed Tito's Middle Eastern policy in early June 1967; to have been sceptical about the priority sometimes given, not least by Tito himself, to links with the newly-independent Asian and African nations, over the need for closer economic and political relations with the EEC countries; and also to have been at least very cautious in his attitude towards the Soviet Union (he was certainly regarded as anti-Soviet in Moscow). Finally he had compounded the offence of an independent stance on matters of foreign policy by expressing doubts about the wisdom of Tito's final steps against the Zagreb 'triumvirate', and about the dangers of Stalinism implicit in using a 'strong-hand' policy against them. One of their most determined opponents in Croatia, Jure Bilić, later wrote in *Politika* (10 February 1974) that 'The Great Serb liberals defended the former fraction in the

Croat Party leadership and demanded that it should not be destroyed'.

Thus in the eyes of Tito and the inner group of LCY leaders there
was a strong reason to get rid of Nikezić. Although the case against him
was presented in terms of preferring 'technocracy' to self-management,
his fall seemed to portend a literal 're-orientation' of Yugoslav foreign
policy and a re-centralisation in Party affairs.

3

'Self-management' was a slogan on which everyone could agree, but it
implied very different ideas to various constituent sections of Yugoslav
society. To the Croat patriot it had meant freedom for the Croat
Republican government and Party from Federal interference. To the
reconstituted Serb Party under Nikezić it had meant freedom for the
'technocrat' to build up the Serb economy with only the minimum of
political guidance. To the dominant leaders of the LCY it now seemed
to mean the liberation of enterprises from the covert rule of the big
economic combines and banks, and the subjection of 'technocrats' to
effective control by workers in their own enterprises. This concept moreover was backed not only by the more official Party ideologists, but
also to a considerable extent by the intellectuals and philosophers of the
Praxis group, who wrote from a radical neo-Marxist standpoint, and
on these points represented many of the more idealistic among the
younger generation.

The bitter truth in 1971–2 was that, even apart from the difficulties
involved in making any important decision at Federal level, the problems which were to have been solved by Economic Reform had refused
to go away. Something had indeed been achieved. Good harvests in
both years were of great help to the economy, and two successive
devaluations of the dinar in January and December 1971 (by 38.6%
in all) had helped to boost exports. The structure of Yugoslav exports
also had been diversified. Raw material exports were much less important than before as a percentage of total exports (1961 24.7%, 1971
11.2%), and this was particularly welcome as a sign that the Yugoslav
economy was no longer of the 'colonial' type. In 1971 57% of Yugoslav exports were in the 'highly finished' category, and their destination
included some of the chief industrial countries. Shipbuilding had
become a particularly important industry with the Soviet Union and
the U.K. as principal buyers.

At home however inflation was rampant. The rise in personal

incomes above any increase of productivity, and the over-free granting of short-term credits to help firms in financial trouble – familiar phenomena in the U.K. – contributed heavily to the rise in prices. Professional economists claimed that they had given adequate warnings from 1965 onwards and were bitter about the lack of economic leadership and expertise at the top. In 1971, the distinguished economist Branko Horvat wrote in *Praxis*:

The question arises: why for a full five years did the judgements of political and state functionaries deviate to such a degree from the judgement of scholars?...The practical problems of controlling inflation, ending the liquidity crisis, and promoting faster economic growth in the less-developed regions are being tackled pragmatically under the immediate pressures of the moment and are often contrary to the principles on which policies are supposed to be based.

Horvat's article appeared in 1971. In 1972 some improvements had occurred in the general economic situation, but even so the crucial agreement on a basis for the distribution of funds to the under-developed areas was not reached until the end of the year, and then only as the result of intervention by the FEC. The essential fact is that from 1971 there was a manifest crisis in the Yugoslav economy, and that the 'liberal' solutions of Reform were subject to heavy criticism not only from 'conservatives' who wanted to take any excuse for re-centralising Yugoslavia and drawing it closer to the Soviet Union.

Such people no doubt existed, but would still have found it difficult to advocate use of the 'firm hand'. For them, as for others, the least divisive way of introducing a new policy for the economic and political development of Yugoslavia was to do so in the name of self-management, thus reverting to the concept preached by the CTY leaders in the late 1950s and revived in the 'Workers' Amendments' to the 1963 Constitution put forward in summer 1971. The essence of this concept was to widen and deepen self-management, and to protect the workers against interference not only by Federal, Republican or indeed Communal bureaucrats (and elected Assemblies), but also by large integrated enterprises and banks which had indeed become considerable and apparently autonomous powers in the land. Even Belgrade newspapers (and the attack on the banks was linked with that against the Serbian Party leadership) admitted in September 1972 some very significant facts about the concentration of their power. The three largest banks in Yugoslavia were in Belgrade, and controlled, together with other Serbian banks, nearly two-thirds of total Yugoslav bank assets – the comparable figure for Croatia, industrially the more important Republic, was only 17%. The proportion of foreign trade business was even more favourable to Belgrade firms, which were involved in over two-thirds of Yugoslavia's foreign trade. Here, it seemed, was a definite and important target for the LCY in their campaign for nation-wide self-management.

They also campaigned vigorously against 'bureaucratising' elements within enterprises – directors who tended to make themselves per-manent, 'technocrats' who blinded ordinary men by science, and even Workers' Councils who lost touch with their own grass roots. Control of such elements should be strengthened, partly by more frequent and better conducted meetings of Workers' Assemblies, partly by ensuring that elected representatives acted more as delegates and less as pleni-potentiaries in their own sphere. And control could best be ensured by more activity on the part of the CTY and the LCY. Such had been the main themes of the second LCY annual conference in January 1972. They were prominently emphasised again in the purge of the Serb LC, and in the course of 1973 they were worked out in more detail.

Again it is interesting to find much of the essence of the Party ideo-logists' case for wider and deeper self-management echoed in rather different terms by the radical intelligentsia connected with *Praxis*, who stood on this issue for a wider public. Mihailo Marković for example, writing in 1972, expressed the disillusion of many young students and academics at what they saw as Yugoslavia's side-slip from Stalinism to market socialism, and at the undesirable consequences of Economic Reform – a policy which deliberately sacrificed certain socialist ideals and achievements in the name of quicker development and more free-dom. To rid the country of equality in poverty, the reformers had permitted a state of affairs in which some remained poor and others enriched themselves overnight. The opening of Yugoslavia to the out-side world had its very bad side: 'It has brought us certain achieve-ments of bourgeois Liberalism – more freedom of speech, for religious propaganda, for travel, for business transactions, for getting rich, for opening foreign currency markets, for entertainment, for pornography, and so on.' But since 1963 there had been no further word of true democracy. Marković and other radical critics of the LCY leaders expressed constant fears about the excessive power which these could easily come to enjoy under the existing system and the dangers of a return to Stalinism. In 1972 however Marxists and neo-Marxists were at one in their criticism of the then existing machinery of self-manage-ment, both at parliamentary and at enterprise level, and about the need for some political reform which would make 'self-management' into a reality. This is an important part of the background for the preparations which took place throughout 1973 for the Xth Congress of the LCY and for the revised Constitution of 1974.

4

Yugoslavia's Fourth Constitution was promulgated on 21 February 1974. It is perhaps the longest and most complicated Constitution in the world,[3] and embodies aspirations (e.g. the right to family planning and a clean environment) as much as it regulates realities – family planning has far to go in the Kosmet, and the realities of Belgrade include an environment very heavily polluted by excessive motor traffic. The most important trends of the new Law are however clear enough. It is intended in the first place to provide a firm legal basis for a type of self-management much more extensive than had been realised in the years of Economic Reform, and particularly to provide safeguards against most imaginable forms of 'technocratic', managerial or financial control over the product of the worker's labour and the method of his work.

The problem in Yugoslav theoretic terms was to prevent 'social property' from being appropriated as 'group property' – a process which, it was implied, had frequently taken place within nominally self-managing firms over the last twenty years. One method of de-privatising 'group property' had been heavy taxation, e.g. on fixed assets or in respect of a peculiarly favourable site; but this method had been discredited as involving too much bureaucracy. Now the principal means of realising a new and genuine form of industrial self-manage-ment was to be the universal evolution of new and smaller self-management units within existing enterprises. These were in fact to be federalised, or indeed confederalised. The new basic unit was to be the specialised branch or 'working unit', which had made its first appear-ance in the late 1950s, and in 1971 had been rechristened the Basic Organisation of Associated Labour (BOAL). The original unit, the enterprise, now rechristened as 'Organ of Associated Labour', was to exist vis-à-vis the outside world as the representative of an association of BOALs; but as such it was to have only delegated powers, and only such income for limited purposes as the BOALs agreed to give it. The BOALs were to co-operate with each other on a contractual basis, and were free to conclude contracts ('social compacts') with BOALs outside their own enterprise (though in practice there were inducements to

[3] The Constitution of India may be longer.

give preference to associated BOALs). It was provided that the BOAL should be so far as possible autonomous, and in particular that, within the terms of its original compacts with the other BOALs and the management of the enterprise itself, it should dispose freely of its own net income (the gross income would still in effect be subject to various Federal, Republican and local taxes or levies). The 'social compacts' had to be in conformity with the Yugoslav Constitution and statutes, and were legally binding on the parties which concluded or acceded to them.

There were further elaborate provisions to separate, so to speak, the 'legislative' and 'executive' branches within the BOALs and within the enterprises, and to subject the executive or managerial machinery to strict control, thus guarding against the emergence of a 'techno-managerial' bureaucracy. Managerial staff were not to be eligible for election to Workers' Councils. Directors were to be re-christened 'individual management organs' and were to be elected (for a term of four years, renewable) from a list proposed by a special commission, in which the local assembly had equal representation.

The reform of the banking structure was of more immediate importance, given the political circumstances under which the new Constitution was prepared. The basic concept was that banks should be responsible only to the enterprises or BOALs which contributed capital to them. In particular the credit committees were to consist of representatives of the shareholders, and to exclude not only bank employees (who were regarded as producing nothing of real value) but also representatives of the local 'socio-political communities' (in particular, Communes). All funds earned by the bank's credit operations were to be distributed among the shareholding enterprises, after deduction of the bank's reasonable operating expenses. Thus the accumulation of power by 'non-productive' committees of financial experts was to be prevented, and a curb was also to be put on 'political' investments by the local Communal authorities.

The area of self-management was also extended under the new Constitution to the social services, with the idea of encouraging more independent activity by citizens, not only as producers, but also as consumers of social services (health and education in particular). This was not by any means a new departure, but previous efforts to work towards, for example, a self-managing and self-financing educational system had given rise to grave difficulties and bitter debates in the early years of the Reform period. In defining the means by which the concept of self-management should be applied to the social services, the

Constitution was more than usually normative rather than definitive.
The essential concept has however remained that services up to a
minimum level should be guaranteed by the Federal or Republican
governments; while above that level needs should be established and
finance provided by agreement between representatives of local government, technical experts in e.g. the health and education fields, citizens
and local enterprises, both as 'consumers' of services and as sources of
finance. These should meet together formally as local 'communities of
interest' in various social fields. The ideal end result would be that such
communities should replace Federal, Republican or local government
over a wide field in collecting revenue and providing services.

To correspond with these extensions of self-management, the whole
parliamentary machinery of Yugoslavia was also to be re-organised, to
make it as representative as possible and also as responsive as possible
to those represented by it. The machinery prescribed by the 1974
Constitution was extremely complicated, but the essential characteristic
was to introduce a delegate system at all levels. The first stage was the
election of delegations consisting of between ten and thirty members,
by the 65,000 BOALs and equivalent working units (such as agricultural co-operatives); all voters (whether or not members of working
units) simultaneously elected similar delegations to represent the 12,000
local communities – the smallest unit of local government. Candidates'
political respectability, from the LCY point of view, was assured by the
constitutional provision that they should be proposed by SAWPY, and
the make-up of the delegations had constitutionally to 'correspond to
the social composition of the basic self-managing organization or community concerned' – i.e. there should be a majority of worker delegates,
and the danger of technocracy should be eliminated from the start.
The delegates at the first level – about a million in all – then elected
delegates to two Chambers in the Communal assemblies – a Chamber
of Associated Labour to represent the citizens as producers, and a
Municipal Chamber to represent them as inhabitants of local communities. A third Chamber at Communal level was formed by delegates elected by 'socio-political organisations' – i.e. the LCY, SAWPY,
the CTY, and others. Thus the LCY assured itself a new and key
position in local government. The Communal assemblies elected delegates from the appropriate Chambers to the second intermediate level –
for the Republics and Provinces. The third and final stage was the
election of delegates to the two Chambers of the Federal Assembly.
Here the confederate principle predominated. Thirty delegates for each
Republic and twenty for each province were nominated by the 'basic

delegations' (i.e. those elected by working units etc. at the first stage) from lists prepared by SAWPY, and were then elected by the Communal Assemblies to the Federal Chamber; the second Chamber, that of Republics and Provinces, was made up of twelve delegates from each Republican Assembly and eight from each Provincial one, elected by those assemblies from among their own members, and responsible to them.

Only at the first stage – the election of 'basic delegations' – did the individual voter have any voice and that only within the limits determined by SAWPY. The system discriminated in favour of the industrial worker, who had at least two votes, one as producer, one as inhabitant of a district – and possibly another as a member of a Trade Union, SAWPY or the LCY. The LCY's influence was further increased by the special position of the 'social-political Chambers', which were not subject, like the others, to the limitation about 'social composition', and by a further constitutional provision that delegates were required to retain their jobs during the time spent in political work. This was designed to ensure that all except the 'social-political' delegates should be part-time politicians, who would not be inclined to develop any professional interest in a political career.[4] Thus at the parliamentary level, as in industry, a serious effort was made to reduce to a minimum the role of the expert, entrenched among his mysteries.

More immediately relevant to the causes of the nationalist crisis of 1971 were the provisions of the Constitution confirming the amendments of that year, which had virtually confederalised the Yugoslav Federation. In particular the amendment was confirmed that listed the subjects on which the agreement of the six Republics and two Provinces had to be secured before Federal legislation was enacted. The principle of Republican equality was further exemplified by the new arrangements for election to both Federal Chambers on a basis of regional parity, and by the provision for a nine-member Federal State Presidency (one from each Republic and Province, and Tito himself).

The promulgation of the 1974 Constitution was followed in April by the Xth Congress of the LCY, which indicated the general sense in which the Constitution would immediately be interpreted. There were some ominous signs here for Western observers. The cult of Tito's personality was more conspicuous than before; the name of Lenin was frequently invoked; Yugoslavia's Stalinist age, 1945–50, was described

---

[4] In the mid-sixties the Federal Assembly had developed its own cadre of professional committee-men, who could often by-pass good LCY men with no very clear idea of what were the proper limits of their activity.

more politely than in the past as the 'period of revolutionary étatism'. The theme of democratic centralism was strongly emphasised, with more stress on the need to carry out decisions uniformly than on the need to reach them democratically. The leading role of the LCY was also a constant theme and it was clear that the LCY organisations in enterprises, reactivated since 1971, should be ready to intervene actively in the selection of personnel and in making key policy decisions.

At the same time there was no sign of open reversion to a 'communal economy', and no open break – as foreshadowed more than once by Tito in previous years – with the crucial decision of the VIth Congress in 1952 that the LCY should play a 'persuasive' rather than an 'administrative' role. There was to be more direction and more political activity by the LCY, but the object was still to remove obstacles to self-management and to curb the power of 'élitist' groups who tried to oppose it for their own limited interests. Indeed the Party statutes were changed to provide for an increased degree of flexibility within the LCY itself, which would enable it to respond to initiatives from the organisations at basic level.

There was nothing in all this which need prevent a return in practice to a much stricter and dictatorial Party rule, but the fact that such rule would still be exercised in the name of 'self-management' was still important. It might be no more than an exhibition of decent hypocrisy – the tribute of dictatorship to democratic principles. It might on the other hand indicate, as the whole evolution of the 1974 Constitution had indicated, that those among the Yugoslav leaders who wished to re-centralise were aware that they would have to do so carefully, and that self-management in a fairly normal sense of the words still meant a lot to others within the LCY. The Party had indeed changed considerably since its IXth Congress in 1969. Of its roughly 1,100,000 members over an eighth had been removed, and about a quarter of these had not been replaced. At the top the Party Presidency had lost twenty-one of the fifty-two members confirmed at the IXth Congress. Only eight of these had been made to resign for ideological reasons, and eleven of those who had left were nominally under no disgrace. But there was a marked difference in political complexion by 1974. The total number was reduced to thirty-nine. Nikezić, Tripalo and other 'liberals' were out. Stambolić and Koliševski, whose political careers had in 1969 seemed to be over, were back, and with them a number of rather inconspicuous new 'conservative' routineers. The Executive Bureau too, now re-christened the Executive Committee, for the first time included members – three in number – who had played no part in the Partisan war. The most formidable of these new men was Stane Dolanc, the Slovene secretary of the Bureau.

A new look, certainly; but there remained either in positions of power, or prominent among ordinary LCY members, many of the veteran initiators of Reform. Kardelj and Bakarić, still very close to Tito, were members of the Presidency; so were Gligorov and Sergej Krajgher. Todorović, Crvenkovski, Tempo and Koča Popović were all still around, not prominent, but not disgraced. Democratic centralism was the order of the day, with the accent on centralism and discipline; but within the small circle close to Tito there remained leaders who were unlikely to forget, even under new political conditions, their vision of a self-managing society as the ultimate goal.

5

The formal framework of the new model Yugoslav democracy was completed in November 1976 by a further important law – the Associated Labour Act of November 1976. This, like the Constitution of 1974, is an enormously long and complicated document, running in the official English translation to 400 pages and 671 clauses. After the new Federal Assembly was set up in accordance with the delegate principles of the 1974 constitution, a special commission was formed to bring the existing laws in the field of labour relations into line with the new constitution, and to prepare new laws for this purpose on 'social property', organisations of associated labour, and self-management agreements and 'social compacts'. Public discussion on the various draft bills was organised on a large scale and completed in summer 1975. It was then decided to codify the separate draft bills into a single Law on Associated Labour. This in turn was subject in draft form to public discussion from BOAL level upwards. As the preface to the final version of the Law makes clear,

The breadth of, the massive response to, and the intensity of, the public discussion of the preliminary draft were closely associated with the socio-political activity of the Socialist Alliance...and of the Confederation of Trade Unions, and particularly with the stands taken at the Third meeting of the Central Committee of the LCY, at which the immediate tasks of the League of Communists in the struggle for the further development of socialist self-management socio-economic relations in associated labour were considered.

It would indeed be hard to imagine that public discussion of such a long and complicated law could end in anything but chaos or apathy without a good deal of explanation in simple terms and firm political guidance.

The 1976 law to some extent confirmed arrangements which had been put into practice since early in 1974. However it was also, to a greater extent even than the 1974 Constitution, a normative law, explaining the framework within which self-management should be instituted, and pointing the main directions in which it should be developed. In his speech introducing the Law to the Federal Assembly, the President, Kiro Gligorov, emphasised both the principal objects of the Law and certain problems connected with it.

Politically, it should now be superfluous in Yugoslavia 'to speak of political power outside the sphere of associated labour'. The new Act made impossible the 'existence of any kind of monopoly by anybody in the disposition of the means of production and surplus labour (neither through private property, state property nor group property)'. The Act was thus meant to guard, though Gligorov did not put it this way, against the revival of capitalism, state socialism, or rule by Republics, Banks or technocrats. Its effect would be reinforced by the delegate system in the Assemblies – 'a negation of formal and representative democracy'.

Looking to the future, Gligorov saw the 1976 Act, with its insistence on the right of workers to dispose of the net income of their own working units, as providing important 'stimuli for economic expansion, while preserving the equality of the nations and nationalities of Yugoslavia'. Under the Act, BOALs would have 'enormous latitude for concluding self-managing agreements and social compacts'.

The implications of Gligorov's attitude were threefold. The new system, if properly applied, would allow the BOALs to make significant net profits; the workers would see that their interest lay in investing a good proportion of these, rather than in the maximum immediate increase of personal income; they would see also that the most profitable sort of investment would be on a nation-wide basis, rather than exclusively in the economically better developed Republics (the third of these assumptions has always seemed the most doubtful).

Subsequent commentaries show that the ideal is a network of 'social compacts', covering not only the whole geographical area of Yugoslavia, but also all stages in production, marketing and foreign trade contracts. Gligorov was insistent that financial autonomy must not remain simply an ideal:

We should develop maximum sensitivity regarding respect for workers' inalienable rights concerning the disposition of income received. We must

put an end to the practice of declaring ourselves. . .in favour of this fundamental principle while forgetting it in actuality in the name of one or
other interest and aim. Respect for the principle should be assured
through full statutory and judicial protection, but we should also make
such practices i.e. any practices contrary to the principle, socially in-
famous.

Even a cursory reading of the 1976 Act is enough to show that there
are many actual and many potential limitations on the financial
autonomy of the BOALs, or putting the same point in a different way,
that it may run counter to other obligations assumed by different self-
managing sections of the Yugoslav Community. At one end of the scale
are certain general obligations laid down in the Act, e.g. Article 47, 'to
ensure conditions for the continuous rise in income', and Articles 43
and 44 about safety measures and the protection and improvement of
the environment. Considerable limitations may again be implicit in the
provisions of Article 20 that the mutual relations of workers and enterprises shall be regulated 'in conformity with the uniform foundations
of the system of social planning, the uniform foundations of the price
system, the uniform foundations of the credit system and the common
foundations of credit policy. . .'

Then there are comparatively precise definitions of charges to be
made on gross income, including (Article 110) obligations 'towards
basic organisations. . .in the spheres of education, science, culture,
health, social welfare. . .' and liability to a special charge on income
resulting from exceptionally favourable natural or market conditions
(Article 111 – which is designed in terms of Yugoslav theory to lessen
the gap between 'social property' and 'group property').

Further general obligations are listed in the definition (Article 116)
of net income:

In allocating net income, workers in basic organisations shall be forced to
allot resources for the promotion and expansion of the material base of,
and for the creation and renewal of reserves in line with the nature of, the
activities performed by basic organisations and the role they play in social
reproduction, with a view to realising social reproduction in the basic
organisations and society as a whole. . .

The sentence, not untypical, continues for another 30 words.

Given the extremely complex nature of the new system, the general
wording of the crucial Articles of the new Act, and the part played by
the CTY since the mid-1950s in promoting the concept of self-management at enterprise level and below, it is not surprising to find that the
position of the CTY as stimulators and watchdogs of self-management

is strongly entrenched in the Act. Article 36 for example provides that Trade Unions 'may institute proceedings. . .to ensure workers their socio-political and other management rights. . .may initiate and propose the conclusion of self-management agreements' and shall take part in the conclusion of agreements 'whose purpose is to regulate mutual relations among workers. . .or to determine grounds and scales for the distribution of income and the allocation of resources for personal incomes, and shall sign such agreements'.

The Associated Labour Act is in sum a very complex and ambiguous document. It does indeed provide a charter in general terms for the extension in breadth and depth of industrial autonomy. It cannot however prescribe in detail how this is to be done. It relies a good deal on the social conscience of the workers to fulfil its more general aspirations. It also contains clauses which could be used by non-industrial self-managing bodies, particularly by delegates in the chain of Assemblies, to limit industrial autonomy. And it provides strong positions for the LCY, and the CTY, from which they may be able, particularly as the power of 'technocratic' influence groups is diminished, to exert a crucial influence on the economic and social development of Yugoslavia. The history of Tito's Yugoslavia suggests that normative political philosophy and legislation is important. It also suggests that practice can quickly change the general direction in which the letter of theory and law is applied, and that the role of political or philosophical watchdog is not easy for Party or Trade Unions to maintain.

17

Recent trends

There were no major domestic crises or drastic changes of policy in Yugoslavia between the Xth Party Congress in spring 1974 and the XIth in summer 1978. However the international context changed considerably. Theoretically indeed Yugoslav foreign policy remained unaltered. Increasing emphasis on 'self-management' at home was accompanied by further insistence on non-alignment and on the independence of Communist parties in the world and European contexts respectively. Non-alignment has been described since the end of 1975 as 'the consistent expression of Yugoslav socialist self-managing practice'; if basic units of enterprises within Yugoslavia are to enjoy independence, so should the basic national units of the international community, regardless of their size, geographical location, and relation to the Great Powers. Non-alignment, it is frequently said, represents a permanent commitment (or non-commitment?) for Yugoslavia.

It remains easier even for Yugoslav theorists to define non-alignment negatively than positively. *Ex hypothesi*, they say, it involves no commitment to any 'bloc', not even to a 'Third World' bloc of underdeveloped countries. Neither should it involve closing one's eyes to the issues between the 'blocs', nor any *a priori* neutrality on such issues. The non-aligned nations must work, particularly in the context of the U.N., for an equitable solution of international problems, both political and economic, on a basis of equality between nations, and each problem should be judged separately on a purely factual basis.

This is the theory of the matter. The practice of non-alignment has become notably more difficult. There have still been occasions in recent years when the Western powers could justifiably feel that non-alignment was little more than a decent mask for the pursuit of an essentially anti-Western policy. Miloš Minić, for example, Yugoslav Foreign Secretary at the time, listed in June 1976 at Algiers a 'chain of focusses of crises', for which the Western powers were generally held responsible, from the Western Mediterranean, through Cyprus, the Middle

East, and South Africa to Korea.[1] Such occasions however have become less frequent. It is doubtful whether, even at the height of their concern with Western neo-imperialism, the Yugoslavs have succeeded very well in fostering 'objectively' pro-Soviet policies under a non-aligned label. And by now circumstances have changed considerably.

The principal common factor between the large number of nations which now participate in non-aligned conferences is some degree of economic under-development. They have a good case for forming a common front at the United Nations and pressing for e.g. a new set of ground rules to cover international trade. They want to ensure that frontiers are as open as possible to Third World exports, that arrangements are made to ensure some stability of markets for 'colonial' raw materials, and that terms of loans and credits to the Third World are not too onerous. At times Yugoslav analysts have admitted that the essence of non-aligned activity lies and should lie in promoting new movements in the field of international commerce and finance – or in official Yugoslav terms 'the process of economic decolonisation is the essential path in the search for a more just exchange of goods between the developing and the developed countries'.

From the third non-aligned summit, held at Lusaka in 1970, onwards through the fourth and fifth summits (Algiers, September 1973, and Colombo, August 1976), the action programmes for economic co-operation provided the main area of agreement for the non-aligned countries. They envisaged first of all accelerated trade and aid between the countries themselves, and in the second place more pressure on the developed countries through the 'Group of 77' at the U.N.

So far as the first objective is concerned, the importance of the economic links between Yugoslavia and the less developed countries of Asia, Africa and Latin America is much smaller than might be deduced either from Tito's visionary statements of the 1950s or from the enthusiasm of Yugoslav participation at non-aligned Conferences. Yugoslav trade with Asian, African and Latin American countries in 1977 amounted to about one-sixth of Yugoslav foreign trade as a whole, with exports at about 20% and imports at about 17% of Yugoslav totals, and a Yugoslav deficit of some 8,000 million dinars on a trade total of 43,000 million. Since 1973 the trend has been towards an increase of Yugoslav exports[2] and over the same years there has also

---

[1] Perhaps this speech strengthened the 'positive assessment' of the activity of the non-aligned on the international scene, given by Soviet representatives to Minić during his visit to Moscow in December 1975.

[2] The figures are increased by the amount of Yugoslav aid in building projects, particularly to Kenya and other African countries.

been a decline in imports, not particularly significant since the 1974 figures were swollen by emergency oil imports from Iraq. Yugoslav pressure within the U.N. for a 'New International Economic Order' has no doubt been more satisfactory to the 'Group of 77' and it is in the effort for redistribution of world resources that the interests of the various non-aligned countries (now more than 77 in number) generally coincide.

In the more strictly political field it has become increasingly hard, as the Yugoslavs officially admit, to find common aims on which the very large and disparate group of non-aligned countries can unite. Disarmament is a safe subject, and pressure within the United Nations may be marginally useful; but the super-powers have to agree with each other on a step-by-step programme if any progress is to be made, and in practice many of the non-aligned countries are more interested in building up their own defences than in taking any steps themselves towards 'General and Complete Disarmament'. Meanwhile, whatever may be said about economic 'neo-imperialism', general expressions of political support for liberation movements have become increasingly irrelevant. Such movements can now be directed against well-established Asian or African governments, and have been so directed by Soviet advisers and Cuban troops. At least from spring 1978 the Yugoslavs have strongly and all but openly opposed Soviet and Cuban attempts to re-direct the non-aligned movement into an old-style anti-imperialist anti-Western policy.[3] Such attempts have tended to split the non-aligned movement, to cause doubt about the political reality of non-alignment, and to give rise to disquiet among many member countries of the Organisation of African States. At the XIth Party Congress, Miloš Minić, still Foreign Secretary and not renowned for pro-Western tendencies, spoke frankly about the dangers to the non-aligned countries. All socialist countries, he said, could not automatically be considered as their allies: 'We cannot understand or accept the stubborn insistence of certain people that it [non-alignment] should be confined only to the struggle against imperialism, Colonialism and neo-imperialism.'

There was no reason why the non-aligned should not also oppose 'hegemonism' (the normal euphemism for Soviet domination) and indeed 'it may happen that hegemonism in a historic sense is a sort of inheritor of those forms of domination and exploitation which, under

---

[3] Early in 1979 the Vietnamese invasion of non-aligned Cambodia and Chinese counter-action have faced the Yugoslavs with similar and very awkward problems in Asia.

pressure..., are disappearing from the historic scene; for example, colonialism...'

Similar doubts were subsequently expressed by the Yugoslav leaders at the conference of non-aligned Foreign Ministers in Belgrade (August 1978).

In this context there has been an important rapprochement between the Yugoslavs and the Chinese, who openly attack Soviet imperialism. The visit of Chairman Hua to Belgrade in August 1978 marked an important movement in Yugoslav foreign policy.[4] This was all the more unwelcome to the Soviet Government, in that Hua had already paid a very well-publicised visit to Bucharest. Tito thus appeared to be associated with a conspicuous gesture of independence by a member state of the Warsaw Pact.

Here was a demonstration of the implications of the Yugoslav doctrine of 'independent ways to socialism'. In the same context the problem of 'Eurocommunism' is extremely important for the Soviet Union and Western Europe alike. If Tito's commitment to non-alignment has in the past worked against the West, his commitment to the independence of national Communist Parties, or self-management in the international socialist context, has begun again to work against Moscow. The most conspicuous instance of this tendency has been Yugoslavia's strong support of the Spanish Communist leader, Santiago Carillo, in direct opposition to Moscow's criticism of him. In its bilateral relations with Yugoslavia the Soviet Government has from time to time been brought to re-affirm the principles of the Belgrade and Moscow meetings of 1955 and 1956, involving equal rights for the Yugoslav Government and the LCY vis-à-vis the Soviet Government and the CPSU. The Soviet attitude to the other Communist Parties of Eastern Europe and elsewhere has been quite different. The Soviet leaders have never abandoned the idea of a 'leading role' for the CPSU; and with the growth or revival of comparatively independent Communist Parties in Western Europe, they have rated even more highly the importance of a common 'party line' co-ordinated in Moscow. It appeared therefore as something of a triumph for Tito when at the Conference of European Communist Parties held at Berlin in June–July 1976, Yugoslav ideas about the free exchange of views among equal partners prevailed, and no attempt was made to issue a binding detailed statement of policy in a communiqué after the Conference.

Yugoslav official commentaries drew the obvious contrast between

---

[4] Formally this visit was the natural outcome of President Tito's visit to Peking a year before.

the Cominform Conference of summer 1948, which outlawed Yugoslavia, and the proceedings at Berlin in 1976. Here was for them a formal turning-point in the relations among Communist and workers' parties on many basic questions. In his main speech at Berlin, Tito emphasised the importance of links and co-operation between Communist Parties and 'the expanded forces of democracy, progress and socialism' in the context of 'the fight against imperialism, vestiges of colonialism, neo-colonialism' [and in the] 'effort to secure radical change in non-equal economic relations throughout the world.' It is no doubt important that Yugoslav ideas about inter-Communist relations have obtained so much theoretical backing in the European Communist world. However in Europe itself and in the Eurocommunist context, the Soviet Government seem no more likely to pay attention to the equality between Communist Parties and the need for a 'popular front' policy than they did to their own declaration of 30 October 1956, about the principles of a Socialist Commonwealth.

As regards direct East–West relations, particularly in Europe, Tito could claim for a time that reality had been catching up with Yugoslav policies. The first important fact for him about the Helsinki Conference of European states in August 1975 was that it took place. Here was a conference at which all European countries were represented, nominally at least 'on an equal basis', and not as members of blocs. Here was a meeting at which the Yugoslavs could at least in limited degree revert to their once-coveted role of mediator between East and West, and in the long-continued preparatory negotiations the Yugoslav delegation played a reasonably independent role. The Yugoslav leaders were glad to see the post-war settlement of Europe effectively confirmed by the Helsinki meeting, even if this did not involve a formal treaty. They were glad to subscribe to statements about the desirability of increased economic and cultural exchanges between East and West, though also sharp enough to know that an increase did not depend primarily on any agreed formulation of general principles. They may well have believed that some further détente, in the literal sense of decreased tension, could lead to some gradual concrete progress in arms control and towards disarmament. Quite as important for them was the calculation, which they made along with other Eastern European countries more closely bound to the Soviet Union, that the obligations assumed by all Governments signatory of the Helsinki Final Act would marginally help to restrain the Soviet Government from further interventions in the affairs of the socialist countries of Eastern Europe, Romania and Yugoslavia included.

The results of Helsinki over three years have included no increase in mutual confidence between the 'blocs' in Europe, much less any of that sense of 'euphoria' about East–West relations which was so much dreaded before the Conference by responsible statesmen and officials not least in Britain. The Yugoslavs have had their particular reasons for disillusion. Less than a year after the signature of the Final Act they were reminded that some ghosts remained unlaid. The Bulgarians discovered in their census of December 1975, that there were no Macedonian nationals in their country (with the implication that others who called themselves Macedonian were in fact Bulgarian) and prepared for the centenary of the Treaty of San Stefano by reviving memories of the Greater Bulgaria which the Russian Government had wished to create in their own interest. On the other side the suggestion by Henry Kissinger's Under-Secretary, Sonnenfeld, in May 1976 that the U.S. administration should tolerate or even encourage tighter Soviet links with the Socialist countries of Eastern Europe evoked very sharp reaction from the Yugoslav leaders. They saw here a reminder that Great Powers might still do deals with each other at the expense of small independent ones, and that the U.S. administration might be prepared either to abandon Yugoslavia to the Soviet sphere of influence or to consent to the break-up of the Federation.[5]

The greatest subject of anxiety for the Yugoslavs has however been the general deterioration of East–West relations in Europe since 1975. For some time they tended to put the greater share of blame on the West, for insisting so strongly on the fulfilment of the human rights articles, and thus endangering the spirit of détente. The implication was that if more progress was made on 'confidence building' measures, arms control, and increased commercial and financial exchanges, a climate would be produced in which more progress could also be made on human rights. Such a view stemmed no doubt partly from the fear that their own record in this respect, however good by comparison with that of the Soviet Union, was not perfect; perhaps a deeper fear was that the Western powers were using the human rights issue as a means of promoting their own ideology and interfering in the internal affairs of Eastern Europe. Above all, there was a desire to preserve the appearances and atmosphere of détente. If these were dispelled, whether by Western insistence on the 'human rights' issue or by Soviet attitudes and actions, the Soviet Government (particularly if involved in a 'succession crisis') might revise its 'Westpolitik', adopt more openly

[5] The 50/50 division of influence agreed between Churchill and Stalin for Yugoslavia in October 1944 was revived as a bogey in this context.

hard-line policies, and apply stricter discipline within the 'Socialist camp'. This could involve at the least less toleration for Yugoslav ideas about an equal voice for all socialist countries, and at the worst a direct attempt to isolate and discipline Yugoslavia. By summer 1978 détente seemed indeed to be at risk; but there were signs that the Yugoslav leaders were distributing more evenly the blame for this state of affairs. Readers of Yugoslav newspapers could learn something of the fate of Soviet dissidents through the reporting of the exchanges between Soviet and American leaders. They could learn something too of Soviet and Cuban interventions in Africa; and there were sharp allusions at the XIth Congress of the LCY to 'hegemonism', which is a hardly disguised criticism of the Soviet Union.

In the meantime, while Yugoslav political relations with the Western world are not the subject of much open discussion, Yugoslavia remains strongly bound by economic interest particularly to the EEC countries. Total trade with Europe as a whole and North America rose from 160,000 million dinars in 1974 to 196,000 million in 1977. Within these figures, the share of Eastern European countries for some time mounted steadily from 36% to 47% in 1976. The high point of these exchanges was reached following a visit of the Yugoslav Foreign Secretary, Minić, to Moscow in December 1975, when agreements were concluded substantially to increase trade. The projected increase in Yugoslav imports would be a particularly important change. Traditionally Eastern Europe has been a good market for Yugoslav exports, and not such an important source of supplies for Yugoslavia. However trade with Eastern Europe fell back to 41% of the total in 1977. Trade with Western Europe and North America rose sharply in the same year from 53% to 59% of total trade with Europe as a whole and North America (44% in 1974). Seven-eighths of the increase was in imports, and the implications of this figure for the structure of the Yugoslav economy are serious. The conclusion of Yugoslavia's trade treaty with the EEC in 1973 was an event in its economic life, and it looks as if this should be renewed on terms quite advantageous for Yugoslavia.

In any case it will not be easy on general economic grounds for Yugoslavia to swing too far eastwards. There are strong non-commercial links with the West, including some half a million Yugoslav workers abroad, mainly in Western Germany and Austria. Remittances from them are an important source of foreign exchange; and the fact that they do not have to be absorbed in the overcrowded towns of Yugoslavia helps to solve what could otherwise be a difficult social problem, even if it may lead to others, for example an excessive brain-drain.

Tourists from abroad are another important source of foreign exchange, though the total number (about 5.6 million in 1976 and 1977) is rather less than the peak of 6.15 million reached in 1973. Here again, while exact numbers are not available, tourists from the Western world predominate and pay more on the average for their accommodation than do those from Eastern Europe. Any re-orientation of foreign policy which imperilled these links would be an expensive one for Yugoslavia.

Another aspect of Yugoslavia's commercial and financial links with foreign countries, largely but not entirely those of the West, has recently grown in importance. By the time of Economic Reform, the practice of manufacturing under licence from foreign firms was well established. In 1967, as already noted, a law was passed permitting the investment of private foreign capital (not to exceed 49% of the whole) in joint ventures with Yugoslav enterprises. In fact there has been no great rush of foreign capital to Yugoslavia. By the end of 1972 links had been established by Western firms with 50 Yugoslav enterprises, and Western capital totalled about $75 million out of their total capital of about $325 million. By mid-1977 there were 150 joint ventures in Yugoslavia, according to official sources, with $20,000 million total capital, of which $3,000 million had been invested by foreign firms – still not a large stake in Yugoslavia's total industrial production. The extension of self-management within Yugoslav enterprises has not appeared to be too serious a discouragement to foreign investors; however it was thought desirable in summer 1977 to introduce a new bill, laying down more precisely certain rights of the foreign investor which were not to be diminished by any subsequent legislation, and stipulating that a joint Yugoslav–foreign committee should be established in each case to supervise joint operations and to see that they were consistent with the terms of the original contracts.

The substance of Yugoslav–Western relations is economic, but in the case of Italy, Yugoslavia's third largest commercial partner and a considerable source of manufacturing licences and joint venture capital, an important new political agreement was concluded in November 1975. The Yugoslav–Italian land and sea frontiers in Istria were thereby finally settled and the 'provisional' division of territory agreed in October 1954 was at last formally confirmed. The process of ratification was not completed on the Italian side until March 1977, but it could then be said that the issue was settled once and for all. It had never seemed very dangerous since 1954 but was still capable in 1974 of serving as a focus for Italian right-wing agitation. The Yugoslavs were glad to see the issue out of the way, and could point to the agreement as an example of how they were putting into effect the policies outlined in the Final Act of the Helsinki European Conference (1975).

In general Yugoslavia's political relations with the West have been a function of other aspects of Yugoslav foreign policy. The permanent commitment to non-alignment has still, but decreasingly, involved certain implications for the Western powers. Much more important however have been the implications of Yugoslavia's changing relations with the Soviet Union. At the beginning of 1976 it looked as if the key factor in Yugoslav–Western relations might be the conscious effort by the Yugoslav leaders to lessen Yugoslav economic dependence on the Western world. This has not been effective. The Yugoslavs have always had to be cautious in their trade with Eastern Europe. They have better reason than most to know that, while the Soviet Government can conclude very large-scale agreements for the export of capital equipment or essential materials, these may even with good will take a long time to materialise. And good will has not always been present; the tap may be turned on and off, as in the years following 1956, or turned off altogether, as in 1948. In 1977–8 Yugoslav support for the independence of Communist Parties, fears for the independence of the non-aligned movement, and renewal of cordial relations with China have combined to make Soviet–Yugoslav relations more difficult than for many years. The importance for Yugoslavia of re-insurance with the EEC and the U.S.A. has correspondingly increased, and was illustrated in autumn 1978 by increased purchases of U.S. military equipment.

Thus, to sum up the determinants of Yugoslav foreign policy, the first ideological commitment remains to non-alignment, to a 'Southern' stance in the North–South world economic debate, and to some identification of the non-aligned and 'socialist' causes. A further commitment is to the independence of Communist Parties, and to 'individual ways to socialism'. On both counts Yugoslav relations with the Soviet Union have become more difficult in 1977–8, and there has been a rapprochement with China. These political circumstances as well as economic necessities have increased the need for good political and economic relations with the Western powers, particularly the EEC countries, and among these particularly with the Federal Republic of Germany and Italy. At the same time fear of more unfavourable developments in the Soviet Union, combined with some residual ideological commitment to Moscow, force on the Yugoslavs a cautious stance on the main issues of East–West dialogue or confrontation in Europe.

2

It is within this international setting that the conscious drive for 'socialist self-management' has proceeded on the Yugoslav internal front. So far as political and social machinery and institutions are concerned, some progress has been made in the directions desired. Kardelj saw the comparatively liberal system of the 1960s as a mask for the strengthening of a technocratic state, and regarded the abolition of it as the first major task of the Yugoslav leaders and the LCY. This has been achieved, and there is no reason to doubt that since 1974 the delegate system has taken root at all levels of assembly. The excitements of public elections like those of 1964 and 1968 are things of the past, and the 'general political deputy' as representative of the people has disappeared.

The new system has of course had its teething troubles. The delegates have tended to be overloaded with masses of paper, and have needed some system of pre-digestion if their attention was to be properly concentrated on the most important issues. Links between them and the 'basic organisations' at the bottom of the representative pyramid have proved hard to maintain in effective operation. It has been difficult for the delegates to pass adequate rather than indiscriminate information down to the BOALs, and the BOALs themselves have had difficulties in organising the assembly meetings which were meant to decide at ground level on the policy matters most important to them. Agenda for such meetings are apt to be too lengthy and unselective, and some factories or units were forced at an early stage to appoint professional administrative secretaries to cope with this problem (the 'expert' creeping back under a new cover?).

The main enemies of extended self-management, in Yugoslav theory, are technocrats and managers. There is no doubt that machinery has been provided to curb their powers. Self-management within enterprises has largely been devolved to units (BOALs) and there have been at least periodic campaigns to keep directors under control at enterprise level. A large number of directors were dismissed, for example, in Belgrade (the principal stronghold of 'technocracy') in 1975 within a year of the introduction of the new constitution, and there were trials in spring 1976 of a number of others for economic offences. One may suspect however that a large proportion of the more successful directors have settled down under the new constitution and either command the full confidence of their workers (which is likely enough if their operations in the past have been demonstrably successful), or have learned how to manipulate the new machinery in order to ensure the continuity necessary for the effective operation of their firms or units.

The machinery of total participation and self-management is indeed likely to function only partially for some time before it is fully used. A Trade Union survey, published in 1977 and covering forty-five enterprises, may be taken as typical. It indicated that average attendance at meetings had risen from 72% to 78% in 1976 (a less official survey might have resulted in lower figures). The heaviest attendance, not surprisingly, was for discussions of income distribution, but the largest number of items on the agenda (22%) referred to the establishment of further self-management bodies, and there was a general feeling that the workers still had insufficient say in decisions on major policy questions. The tendency to concentrate on working conditions and leave policy to the expert clearly remains a strong one. It has perhaps been reinforced by the introduction and extensive use of 'self-management' courts at Communal level, to arbitrate, or if necessary take legal decisions, on workers' rights, particularly on questions of comparative salaries and the allocation of living quarters. These naturally remain the workers' main concerns and there have been difficulties in interesting them seriously in the need to introduce self-management outside their own enterprises, or to participate in the local 'communities of interest' dealing with public health, education, etc. There has also been, as Gligorov told the Assembly at the end of 1976, 'considerable misunderstanding' about the position of trade and banking organisations, formerly the best-defended stronghold of 'technocrats' and managerial experts, as self-managing units under the Associated Labour Act.

Not even the most optimistic proponents of the new system could be surprised by the fact that growing pains have been prolonged. It is indeed surprising that a change of system on such a large scale has not had more disruptive effects on the Yugoslav economy as a whole. Many of the larger and more efficient firms which had flourished during the pre-1974 years were no doubt content to adapt themselves at a modest pace to the internal extension of self-management and the control of directors by Workers' Assemblies. Firms such as those of the large 'Petrokem' combination of fourteen enterprises in the chemical and petroleum industry (established in 1974) have probably been mainly interested in seeing that there is not too much 'rotation' of efficient executives, and that existing plans for expansion and integration can remain; but such plans will be presented as resting on a basis of agreements for pooling resources by the constituent BOALs of the member enterprises. The same argument applies to other industrial success stories in Yugoslavia – for example, the Gorenje household-appliance factory at Velenje, which can now advertise itself as an association of eleven BOALs. So far as such arrangements have increased workers' interest in the success of their units and enterprises, they serve in the long run to increase efficiency and profits; but it is unlikely that over the last four years the successes of efficient enterprises have depended on the new constitution. On the other side of the account grave economic problems have arisen or recurred in the economy as a whole; but these seem to have had little direct connection with the Yugoslav management system. One may therefore arrive at the largely *a priori* conclusion that up to date 'extended self-management' has probably not had more than marginal economic results in Yugoslavia.

3

Such a conclusion is reinforced by a study of the general statistics available about production, prices and trade over the last three or four years. The basic problems in Yugoslavia since Economic Reform in 1965 have been familiar, interlinked and persistent. The growth rate must increase, but the economy must be re-structured towards productivity and competitiveness in a world market. At the same time the social and political cost of closing down non-competitive industry, or of drastically reducing the agricultural population, is too large to be borne.

The general growth rate for production envisaged for the five-year period 1976–80 is comparatively modest – 7% in all, with a rather higher figure for industry and about 4% for agriculture. Industrial growth as a whole is probably on target, but this in itself means little in the light of the structural problems in industry. Agriculture still constitutes a special problem. It remains largely in the hands of private farmers on small holdings; quite apart from the ideological factors involved, the social cost of collectivisation would be intolerable, since it would entail a further large migration from the countryside to the cities. Agricultural productivity has increased over the last 10 years at an annual rate of about 2%; but the rate must be doubled if the urban population is to be supplied adequately and cheaply with large imports from outside Yugoslavia, and if Yugoslavia is itself to export again as it did before the war. Harvests have been good in 1974, 1976 and 1977; from 1976 to 1977 growth was about 3%. This did something to foster confidence in the general plan that productivity in the private sector of agriculture should be increased by infection, as it were, from the socialised sector. It is hoped to hasten this process by a series of new 'self-management agreements' between private farmers and working units on the socialised farms, and by long-term supply contracts between private producers and consumers' associations in the cities. The price of food however remains a serious problem within the context of consumer prices as a whole, which until the end of 1975 was rising at an annual rate of about 20%. The pace slowed to 12% during 1976 but increased again to 15% in 1977.

Food prices are no doubt the main concern of normal consumers, though many of them even in the main Yugoslav cities have their own private sources of supply in the country outside. It is however the general price and investment structure which still causes most anxiety to Yugoslav economists and planners, and indirectly to the proponents of extended self-management. From 1975 on there were many indications in the Yugoslav press that extended self-management, with greater financial autonomy, was producing some unexpected results. It had not led, as might have been feared, to an excessive growth of wage payments in proportion to 'accumulation' (investment). On the other hand it had not generally stimulated productivity, as had been hoped. In his speech introducing the Associated Labour Act to the Federal Assembly at the end of November 1976, Kiro Gligorov gave vent to his disappointment. He had been one of the main proponents ten years earlier of Economic Reform and of restructuring the Yugoslav economy in order to adapt it to the world market. He evidently hoped that the new system might achieve the same ends more efficiently, and he expressed disillusion about its functioning during the two and a half years since spring 1974. The slogan of 'self-management', he said, must not be made into an excuse for economic insufficiency. Inadequate results could not be justified in its name, and much less losses. His main point however was that the current system of income distribution did not provide enough incentive:

It is a fact that in this respect we have not made any progress, and there are even indications that we may have made a step backwards...that there are serious problems in this sphere is shown by the insufficient rise in labour productivity, insufficiently rational utilisation of social resources, unused capacity, etc., an open-handed approach to accumulation, etc., and also by poor economy in current human labour...

The first obvious weakness of the new system in fact proved to be excessive equalitarianism in the share-out of the income distributed. At the end of 1975, Mika Spiljak, President of the CTY, had publicly emphasised the need for greater wage differentials and for the abolition of any limit on earnings. A year later Gligorov said that it was 'indispensable fully to respect everyone's contribution to a rise in an enterprise's net income and politically and economically to expose false slogans about solidarity at a low level of income and low productivity'. Here was a new and seemingly unexpected consequence of the anti-technocratic, anti-élitist attitudes encouraged at the Xth Congress of the LCY.

By 1978 the problem of productivity was still serious, but the main emphasis of Yugoslav economic analysts was on the increasingly unsatisfactory structure of investment. Theoretical diagnosis pointed to the prevalence of 'group property relations' within enterprises, which led them to achieve and enjoy where possible monopoly positions. In more practical terms there were too many cases in which enterprises pursued their own immediate economic interests within a limited area where they were subject to comparatively little competition. With this end in view they had spent valuable foreign exchange in importing machinery which they might have obtained from elsewhere in Yugoslavia, and had competed with other Yugoslav enterprises in exporting, rather than planning a joint export campaign with them. The sum of criticism was that, for all the talk about the need for extended self-management agreements and associations within a unitary Yugoslav market, it had led in practice to inadequate results and little coordination. The worst case of overlapping and lack of long-term joint planning was in the field of energy, where each Republic or region, it was said, had to have its own refinery (often operating at low capacity) for crude oil imported at great expense, while Yugoslav coal production was insufficiently encouraged and its price and wage structure were still out of date. The historian may see in this a recrudescence, at a different level of economic development, of the 'localism' and 'political investment' of the decade from the mid-1950s to Economic Reform, and a repetition of a number of the arguments used against the unreformed economic system in 1964–5.

In 1978 as in 1965 there were two areas in which action seemed urgent. In Yugoslavia as well as in the countries of Western Europe the balance of payments deteriorated sharply after the world oil crisis of 1973. In 1972 Yugoslav exports covered nearly 70% of imports, in 1974 little more than 50%. In 1975 and 1976 the trend was upwards. The export–import proportion reached over 66% in 1976, and a fair proportion of the deficit was still met by receipts from tourism or remittances from over 500,000 Yugoslavs working in Western Europe. In 1977 however there was a sharp deterioration. Total exports increased very little (from 83 million dinars to 86 million) while total imports rose from 125 million dinars to 160 million. Thus exports covered only 53.7% of imports. Within this total figure, figures for trade exchanges with the EEC countries showed a marked deterioration. Yugoslav exports to the EEC rose only from 31,200 million dinars to 33,000 million; while imports increased from 47,500 million to nearly 62 million.[6] At the beginning of 1978 an effort was made to economise on imports by establishing offices at Republic level for the acquisition of foreign exchange. No doubt some co-ordination is better than none, and a Republican system is more in the interests of Yugoslavia as a whole than a free-for-all by individual enterprises. However the dangers of such a system are obvious in the light of past 'nationality crises'.

A second important consequence of the defects in Yugoslavia's investment structure and of the deterioration in the balance of payments has been a failure to improve the economic relations between the more and the less developed Republics and Provinces. In the Kosmet particularly, industry is said to have been financed mainly from the central fund for industrial development and to have attracted little finance direct from enterprises in other areas. There have been familiar criticisms too of the structure of investment there – too much money devoted to basic industries which take long to bear any fruit, too little to processing industries or agriculture. The net result has been that, while production may increase, the level of development relative to other regions still falls; and this is unfortunate not least in relation to the birthrate, which at an annual level of twenty-eight per 1,000 inhabitants is very high, and results in the increase particularly of the Albanian part of the population (about 75%). Thus economic stagnation in 1978 as in 1965 compounds the political problems involved for the Yugoslav leaders in the 'nationalities question'.

4

The official solution for economic stagnation and structural problems has been more integration of the right kind, to be achieved by enhanced 'political consciousness', and more intensive activity by the LCY and the CTY at all levels. In November 1976 Gligorov underlined the role

[6] There was also quite a sharp increase from 1977–8 in Yugoslavia's deficit with the COMECON countries, but the rate was not so startling as for the countries of the EEC.

of the CTY. They had to combat levelling tendencies 'with a view to changing existing relations in income distribution within the organs of associated labour enterprises. . .Without this we shall only talk in vain of the levelling of income, of over-emphasising social criteria in the distribution of personal incomes, etc. . .'

Stane Dolanc emphasised more strongly in March 1977 the key role of the Party: 'The LCY confirms itself through action as the fundamental internal motive and directive force in the struggle for self-management and as an irreplaceable factor of the ideological cohesion and political stability of Yugoslav society.' Kardelj put the essential problem and the proposed solution comparatively clearly in his report of June 1977 to the Presidium of the CC, LCY: 'There are still some self-managing units whose members are not yet able to determine and control from below what is being decided in society.' It was at these points, he said, that economic failures occurred, and it would be 'a matter for the membership of the LCY to fight for their attitudes on the spot, i.e. from within self-managing bodies and assemblies of delegates'.

At this point the question of 'persuasive' as against 'administrative' methods appeared again. The LCY is not meant officially to exercise a political monopoly or to represent the authority of the state. Under 'socialist self-management' it has a leading role as 'a component of the democratic pluralism of self-managing interests, while it is effective in proportion to the ability of Communists to make their attitudes prevail in society'.

There remain alternative and opposite dangers for the LCY in fulfilling this role. Either members give up trying, and become local patriots for their particular working organisation; or they try too hard and self-management in its most devolved form becomes a cover for Party dictatorship. Given the history of national dissensions in Yugoslavia, and the recent evidence about the revival of 'localism' and the pursuits of 'group interests' in the economy, the dangers of fragmentation of the LCY into a confederation of Parties, divided along Republican lines, or of its infection on a large scale by local economic interests, is probably the greater in the long term. It may indeed be increased by two facts which were cited with satisfaction at the XIth Congress of the LCY and in the preceding Republican Congresses. The total number of LCY members has greatly increased since the Xth Congress, from 1,150,000 to 1,600,000; and within this total the proportion of young members has also grown. It is possible that the system of directives within the LCY as a whole is good enough to maintain co-ordination within such a large Party, and (theoretically) that the 'political consciousness' of members is so strong that a system of directives is not necessary. However it seems equally likely that Republican and localist tendencies within the LCY will become stronger as it increases in size. The higher proportion of young members may also work in the same direction, since it is among the older generation that the staunchest supporters of a centralised policy and a 'firm hand' are likely to be found.

Nevertheless it is a return to the 'firm hand' which has appeared the greater danger at various times and in various spheres since 1974. The evidence for this statement does not come from the field of industrial self-management, where indeed it should be hard, if the LCY is paying due attention to its own directives, to find evidence of co-ordinated LCY pressure in self-managing units. In other areas of Yugoslav society the case is rather different. The impression gained by a foreigner revisiting Yugoslavia after the high tide of 'liberalism' following Economic Reform is that outside the economic field Party control is stricter and Party influence more perceptible than it was ten years ago, though this has generally not attracted much attention and comparisons with other East European countries are still quite out of place.

The directive laid down at the Xth Party Congress in spring 1974 was to combat both 'bureaucratic-dogmatic' and also 'anarcho-petit-bourgeois and pseudo-liberal' trends. As regards 'bureaucratic-dogmatic' tendencies, there have been some well-publicised actions against 'Cominformists'. A small Montenegrin group was accused in autumn 1974 of having tried to found a pro-Soviet Communist party at Bar, and of forming connections both with similar groups in Serbia and Croatia and with the Soviet and other Embassies in Belgrade. Early in 1976 there were further trials of and sentences against some thirty 'Cominformists', including Colonel Vlado Dapčević, brother of a famous Partisan General, who had tried to escape from Yugoslavia in 1948.[7] Tito was no doubt genuinely upset by their activities, but it is hard to think that they represented any serious threat to the stability of his régime. The cases probably served as a warning by the Yugoslav leaders to the Soviet Government against meddling in any succession crisis, and as evidence for Western observers that Tito was even-handed in dealing with Eastern and Western sympathisers.

Certain official actions on the other front against 'anarcho-petit-bourgeois' and 'pseudo-liberal' representatives have indeed caused

[7] He was allowed to leave Yugoslavia in 1955, but was recaptured and brought back in 1976, with Romanian co-operation.

concern in the West. Neo-Marxist academics and writers critical of the Yugoslav régime were gradually (very gradually by East European standards) put out of business, and repression in such cases corresponded to the convictions or prejudices of Tito himself. The earlier stages of action taken against Mihajlo Mihajlov and against the theoretical neo-Marxist periodical *Praxis* have already been mentioned. At the beginning of 1975 Mihajlov was re-arrested and put on trial for publishing in the Russian émigré periodical *Posev* articles critical of the Yugoslav régime. He was sentenced in February 1975 to a further term of imprisonment, but was released under the amnesty of November 1977. *Praxis*, which had been in more or less hot water with the Yugoslav régime for many years, finally closed down, also in February 1975, because the printers with impeccable political orthodoxy refused to produce it any longer. This was part of a wider action against neo-Marxist academics. In particular a purge of the Belgrade University Philosophical Faculty was started in January 1975. The legal proprieties were observed, but the limits of self-management within the University became apparent. At this time the Serbian Assembly voted, under legislation specially amended for the particular purpose only two months before, to suspend indefinitely from their teaching posts Mihailo Marković, Svetozar Stojanović, and six of their colleagues. They were charged generally with having used their positions in the Faculty to further their own political pretensions, and more particularly with having inspired the protest action by Belgrade University students in summer 1968. By the standards of other Communist countries the purge was a very gradual and mild one. The philosophers continued to receive full pay until new jobs were found for them, or until they retired.[8] However the political nature of the Serbian authorities' intervention was shown up when in March 1975 the periodical *Filosofija* published the reports of eight special commissions of the Belgrade Philosophical Faculty, which had investigated fully and rejected the official accusation against the Professors that they were morally and politically unsuited to teach.

The early months of 1976 also witnessed a campaign which could be taken to portend a general tightening up of social discipline, by encouraging social self-protection in Yugoslav self-managing society and reinforcement of the secret police through 'do-it-yourself' activities in BOALs and residents' associations. 'Social protective activities' were to be transferred 'from the professional to the public sphere', where

---

[8] It was virtually impossible for them to get similar jobs in Yugoslavia, but Stojanović was already in the U.S.A. at the beginning of 1975.

people were to guard themselves and their fellows against 'various deviatory phenomena of a political, criminal and anti-self-management character'. The last qualification could be interpreted very widely and could lead to a disagreeable increase in denunciations and suspicion, but does not seem to have done so.

In fact since early in 1976 there has been little suggestion of the LCY generally reverting to the 'firm hand'. While their policy has been rather more restrictive than in the late 1960s, the pattern has remained much the same. Since the LCY has such a difficult and delicate role to play in guiding the economy and social services, their leaders have been all the more inclined on occasion to prove their virility, so to speak, by intervention of a more active nature against neo-Marxists and liberals. Such action corresponds to Tito's own temperament, and might incidentally reassure the Soviet Government that the Yugoslavs are still good communists. It has probably seemed the more necessary since, in respect of the market elements in its economy, of the freedom of movement and contact accorded to foreigners, and of the circulation of non-Marxist ideas, Yugoslavia has remained an open society by any standards, and remarkably open by contrast with its East European neighbours. The Yugoslav leaders can for example claim with justice to have done more than most to fulfil the clauses of the Helsinki Final Act about exchanges of information and the sale of foreign newspapers. No doubt this is partly a function of the continuing large inflow of Western tourists; but it would be news indeed if for example Moscow were able to report, as Belgrade can, the sale of 2.5 million copies of the anti-communist West German tabloid newspaper *Bild Zeitung* in a single year. The maximum flow of information has not always been encouraged, especially on matters connected with the Soviet Union, but any alert Yugoslav reader could find a lot between the lines of his newspapers on internationally delicate subjects, such as the activities of Soviet dissidents; he could also test his faith in Communism by reading translations of George Orwell, most of Solzhenitsyn's works, and the memoirs of Nadezhda Mandelstam. It is against a general background of free circulation of ideas and people that the more notorious examples of restrictions by the LCY should be seen.

5

An important occasion for stocktaking and trend-setting by Tito and the Party leaders was the XIth Congress of the LCY, held in June 1978. This was officially represented as a Congress of consolidation, at which no great changes would be made. The main task was to work out more precisely the guidelines for socialist self-management laid down at the Xth Congress in 1974; and these were themselves represented as stemming logically from the conclusions of the VIIth (Ljubljana) Congress of 1958. Thus the emphasis was on continuity, and on the role of the LCY in executing more efficiently a stable policy.

Nevertheless the Congress was important in and beyond Yugoslavia. It could easily have witnessed President Tito's last major public appearance, and though this aspect was dismissed by Tito himself as unimportant, the Congress ratified the proposed re-organisation of the Party Presidency to ensure its more efficient functioning – clearly against the day of his disappearance. It was now to consist of twenty-four members only (as opposed to fifty-two in 1969 and thirty-nine in 1974), three from each Republic, two from each Autonomous Province, one representing the Army and Tito himself. Day-to-day executive decisions would be largely in the hands of Stane Dolanc, the Secretary.

Of more obvious interest to Yugoslavs were the international setting of the Congress as part of the European Communist or socialist movement, and the Yugoslav internal context – one of growing economic difficulties with obvious political implications. These factors, in the shadow of President Tito's departure, combined to give a special interest to the conclusions of the Congress and the way in which they were formulated.

The Yugoslav leaders were acutely conscious, at a time when 'Eurocommunism' was becoming a political reality, of their own place in the international socialist movement. Theory therefore bulked large at and before the Congress. A new challenge, they said, was presented to the world by the XIth Congress, and embodied in the formula 'democracy and freedom in socialism'. In this context the theoretical preparation for the Congress was considered especially important, and was entrusted to Kardelj. The result was a very full report on *Directions of the Development of the Political System of Socialist Self-Management*, Kardelj's last major work before his death in February 1979. This was published in Yugoslavia in autumn 1977, and subsequently translated in abridged form for international consumption under the title *Democracy and Socialism*.

Some of the main themes of this work must be briefly mentioned here. The essence of Kardelj's argument was that a Yugoslav-type system of economic and social self-management provides the working class with far more control over their own environment than they could ever enjoy under 'bourgeois' parliamentary democracy in which, however much freedom of speech there may be, the vital controls over the economy are exercised in the interests of the capitalist class. Thus under the 'bourgeois' multi-party system there is no effective representation of any interest which wishes to change the capitalist system fundamentally. In Yugoslavia on the other hand, there is within the socialist system a 'plurality of self-managing interests' which gives working-class individuals effective control over most aspects of their lives.

At the same time in Yugoslavia as elsewhere the state is a necessary evil at the present stage, when class enemies still exist and much remains to be done in facilitating economic development. In so far as a state exists in any country, it involves the use of power and elements of dictatorship; thus (and here Kardelj was clearly sensitive) the association by 'bourgeois' theorists of socialism or communism with dictatorship is hypocritical, since the bourgeois state is inevitably a dictatorship of the bourgeoisie. In Yugoslavia the working class is supreme, and the LCY exists to ensure that 'self-management' does not allow opportunities to its enemies.

Socialism is not conceivable without democracy. It cannot make progress unless it fosters democratic relations among people. However, what a socialist society wants is democracy in socialism, and not democracy used as a weapon against socialism. Therefore we must preserve the class nature of our democracy. What this means is that the interests of the working class, closely aligned with all other working people, must be guaranteed undisputed predominance in this democracy, and that everyone acknowledging this fact will enjoy democratic rights.

The formulation is rather chilling to 'bourgeois' eyes and ears, even though Kardelj said elsewhere that the Yugoslav system is a plurality of self-managing interests and not a one-party state. Evidently too it is not only Western 'bourgeois' analysts who ask the obvious questions 'who defines the working class? who guards the guardians, or controls the Party which protects the plurality of interests?' Among the most interesting sections of Kardelj's book are those in which he criticises those 'ultra-left' intellectuals who themselves criticise the practice of the LCY and current trends in Yugoslav society. The charges brought by the intellectuals are, in Kardelj's version, familiar enough from the years immediately following Economic Reform; excessive materialism all round, excessive differentials in earnings, the transformation of the political leaders into a 'New Class', the lack of 'spontaneity' in politics (i.e. the existence of too rigid a Party line) and the absence of 'bourgeois' freedoms. The substance of Kardelj's counter-criticism is that the 'ultra-left' intellectuals are sore at being deprived of a privileged position, that 'spontaneity' in politics would involve anarchy, and that more economic equality could only be imposed by a revived state-bureaucratic apparatus; this would result in economic stagnation which would seriously check the further development of self-management. Kardelj charged the intellectuals with simultaneously attracting the support of 'bourgeois political pluralists' in the West and working 'objectively' for the re-imposition of 'technocracy' and/or state socialism of a Stalinist type.

In his report to the XIth Congress, Tito pursued the same themes and dwelt on the need for preserving the 'leading role' of the LCY by seeing that its policy is not identified with 'various demagogic, liberalistic, ultra-left, sectarian and similar phrases and "promises"'. Tito's emphasis on the need to counter these was no doubt motivated in part by the desire to give some satisfaction to Moscow orthodoxy. However the balance between right and left-wing heresies was held fairly even, as in the past. A reversion to state socialism and the 'firm hand' policy was still regarded as highly undesirable. Tito warned the LCY against any attempt to preserve its own power by force, and the resolutions of the XIth Congress included an interesting warning to members of the LCY against pursuing sectarian policies in relation to religion, and trying to prevent believers from taking part in the work of SAWPY or other social organisations. There have also been semi-official suggestions in the Yugoslav press to the effect that increased agricultural production and even collectivisation is being hindered by too doctrinaire an attitude towards private peasants.

This suggests that at something less than the highest level LCY members may still be too ready to pursue an 'administrative' policy; and such a conclusion is reinforced by the results, published just before the Congress, of a semi-official public opinion poll on the general problem whether the Yugoslav worker was in general ripe for self-management. In this context answers to a question about the greatest hindrances to self-management were in the main indecisive, but only 8% of those questioned plumped for 'technocrats' (which would have been the 'correct' official answer); 9% saw the greatest danger in the activities of the state and the LCY (i.e. the 'firm hand' policy).[9] Either this or technocracy may have been the target in Tito's sights, when in November 1978 he campaigned against 'leaderism' and 'professional-

[9] In answer to another question, one-third of the respondents thought that a 'firm hand' would be necessary to increase general 'political consciousness' and another third answered 'yes, but. . .' The details of this survey are taken from the Yugoslav weekly, *Nin*, nos. 1422 (9 April), 1426 (7 May) and 1427 (14 May) 1978.

ism', and introduced one-year rotation of Chairmanship into the LCY and CTU hierarchy, starting with the Presidency of the Party.

The Yugoslav leaders must indeed have reflected on the need for the 'firm hand' in connection with the economic situation which had developed in the months preceding the Party Congress. The structural problems of the Yugoslav economy featured very largely in Tito's own report. He mentioned particularly continuing inflation, insufficient productivity, the importance of developing domestic sources of energy, and the need to survey the 'regional components of external economic relations', particularly in the light of the EEC countries' reluctance 'to conduct a policy of balanced trade exchanges with the Yugoslav economy'.

Some account of the background to these statements has been given in §3 above. The existence of major economic problems was amply confirmed both by many principal speakers at the Congress and by press commentary on its proceedings. The problem of the under-developed regions or Provinces of Yugoslavia appeared to demand the most urgent and concrete consideration. It was agreed that at its autumn session the Federal Assembly should reconsider, on the basis of the findings of a number of technical institutions, the membership of the 'under-developed club', and should decide which regions should receive aid from central funds during the coming five-year period, and in what form. Other specific problems under discussion were the increase in unemployment, the number of firms operating at a loss, and the excessive amount still being spent by consumers. The principal solution advanced for this formidable set of problems by Tito and others was that 'Communists must apply themselves to the very serious structural problems of the economy much more boldly, with more co-ordination, and with much more ideological knowledge.'

It would not be difficult to conclude from this that the application of a much 'firmer hand' may be under serious consideration.

Such a policy however would not necessarily involve a general east-ward swing by the Yugoslav authorities. A 'firm hand' in the domestic economy and an attempt at some literal 're-orientation' of Yugoslavia's trade relations could go together with a determination to preserve a good deal of freedom of discussion. In the chapter of his report to the Congress devoted to the development of Marxist theory, Tito inveighed against sectarian groups who try to achieve a monopoly position in the field of ideology, instead of permitting an honest conflict of opinion. The reference could here as well be to the 'ultra-left' as to those who favour 'administrative' methods, but there was no doubt of the trend

of Tito's remarks when he criticised those who pressed for severe censorship regulations in order to preserve or restore Yugoslavia's image
abroad.

Thus Tito's dislike of neo-Marxist theory is balanced by his desire to
avoid Soviet-type 'state socialist' practice, and the economic need for a
'firm hand' is offset by what are essentially foreign policy considera-
tions. The combination of economic difficulties at home and Soviet–
Yugoslav tensions within the world communist and non-aligned contexts is likely to leave Tito's successors, as it gives him, a very difficult
hand to play.[10]

[10] In May 1979, while this Chapter was at the printer, Stane Dolanc was removed
from his post as Secretary of the Party Presidency, for which he had been given
a four-year mandate by the XIth Party Congress. His successor, Dušan
Dragosavac, a Serb from Croatia, was appointed for two years only. Dolanc, who
accompanied President Tito on an important visit to Moscow also in May 1979,
seems not to have lost all influence; but his removal from a key post is probably
part of some active manoeuvring in anticipation of Tito's leaving the political
scene.

18

Conclusions

If any description of current trends in Yugoslavia is subjective enough, any attempt to project them into the future must be even more dangerous. Some reasons have been given in the previous chapter for doubting whether the Yugoslav leaders can combine economically effective self-management with a monopoly position of the LCY, and for thinking that the problems of nationalism and economic 'localism' will be with them for a good time yet. There is no use in pursuing such speculations further. However a view must be offered on the one aspect of Yugoslav affairs which is of most immediate interest to the foreign observer. Has Yugoslavia achieved stability over the past thirty years? And, if so, how much does it depend on the continued presence of Marshal Tito at the head of affairs?

In attempting an answer to the first question, it is important first to identify certain elements of continuity in the post-war history of Yugoslavia. This has been eventful indeed, but not simply a succession of crises, with a 'great helmsman' avoiding the most obvious shoals on each occasion by sharp changes of course which lead him inevitably towards the next snags. The truth is rather that each change of course has shaped the outlook of certain key people and produced certain institutions which at least in modified form have survived the next change. To this extent indeed Yugoslavia can be regarded as a pluralist society.

To put the matter more correctly, the period of 'war communism' from 1945–8 produced a certain type of Communist Party and a certain style of Communist leadership which relied on strict discipline and what afterwards became known as 'administrative methods' – the habit of direct command through the machinery of government, which was identical with, or duplicated by, that of the Party. The style of LCY action has changed, and 'administrative action' is officially deplored. None the less Tito himself has felt bound on certain points to issue what are virtually commands (as in the case of the Belgrade

Professors of Philosophy). There is plenty of evidence of the persistence of a conservative communist outlook in certain fields. The LCY could still be used as as instrument to enforce it, and one important incidental effect of the 'enlarged self-management system' is that it leaves very large scope for action by Party members at the level of BOALs and Workers' Assemblies.

Historically the 'command period' of the Party was followed by a system of devolution from state to Republican and district levels of parliamentary representation and administration. This could over-encourage nationalism at the Republican level and 'localism' at lower levels, tendencies against which the LCY itself proved by no means immune. The period of decentralisation as well as that of command has had lasting repercussions. These assumed a form dangerous to Yugoslav unity at the time of the 'nationalities crisis', 1971–2. The delegate system in operation since 1974 was designed to ensure that Communal Assemblies and others should be responsive to pressures from factory units and from the Party, and thus be protected from the infection of nationalism. It would however be unwise to assume that nationalism is dead even within the LCY, especially since it has become a 'mass party' of over 1.6 million members. As for economic 'localism' (once summarised in the ironic slogan 'a swimming pool for every Commune'), this is clearly alive and causing very considerable difficulties for economic planners and others.

There are other constant economic factors, which arose partly from the devolutionary process started in the 1950s, but mainly from the attempt to restructure the Yugoslav economy under the slogan of Economic Reform in 1965. This confirmed the official respectability of the 'principle of profitability' and of the attempt to adapt the Yugoslav economy, as enterprises became cost-conscious, to world market conditions. The indirect results of both reforms and Reform included the growth of a caste of expert directors and managers, and also of specialist institutions in the economic field. Since 1974 these may be under tighter control by Workers' Assemblies, Workers' Councils and LCY representatives; but the experts and specialist institutions exist and continue to exercise an important influence on the development of the Yugoslav economy. Indeed the economic stagnation of 1977–8 may serve to increase their importance, even if the blame for it is officially attributed to narrow technocratic influence.

A new layer of institutions and a large sediment of continuing practice has been left by the 'nationalities crisis' of 1971–2. This has resulted in the conversion of Yugoslavia from a fairly tight to a very loose Federation, with a minimum of Federal State apparatus. Para-doxically, the best guarantee of the continuing unity of the Yugoslav Federation is the machinery evolved in 1972 for securing agreement at Republican level before any important legislation can be enacted at the centre. The stability of Yugoslavia as a whole has probably increased by virtue of the maximum possible devolution – and of the application of the 'national key' concept to the most important posts in the Yugo-slav Government and Committee structure. Under this concept either equal representation for the Republics is built into the system formally, as in the case of the Presidency, or, when this is inappropriate, great care is taken to see that no Republic is seriously underrepresented at any high level. A very important point at which this procedure applies is the military section of the Presidency of the Federation, which includes the Supreme Commander of the Armed Forces, the Chief of Staff, the Secretary of the Council of National Defence, the Secretary of the Council for State Security and the Secretary of the LCY of the Yugoslav Army.[1] The loyalty of the Army to the Federation is of course particularly crucial, as was proved in the Croatian crisis of 1971, and every step has been taken to ensure that it remains un-impaired.

Finally there is the latest layer of institutions created by the Consti-tution of 1974 and the Associated Labour Act of 1976, designed to bind the working people of Yugoslavia in a perpetual league against State bureaucracy, Republican nationalism, abuse of power by eco-nomic experts or political functionaries, and 'rotten liberal influences' from the West. The new system of direct self-management operates on something that is very much not a *tabula rasa*, as is shown by the preceding paragraphs. Neither is it in itself a new concept in Yugo-slavia. The idea of more direct power to the workers has been actively discussed since 1957. Total self-management in Yugoslavia implies the existence of a large and effective political party.

It is the LCY which is meant to reconcile the various conflicting tendencies, ideas and institutions inherited by the Yugoslav leaders today – to see in sum that the self-managing element of 'socialist self-management' does not submerge the socialist element, that neither economic self-interest nor 'rotten liberalism' flourish unduly, and at

[1] In 1973 these posts were occupied by three Croats, one Slovene and one Moslem; the senior personnel of the State Secretariat for National Defence comprised four Serbs, four Croats and one Macedonian; and the senior operative posts in the command of the Army, including the commands of Army districts, were shared between four Serbs, two Croats, two Macedonians, two Montenegrins and one Slovene.

the same time that they should not be repressed by too obviously 'administrative' means.

However, the LCY itself, the great co-ordinator, is not a constant. It has been affected by all the main historical tendencies described above. It is not the same sort of instrument that it was thirty years ago, yet the principal problem for its leaders was set by themselves to themselves at their own VIth Congress in November 1952, when the CPY decisively rejected the State socialist system and transformed itself into the League of Yugoslav Communists. The problem of how to exercise a decisive influence without taking 'administrative action' persists since then. Theoretically the LCY is meant to operate at every level of economic and social activity mainly through individuals, who are politically educated and can point to wider social duties as well as to group interests. Such individuals may operate on the basis of instructions from higher Party instances. But from 1952 on there has also been a tradition of non-interference by the LCY as such, and there has often been doubt among LCY members about what specific action they are meant to be taking.

Parallel with these traditions and doubts, the opening of Yugoslav frontiers and development of information media which are interested in 'self-management' and profits as well as in socialism, have made Yugoslavia into far the most liberal of communist countries. Even after some tightening of social discipline in 1974, there is a wide variety of information available, public debate is possible on a considerable variety of subjects (with one or two taboos), and most human rights, in a Western liberal sense of the words, are respected much more widely than elsewhere in Eastern Europe,[2] even though Yugoslav theorists profess to regard the liberal concept of human rights as unduly limited and transcended by their own practice.

As regards the future, it is clear that the LCY's dilemma will persist – how to be the only party in a State embodying a 'plurality of self-managing interests' without either turning it into a one-party State (in the sense of exercising a political monopoly) or allowing certain 'self-managing interests' to act in a non-socialist spirit. This is in itself one source of instability which could be increased by pressures within the LCY for the application of the 'firm hand' in the face of economic or

[2] This judgement is made in the full knowledge that there are obvious restrictions on political activity in a non-socialist sense, and on any attempt at wide educational activity by the Churches. There are also a number of 'political prisoners' still in jail, though I do not know what data Milovan Djilas had for a statement (1977) that proportionately there were more political prisoners in Yugoslavia than in the Soviet Union.

other crises. If such pressures arise, it is in this connection that the absence of Tito from the political scene will be most keenly felt. It is he who still has the prestige to put the political clock back or forward without causing serious rifts in the fairly 'pluralist' LCY. Without him there may be a greater need than before for a 'firm hand'; and it will be that much harder to apply it.

2

Each stage in the history of Communist Yugoslavia has thus contributed something substantial to the institutions, practices and habits of thought of Yugoslavia today. The resulting mix does not at first look a particularly stable one. Of the divisive factors once present in 1948, some indeed have disappeared and some are diminishing in importance. It is hard to think that there could be any support for a direct revival of the Yugoslav monarchy or for the sort of bourgeois rule or liberal democracy that prevailed between the wars. A conservative-communist coup re-establishing throughout Yugoslavia a simple Communist dictatorship, of the type that existed from 1945 to 1950, is more likely but not the most pressing danger. The present rough equilibrium of forces is most likely to be upset by some revival of Croat or Serb nationalism, in reaction either to external pressures, or to an attempt by the leaders of the LCY to use the 'firm hand' against the revival of 'localism' and 'technocracy'.[3]

Economic policies are indeed likely to cause plenty of trouble, directly or indirectly. A conscious and sustained attempt to increase the share of other Eastern European countries in Yugoslavia's foreign trade, in view of the precarious Yugoslav balance of payments, could affect seriously the Croat and Slovene industries in particular, which have had special links with West Germany, Austria and Italy; this could lead to the re-emergence of strong nationalist trends in the Croatian and Slovenian LCs, as well as among the general public. Again pressure to hasten the build-up of industry and communications in the less developed Republics could produce the same results. Any attempt to enforce more widespread investment by prosperous enterprises over the whole area of the Yugoslav market could not succeed without more use than at present of the 'firm hand'. This would involve in effect over-riding the present virtual Republican veto on

[3] The influence of neo-Marxist intellectuals might also gain strength from a drift towards 'dinar socialism' and economic policy. In such a situation they might even conclude a temporary alliance with conservative communists in favour of a 'firm hand policy'.

controversial economic policies (the 'national key' system) and would provoke strongly nationalist sentiments in Croatia and Slovenia. A reaction by Serbian nationalists would inevitably follow; and if Serbian nationalists began again to back LCY centralists, a very undesirable chain reaction would result. It would spread all the quicker if, as has been argued, the growth in the total size of the LCY eases the spread of nationalism within the Republican branches.

One assumption underlying this speculation is that national and political sentiments remain much as they have been in the past. This is of course a large assumption. A whole generation has now grown up since the war, and is beginning to attain responsible positions. Many of them react apathetically against much of the routine political indoctrination to which they have been exposed in the newspapers, in radio and TV programmes, and in classes on Marxism at school and University. Young people have been growing up in Yugoslavia as elsewhere with mainly material ambitions and little interest in ideals. Political apathy could apply not merely to Marxist but also to nationalist ideas, and the younger generation could find the local patriotism of their grandfathers as tedious as the socialist heroics of their fathers. Thus if in Yugoslavia a high proportion of the young are politically apathetic, this may make for a certain stability. In the Yugoslav context however such an argument is only doubtfully valid; politically passive crowds can provide good material for the eloquent political agitator, not least the nationalists who can play on economic grievances.[4]

There may however be other forms of protection for Yugoslav society against the renewal of nationalist tensions. One of these could lie in the much increased mobility of labour, starting with the steady migration from the countryside to the towns and the increase in the number of industrial workers. This resulted in a large and till recently self-renewing (if in most individual cases temporary) migration of Yugoslav workers, mainly unskilled, to Central Europe, and later within Yugoslavia from the less to the more developed Republics. The movement, it could be argued, has tended to alert Yugoslav workers in general to the possibilities of higher standards of living, to strengthen materialist ambitions, and to weaken national ties.

Officially too it is considered that the extension of self-management and the spread of 'socialist consciousness' should in themselves

---

[4] The author must confess too that in 1967–8 when many of the same inducements to passivity were present, he underestimated the immediacy of the nationalist danger in Yugoslavia.

immunise the Yugoslav working class against nationalism, which, it is officially argued, infects primarily bureaucrats and technocrats anxious to preserve monopoly positions. Released from bondage to technocrats, the Yugoslav workers will use their common sense and see their own long-term material interest as lying in the conclusion of a network of 'self-management agreements' and 'social compacts' which transcends local and Republican boundaries. At the same time, the LCY will foster the sense that all nations within Yugoslavia should have equal rights and that special efforts should be made to hasten the economic progress of the less developed Republics and Provinces.

This is certainly not the case at the time of writing, and one may well be sceptical for the future too about the effects of introducing a complete and elaborate system of participatory democracy, or the speed with which it can make itself felt. The machinery of self-management may be, and clearly often is, misused for 'localist' rather than for Yugoslav political purposes. This is not to say that the whole self-management system is nothing but an elaborate charade, or that a new 'self-management culture' may not eventually be evolved. In the longer term the evolution of a 'culture of self-management' could be an important factor for unity in Yugoslavia. Whether it is given time to develop as such depends greatly on the role played by or forced upon the LCY. The LCY is of course intimately connected with the whole committee and delegation system. Inevitably membership of the LCY coincides largely with membership of committees within enterprises and of delegations all the way up the ladder of representative government. No attempt is made to conceal that the LCY and the CTY are to play a particularly active part in self-management at all levels. Theoretically members should do so individually and not on the basis of particular directives from above, which must certainly exist. This theory is no doubt advanced in good faith and, if it can be applied over some time, then a genuine social conscience could grow to counteract both particularism, nationalism and one-party control. If, as seems more likely, social conscience continues for some time to be overlaid generally by particularism – a strong group or local loyalty – then there would be renewed demands for a 'firm hand' and tighter Party discipline from the centre, with the results already envisaged. There is the further possibility, involving equal dangers, that Party discipline will be applied, if at all, on a Republican rather than a central basis, with results similar to those apparent during the 'nationalities crisis' of 1971–2.

At present therefore the best that can be hoped for is a continuance of the present uneasy equilibrium in which the ideal of self-management plays its part. Yugoslavia has survived many internal crises in the past thirty years, and however strong the feeling between Serbs and Croats or between Party 'liberals' and 'conservatives', in their more reflective moments they should be able to sense that their true long-term interest is in a Yugoslavia somehow united, and that a Yugoslavia split up, or reconstituted according to their particular interests, would find it very hard to survive in the harsh world of power politics.

3

So far Yugoslavia has been treated in isolation from its international context, and an attempt has been made to judge the stability of the present regime and society there on the basis of internal factors and history alone. Such an attempt is of course unrealistic. Yugoslavia exists in an international environment which can itself be affected to some extent by Yugoslav internal developments, but is likely also to influence them very considerably. It is the Soviet Union, and the Soviet Union alone, which can directly upset the present balance in Yugoslavia. The Yugoslav leaders are well aware of the situation, whatever may occasionally be said about the dangers of Western intervention. In relation to Yugoslavia, there is one very simple difference between the interests of the two 'blocs'. The Soviet Government has a strong strategic interest in controlling the Adriatic coast, while it is hard to see why any Western statesman or general should wish to advance NATO's front line to Subotica or Dimitrovgrad.

On the probable assumption that the government of the U.S.S.R. remains in the hands of men essentially hostile to liberal democracy and extremely reluctant to forego any part of their political monopoly at home or of their dominance in the countries of the Warsaw Pact, the Soviet interest is in the disappearance of an independent Yugoslavia which can act as a source of political infection in Eastern Europe, can flirt with China and encourage the Romanians to do so, and can hamper Soviet attempts to harness the non-aligned to the 'anti-imperialist' cause. A nominally independent Yugoslavia, which de facto furthered Soviet interests among the non-aligned countries, could still be useful to the Soviet leaders. It would however be much safer for them to see Yugoslavia rejoin the 'Socialist camp' as an obedient satellite, and this has been the medium-term Soviet aim since 1955.

For over twenty years, the Soviet leaders have been willing to pursue their aim with caution. Any direct intervention, or too obvious an attempt to foster some political coup, might have caused and could still cause a confrontation with the NATO powers. And, while the Soviet Government would prefer a dependent Yugoslavia, they have lived not too unhappily for some time with an independent one under Tito's leadership. Both on Yugoslav internal matters and in Soviet–Yugoslav relations, Tito for long achieved a sort of equilibrium based on implicit bargains with his own Party and with the Soviet Union. Internally a considerable amount of freedom was allowed to market forces, to private economic initiative and to the satisfaction of consumer needs, even before these were presented as part of the practice of systematic 'total self-management', as defined in the legislation of 1974 and 1976; however there has always been the condition (indirectly important for the Soviet leaders) that the LCY retains its party-political monopoly and exercises it from time to time in a restrictive sense against those who deviate too conspicuously from 'socialist' norms.

In the field of foreign affairs the implicit bargain seems to have been as follows. Yugoslavia might follow its own 'way to socialism'; it might keep on reasonably good terms with the West, proclaim the prime importance of non-alignment for its foreign policy, and continue to preach the equal rights of socialist countries, as laid down at the Berlin Conference in 1976. On the other side the Soviet leaders have had to be convinced that the Yugoslavs will not propagate the doctrine of national independence too actively among the member countries of the Warsaw Pact; that their concepts of non-alignment should not work against Soviet interests; that an effort should be made to maintain or improve Yugoslav economic relations with the 'Socialist camp', in order to balance the Western economic connection; and that on some important issues of inter-state foreign policy the Yugoslav Government should back the Soviet line (the most conspicuous example has been the provision of over-flight facilities between the Soviet Union and the Middle East in 1973 during the October war between Egypt and Israel).

This state of affairs was for long tolerable to the Soviet leaders and has ensured reasonable stability for Yugoslavia. However after Tito's (and/or Brezhnev's) disappearance from the political scene, they might well demand new terms for a bargain, explicit or implicit, over letting Yugoslavia alone. The Yugoslav–Chinese connection and difficulties within the non-aligned movement could be sufficient reasons in themselves. Moreover within the general East–West context, the Soviet leaders may see greater need for more open Yugoslav support, and greater opportunities for securing it. If East–West tension increases, the need for ideological uniformity within Eastern Europe will be all the greater, and the need for attracting Yugoslavia back to the 'Socialist camp'.

The Soviet leaders, like others, will be reckoning carefully the results for them of Tito's disappearance. On the one hand his personality has been for them a sort of guarantee that the Yugoslav way to socialism will not deviate into liberal democracy. At the same time they must reckon that Tito could do better than any successor in rallying external support for his country against any threat of Soviet intervention and in mobilising it against internal disintegration. On these grounds alone the balance for them has been against active intervention. Tito's disappearance must remove some Soviet inhibitions. However even after he has left the political scene, the Soviet leaders would have to think carefully about the extent of the pressure to be brought on Yugoslavia. A take-over, involving invasion, may be considered desirable, but they could not count in present conditions on a walk-over, as in Czechoslovakia; the system of 'People's Defence' might work well enough to attract Western support. If they resolve to take overt action against Yugoslavia, they must be prepared to do so as part of a wider operation, or alternatively have written off completely Western will to resist aggression. For some time they may well not be prepared to take such risks and may prefer to see what disintegrating effect the passage of time has on post-Tito Yugoslavia.

Meanwhile even heavy political pressure from Moscow might be counter-productive. Yugoslavia, with all its potential sources of internal differences, could well be re-united by too obvious Soviet interference or threats to national independence. This was amply proved in 1948 and 1968. The immediate Soviet interest might seem to lie in at least political support for LCY leaders determined for example on a new application of the 'firm hand' from Belgrade. Even this however could backfire if it led to a renewed confrontation between Serb centralists and Croat devolutionists. The Soviet Union might indeed gain a new foothold in Serbia; but this in turn might lead to Western support for Croat nationalists; and a renewed attempt at Croat separatism could imperil Soviet strategic objectives on the Adriatic coast.

For a time therefore the Soviet leaders are likely to be content with comparatively cautious efforts to build up a position of strength in the Balkans. There are many forms of political warfare, short of direct threats, in which they can indulge. Pressure via the Bulgarian Government over the Macedonian question is an obvious example, and this could be used indirectly to stir up dissension between Serbs and Croats.

Macedonian troops were unwilling in 1945 to serve on the Srem front, and there could well be mutterings in Croatia about getting involved in a major international crisis over Macedonia. Indeed for the present the state of Yugoslav–Bulgarian relations is the most obvious measure of Soviet–Yugoslav tension.

4

Reasons have been given earlier in this chapter for thinking that the present internal system of Yugoslavia rests on a fairly solid and adaptable basis of institution and habit, whatever troubles may lie ahead in a combination of economic and 'national' crises. If this is so, it is largely due to the personality and sheer power of survival of President Tito.

One of his greatest strengths has been his pragmatism. He has not been a doctrinaire intent on imposing his views about the ideal political structure, in conditions where they clearly could not be realised. He has held firm to his faith in the ultimate victory of 'socialism', but the strength of this faith has enabled him to accept a *de facto* alliance with European social democrats and those Asian and African leaders whose real dislike has been of Western imperialism rather than of Western capitalism. Tito has also held firm to the concept of the 'brotherhood and unity' of the races of the Yugoslav Republics and this has allowed him, after the very painful Croatian crisis of 1971, to accept the loosest possible structure of federalism. Within such a limited framework of doctrine, Tito has accepted, often with reluctance, a remarkable series of innovations – decentralisation and the introduction of the profit motive with the attendant risk of anarchy or at least excessive particularism, Economic Reform which had profound effects on the whole structure of the Yugoslav economy and social life, the transformation of the Party into a 'persuasive' rather than 'administrative' machine, the retreat from collectivisation in agriculture, and a considerable amount of toleration in the religious, artistic and intellectual field. His very reluctance to abandon the firm ground of 'democratic centralism' and some degree of intellectual regimentation has ensured that, when he has done so, he has carried 'conservative communists' with him and that the unity of Yugoslavia has suffered the minimum damage. And however much he has hankered to revert to the use of the 'firm hand' after 1972, he has accepted that it could only be applied indirectly, given the hold that ideas of 'self-management' had already gained in Yugoslavia.

Tito's style of leadership has in fact been mainly from behind, with long-delayed but firm interventions at crucial points; such interventions have been determined more by the course of events and of previous argument among other Yugoslav leaders than by his own preconceived ideas. He allowed Djilas in autumn 1953 to publish unchecked for two months articles subversive of one-party rule. He made up his mind in favour of Economic Reform only after an experiment in re-centralisation had failed. He allowed Ranković and the Serbian 'conservative communists' a great deal of rope before moving against them in 1966, and he attacked the Croat Party leaders decisively in 1971 only after backing their flirtation with nationalism for an unaccountably long period. Tito has in fact been reluctant to use his great individual prestige until the ground has been well-prepared or action has clearly become inevitable. His power has been used in the last resort to iron out differences among the rulers or dominant interests of Yugoslavia. He has evolved a political system which leaves his successors some room for manoeuvre. It is admittedly complicated and embodies many potentially conflicting elements. It can nevertheless be seen as representing the maximum consensus possible under present Yugoslav conditions. The consensus moreover has been embodied in institutions for the exercise of power, and not least for the succession to himself as President.

So far as the succession itself is concerned therefore there is little cause for immediate concern about the stability of Yugoslavia. Of course, economic conditions may produce a speedy demand for the 'firm hand' and by extension a nationalist reaction. This is where Tito's personal prestige and experience would be most sorely missed, but the situation will not necessarily arise before his successors have had time to acquire some authority.

On foreign policy, the essence of 'Titoism' has been a formal commitment to non-alignment as the counterpart of socialist 'self-management' at home. If under Cuban and Soviet pressure the non-aligned movement is split between anti-imperialist 'activists' and others, the whole concept of non-alignment will be devalued. The same result might occur if within the U.N. the non-aligned 'Group of 77' pressed their demands for a 'New International Economic Order' to the point of totally disrupting the U.N. But Tito and his successors are likely to be wary on this point while the Yugoslav economy depends so much on relations with the Western world. Non-alignment up to a certain point is likely to remain a pillar of Yugoslav foreign policy, and to be cherished as a means for enabling Yugoslavia to pursue an independent foreign policy and if necessary for mobilising world opinion (likely to prove a frail reed) in favour of Yugoslavia, in case of aggression against it.

The 'Western' link in Yugoslav foreign policy will be little affected by Tito's disappearance from the political scene. For Yugoslavia it is, and is likely to remain, a matter of economic necessity. It is important for the Yugoslavs and the West alike as providing the maximum re-insurance against possible dangers from the East. Whatever Yugoslav statesmen may say in public, such re-insurance must remain of primary importance to them. And whether or not Tito is present, any extensive penetration or domination of Yugoslavia by the Soviet Union is strongly against Western interests in anything like the present international situation. Here then is a comparatively constant element in inter-national relations.

It is Yugoslavia's relations with the Soviet Union which are likely to be most affected when Tito is no longer at the helm. This is not simply because only Tito can maintain the sort of implicit bargains on policy discussed in the previous section. Paradoxical as it may seem, the Soviet leaders may well regret the disappearance of Tito, the man who quarrelled with Stalin during and just after the war, who broke with him (however reluctantly) in 1948 and acquired world-wide prestige by doing so, who showed himself ready for a fight after the invasion of Czechoslovakia, who more recently has achieved cordial relations with China and opposed Soviet attempts to nobble the non-aligned move-ment.

Other Yugoslav leaders were or are firmly behind Tito on all these issues; but no other Yugoslav leader has felt the strong emotional ties which bound Tito to the idea of the Soviet Revolution from 1917 onwards, or has set so much hope as did Tito after Stalin's death on the possibility that the Soviet Union might evolve on entirely anti-Stalinist lines. This hope may have faded even for him, but some hankering for Mother Moscow has remained. Tito has shown himself a Moscow man in his reluctance to deviate from 'democratic central-ism' or to tolerate aberrations by intellectuals. With his successors there will be more calculation, but less emotion. In a Middle Eastern crisis, for example, or in an attempt to discipline neo-Marxist intel-lectuals, the Soviet leaders could not have been so sure of Kardelj, nor could they be so sure now of the younger generation of Yugoslav leaders. Of course they will hope sooner or later to profit from the disappearance of Tito, with his unique ability to settle internal crises in Yugoslavia, and may hope to provoke such crises in order to give their agents or supporters a position of increased influence. They may none the less regret the passing of a man to whom the Russian Revolution meant so much and whom they could regard as, at worst, a calculably reliable opponent.

This is one measure of Tito's achievement. A more immediately important measure of it for the West is the conclusion that, unless the present balance of East–West power in Europe is changed soon and drastically in favour of the East, the internal structure and external position of Yugoslavia could remain for some years at least on a reasonably firm basis. Tito has proved to be a remarkable statesman, whose deliberate policies, pragmatic leadership and fortunate star have enabled his country to survive great dangers and to build a system which, just because of its ambiguities and the extent to which it incorporates previous institutions, practices and habits of thought, has considerable survival value. Whether the system will prove to be an effective model of participatory government is a different question, but also one which should not be dismissed at once in a cynical spirit. Time will provide its answer. Meanwhile, long may the peoples of Yugoslavia flourish in brotherhood and unity, and in increasing prosperity and freedom.

Note on sources

It does not seem appropriate to furnish this book, intended for readers generally interested in contemporary history and international affairs, with a detailed bibliography or source list. The following is a selective list of books which they may find useful both in themselves and for indications of further reading.

Dennison Rusinow's *The Yugoslav Experiment 1948–1974* (Royal Institute of International Affairs, London, 1977), has been for me in a class by itself; it covers much the same ground as this book, usually in considerably greater detail and with a full apparatus of footnotes and bibliography. I owe a great debt to the author.

Fred Singleton's *Twentieth-Century Yugoslavia* (London, 1976), goes further back into history, gives more data about geography and resources, and contains a lot of material for those who prefer a 'thematic' form to that of a historical narrative.

Steven K. Pavlowitch, *Yugoslavia* (London, 1971), an anti-Communist view, has interesting chapters on the Yugoslav lands before unification and on the inter-war period; and Stephen Clissold (ed.), *A Short History of Yugoslavia* (Cambridge, 1968), is convenient, scholarly and available in paperback.

On Marshal Tito, Phyllis Auty's biography, *Tito*, was last issued by Penguin in a revised edition, 1974; Fitzroy Maclean, *Disputed Barricades* (London, 1957) is still very much worth reading, as is Vladimir Dedijer, *Tito Speaks* (London, 1953) (invaluable for the earlier period of his life).

The history of the Partisan War is very amply covered. M. Djilas, *Wartime* (London, 1977) is a remarkable book. Vivid personal impressions are also recorded by Stephen Clissold, *Whirlwind* (London, 1949), F. W. Deakin, *The Embattled Mountain* (London, 1971), and Fitzroy Maclean, *Eastern Approaches* (London, 1949); for those who want more detail, there is Walter Roberts, *Tito, Mihailović and the Allies* (Rutgers, 1973), and Jozo Tomasević, *The Chetniks* (Stamford, 1975).

It is much harder to make a short selection for the post-war period, apart from the general books already mentioned. I have found the following particularly valuable:

Rudolf Bićanić, *Economic Policy in Socialist Yugoslavia* (Cambridge, 1973).

Stephen Clissold (ed.), *Yugoslavia and the Soviet Union* (London, 1975).

Bogdan Denis Denitch, *The Legitimation of a Revolution* (New Haven, Conn., 1976) (particularly on the urban/rural problem, the nationalities question, and self-management).

Milovan Djilas, *Conversations with Stalin* (London, 1962).

A. Ross Johnson, *Yugoslavia in the Twilight of Tito* (Washington Papers, Washington, D.C., 1974) (a good short general survey).

Paul Lendvai, *Eagles in Cobwebs* (London, 1969) (a vivid survey of Yugoslav problems after Economic Reform and before the Nationalities Crisis).

Deborah D. Milenkovich, *Plan and Market in Yugoslav Economic Thought* (New Haven, Conn., 1971).

Paul Shoup, *Communism and the Yugoslav National Questions* (New York, 1968).

Carl Gustav Ströhm, *Ohne Tito* (Graz, 1976) (lively journalistic impressions, with a strong historical bias, for readers of German).

For readers of Serbo-Croat of course the field is much larger. Rusinow's book contains a full bibliography down to 1974. Since then perhaps the most important book – certainly the most important on Yugoslav foreign policy – has been the Memoirs of Veljko Mićunović, Tito's Ambassador in Moscow 1956–8 and 1969–71, *Moskovske Godine 1956–8* (Zagreb, 1977) (this is being translated into English).

Apart from the sources listed in Rusinow (by no means all of which I can claim to have read), I have found invaluable the speeches and interviews of Marshal Tito (in the official edition published from 1962 onwards in Zagreb), and the columns of the weekly *Nin*.

Index

This index covers mainly the personalities mentioned substantially in the text, along with certain Yugoslav 'enterprises' and newspapers, and a few geographical and subject headings mainly bearing on Yugoslavia's foreign relations and some particular problems of its Republics and Provinces. Yugoslav political and economic institutions, Federal, Republican and local, have not been indexed. Readers wishing to trace the origin and development of these can do so most easily by using the analytic table of contents, pp. vii–xii.

The same applies to those who wish to study the role of Marshal Tito in relation to Yugoslav history during the period of his reign. The short entry under his name in the index refers only to aspects of his life not directly relevant to this. A comprehensive entry would cover most of the subject-matter of the book.